To Jack
Merry Christmas
2006

Love you.
Annette

Hail Victory

Hail Victory

An Oral History of the Washington Redskins

Thom Loverro

WILEY

John Wiley & Sons, Inc.

Published by John Wiley & Sons, Inc., Hoboken, New Jersey
Published simultaneously in Canada

Design and composition by Navta Associates. Inc.

For general information about our other products and services, please contact our Customer Care Department within the United States at (800) 762-2974, outside the United States at (317) 572-3993 or fax (317) 572-4002.

Wiley also publishes its books in a variety of electronic formats. Some content that appears in print may not be available in electronic books. For more information about Wiley products, visit our web site at www.wiley.com.

Library of Congress Cataloging-in-Publication Data:

Loverro, Thom.
   Hail victory : an oral history of the Washington Redskins / Thom Loverro.
      p. cm.
   Includes index.
   ISBN-13 978-0-471-72510-7 (cloth)
   ISBN-10 0-471-72510-2 (cloth)
   1.   Washington Redskins (Football team)–History.   I. Title.
GV956.W3 L678 2006
796.332'6409753–dc22

                                                                  2006004491

Printed in the United States of America

10   9   8   7   6   5   4   3   2   1

CONTENTS

FOREWORD

Before the start of the 2005 season, Joe Gibbs invited me to come to Redskin Park and talk to his players about what it can mean to be a Washington Redskin. He was trying to get the message across to this new group of players how great it is to play football for the Redskins.

I told them that when you start winning, you have no idea what this town can be like. You can't imagine how people will take you into their hearts when you lay it on the line and give all you have for the team.

We had a lot of guys who came here and sacrificed their individualism for the good of the team, yet they still were successful individually because of the success of the team. The rules have changed from the time we played because of free agency and the salary cap, but the concepts haven't changed. You still have to sacrifice and do things you might not normally do, for the good of the team, and then hopefully reap the rewards at the end. Quite a few of us did.

We laid it on the line and sacrificed for this franchise, this town, and these Redskins fans, and we were rewarded for it not just with money, but by being part of a community that can embrace you far beyond your playing years.

To this day, I still have people approach me and talk to me about a game that meant the most to them, a time that they shared with family and friends and the entire Washington community, because being a Redskins fan was something that cut across all sorts of dividing lines.

Washington is such a transient place. You have people in high-stress jobs here, and football is a way for people to go back to the time when they were in college going to football games. But the Redskins cut across class lines. You have delivery men and lawyers who connect with one another through the Redskins. Economic or social barriers seem to disappear when you talk about the Redskins.

Here you have the city of Washington, where you have the White House and Congress and all this power, yet it almost seems as if you are more revered by people here as a Washington Redskin, especially if you are winning. It's an amazing feeling.

We did win, going to four Super Bowls and winning three of them in the years spanning 1982 to 1991. We were held in such high esteem in this town, and we appreciated it. It is amazing how everyone here embraced us, and it still continues to this day.

The connections we made, though, went beyond the playing field. We would be in the parking lot at Robert F. Kennedy Stadium after a game drinking and eating with the fans. They would come into our parking lot, which was open, and they would bring us food and drinks, or we would offer ours to them when we would be out there after a game.

We had something special. We were the Washington Redskins, and we still are. That is a very special reward.

Joe Jacoby

Joe Jacoby played offensive tackle for the Washington Redskins from 1981 to 1993. He was part of the famous offensive line known as the "Hogs," who blocked for three different quarterbacks and running backs during that time on their way to three Super Bowl championships. He was selected for four consecutive Pro Bowls, from 1983 through 1986.

ACKNOWLEDGMENTS

It may be obvious, but any acknowledgment for an oral history starts, of course, with all the Washington Redskins players, coaches, and team officials, past and present, who cooperated with this effort to tell the stories that have made this franchise such a devoted part of so many fans' lives.

There are others, though, who made these stories become part of the record of the Washington Redskins and made this book possible. My sincere thanks to my editor at John Wiley & Sons, Stephen S. Power, who had a passion for the project and an instinct for what was important for readers.

Also, I would not have had a chance to be involved in such a project if not for the work of Greg Dinkin of Venture Literary, who saw the potential for a detailed oral history of this cornerstone franchise in the National Football League, and my agent, Jake Elwell, of Wieser & Elwell, for working to put this project together.

Dick Alban   A defensive back for Washington from 1952 to 1955, Alban roomed as a rookie with Sammy Baugh at the Shoreham Hotel in the quarterback's last year in football.

Mike Bass   A cornerback in Washington from 1969 to 1975, Bass will forever be known by Redskins fans as the one who ran back the botched field goal attempt by Dolphins kicker Garo Yepremian for a touchdown in Super Bowl VII, the lone Redskin score in a 14–7 loss.

Sammy Baugh   The tall, lanky Texan put football on the map in Washington when, as a rookie quarterback in the Redskins' first year in town in 1937, he led the franchise to the NFL championship, the first of two league titles with Baugh at the helm. He was a six-time NFL passing leader who from 1937 to 1952 threw for 21,886 yards and 187 touchdowns.

Jeff Bostic   The center of the great Hogs offensive line, Bostic came to Washington in 1980 and put the ball in the hands of Redskins quarterbacks until 1994. Along the way, he had consecutive game streaks of 64 and 52 games.

Mike Bragg   The Redskins punter from 1968 to 1979, Bragg holds a number of the franchise punting records, including most career punts, with 896, and second with the most punts in a season, with 103 in 1978.

Larry Brown   Brown broke in as a rookie in Washington in 1969 with the legendary Vince Lombardi, who discovered Brown had difficulty hearing and had a hearing aid installed in his helmet. Brown had no problem seeing, as he was perhaps the toughest running back ever to carry the ball for the Redskins, gaining 5,875 yards rushing over eight seasons and being named NFL Player of the Year in 1972.

Dave Butz   As one of the rare players who was a free agent back in the days when there were very few such players, Butz signed with the Redskins in 1975 and, as the immovable force at defensive tackle, became the anchor for Redskins defenses until he retired in 1988. In 1983, his All-Pro season, the 300-pound Butz led the team that year with 11.5 sacks and forced a team-high 5 fumbles.

Charley Casserly   A former Massachusetts high school football coach who came to work for George Allen in 1977 as an unpaid intern, Casserly rose up in the organization from scout to assistant general manager to general manager of the squad that won Super Bowl XXVI.

Gary Clark   Clark teamed with Art Monk and Ricky Sanders to make the most lethal trio of receivers in Redskins history, as Clark made four Pro Bowls and pulled down more than 1,000 yards in pass receiving yards five times over his nine seasons in Washington.

Monte Coleman   The ageless Redskins linebacker who played sixteen seasons for Washington, from 1979 through 1994, Coleman was second in franchise history for most games played, with 215, and was among the leaders in defensive records, including third in fumbles recovered, with 15.

Andre Collins   A linebacker picked second in the 1990 draft out of Penn State, Collins was one of only two rookies to have started every game while playing for Joe Gibbs. His 6 sacks in 1990 tied the club record for sacks by a rookie.

Vernon Dean   A cornerback for the Redskins from 1982 to 1987, Dean had a nose for the ball, pulling in 20 interceptions in his first four years with the team and leading or tying for the team lead in interceptions for three of those seasons.

Al DeMao   A center from Duquesne who hiked the ball to both quarterbacks Sammy Baugh and Eddie LeBaron, DeMao played for the Redskins from 1945 to 1953.

Bill Dudley   A Hall of Fame back, "Bullet Bill" Dudley came to the Redskins near the end of his career in 1950. He was a first-round draft pick of the Pittsburgh Steelers in 1942 and was the league's Most Valuable Player in 1946.

Pat Fischer   One of the hardest hitters of any Redskin to ever put on a uniform despite standing at 5-foot-9, 170 pounds, Fischer was a mainstay at cornerback for Washington from 1968 to 1977, pulling down 27 interceptions, playing in the 1969 Pro Bowl, and being named second team All-Pro in 1972.

Joe Gibbs   The most successful coach in the history of the franchise, leading the Redskins to four Super Bowls and winning three of them, from 1981 to 1992. He retired after the 1992 season to manage his successful NASCAR racing team full time, but returned to coaching the Redskins and serving as team president in 2004.

Chris Hanburger   One of the greatest linebackers in the history of the Redskins, Hanburger played fourteen seasons in Washington, from 1965 to 1978, made nine Pro Bowls, and was the NFL Defensive Player of the Year in 1972, when he intercepted 4 passes, returning 1 for a touchdown.

Ken Harvey   A four-time Pro Bowl linebacker who came to Washington as a free agent in 1994, Harvey became the first Redskin to lead the NFC in sacks, with 13.5 in 1994, and just the fourth linebacker in NFL history to do so.

Len Hauss   The anchor of the Redskins offensive line from 1964 to 1977, Hauss was the iron man of the franchise, playing in a team record 196 consecutive games, also with a record 192 consecutive starts.

Sam Huff   A five-time Pro Bowler, Huff remains one of the most recognized faces of the franchise, even though the legendary linebacker played the bulk of his career (from 1956 to 1963) for the New York Giants. In 1964 he was traded to the Redskins, where he became a fan favorite, and he has been part of the Redskins radio announcing team since 1981.

Joe Jacoby   As one of the mainstays of the Hogs offensive line, Jacoby played tackle on all three Super Bowl championship squads. A free agent out of Louisville, Kentucky, Jacoby played his entire career for the Redskins, from 1981 to 1993, and was a four-time Pro Bowl selection.

Dick James   A running back from Oregon who played for the Redskins from 1956 to 1963, James set a single-season scoring record by rushing for 4 touchdowns in a 1961 game against the Dallas Cowboys.

Roy Jefferson   As one of the league's top wide receivers brought in by George Allen when he arrived in 1971, Jefferson joined with Charley Taylor to make one of the most potent one-two receiving combinations in the NFL. Jefferson caught 44 passes, averaging 17 yards per catch in his first year with the Redskins.

Jimmy Jones   A backup defensive end from the New York Jets, Jones was a favorite of George Allen's, not only because he convinced Allen to bring his former teammate from the Jets, Verlon Biggs, to Washington, but also because of his outstanding ability to get to the quarterback. He became Allen's designated pass rusher.

Sonny Jurgensen   One of the greatest passers in NFL history, Jurgensen is probably the player most identified with the franchise, as he, along with Huff, have been part of the radio broadcasting team for twenty-five years. After being traded by the Philadelphia Eagles in 1964, Jurgensen led a high-powered Redskins offense and won three NFL passing titles. Over a seventeen-year career that began in 1957, Jurgensen completed 2,433 passes for 32,224 yards and 255 touchdowns.

Dave Kopay   The running back brought to Washington in a trade by new coach Vince Lombardi in 1969, Kopay later made sports history when, in 1977, he revealed that he was gay in the book *The Dave Kopay Story*.

Jim Lachey   Lachey came to the Redskins in a major trade with the Los Angeles Raiders in 1988 for quarterback Jay Schroeder and became one of the premier offensive tackles in the league. He was named to four Pro Bowls and was a three-time All-Pro selection.

Larry Lucchino   A former teammate of Bill Bradley's at Princeton University, Lucchino joined Redskins owner Edward Bennett Williams's law firm in 1974 and became a partner four years later. He served as general counsel to the Redskins and was a member of the board of directors from 1979 to 1985. He is currently one of the owners of the Boston Red Sox.

Dexter Manley   Manley could have been one of the greatest pass rushers of all time, but his career was cut short by his struggle with drug abuse. The defensive end was a cornerstone of the Redskins defense that won Super Bowl XVII. He is the Redskins all-time leader in sacks with 97 and the single season record holder with 18.

Charles Mann   A remarkable physical specimen who quietly complemented his cohort at defensive end, Dexter Manley, by playing ten seasons from 1983 to 1993 and recording 82 career sacks, was second behind Manley on the team all-time list. Mann was a four-time Pro Bowl selection over a span of five seasons.

Eddie Mason   A linebacker who excelled on special teams for the Redskins from 1999 to 2002, Mason led special teams in tackles in 2000.

Ron McDole   Nicknamed "The Dancing Bear," McDole came to Washington in 1971 after a brilliant career as defensive end with the Buffalo Bills in the American Football League. He was part of George Allen's "Over the Hill Gang" and played for the Redskins until 1978.

Tony McGee   One of the anchors as a defensive end of the great New England Patriots defenses of the 1970s—he ended his career with 106 sacks—McGee came to Washington in 1982 and over the next two years helped work with young defensive ends Dexter Manley and Charles Mann.

Raleigh McKenzie   McKenzie played both guard positions, center, and left tackle for the Redskins from 1985 to 1994, earning all NFC honors on the United Press International squad during Washington's 1991 Super Bowl season.

Ron Middleton   A tight end out of Auburn, Alabama, Middleton came to the Redskins first in 1988 and then in 1990 as a free agent and was one of the key components of the team's run blocking whose presence in the lineup added nearly 20 more yards per game to the rushing attack in the 1991 Super Bowl season.

Rich Milot   A versatile defender who came in under Jack Pardee, Milot played all three linebacker positions and was part of defensive coordinator Richie Petitbon's underrated defenses under coach Joe Gibbs until he retired after the 1987 season.

Bobby Mitchell   The first black player to wear a Redskins uniform, Mitchell was a Hall of Fame halfback and wide receiver who played in four Pro Bowls and amassed 14,078 combined net yards and 91 touchdowns during his career, which began in Cleveland in 1958. He was traded to Washington in 1962.

Brian Mitchell   Perhaps the greatest kick returner in NFL history, from 1990 through 1999, Mitchell set nearly every franchise return record—including 9 touchdowns on punts and kickoffs—and ten NFL records over his fourteen-year career. He is the NFL's career leader in return yardage and also in total yards, with 23,330.

Mark Moseley   Moseley had one of the greatest years any placekicker has had in the NFL in 1982, when he hit his first

20 field goal tries, including a number of game-winning kicks, putting the Redskins in position to reach Super Bowl XVII. In the strike-shortened season, Moseley had 76 points and was named the league's Most Valuable Player. From 1974 to 1986, he led the league four times in field goals.

Mark Murphy   A safety for the Redskins from 1977 to 1984, Murphy was one of George Allen's last personnel shenanigans in his final year as coach, keeping Murphy under wraps during the draft at a Dulles Airport hotel and then signing him as a free agent. Murphy was active in the NFL Players Association throughout his career.

Mike Nelms   As one of the greatest kick returners in franchise history, Nelms led the Redskins in punt returns from 1980 to 1984, scoring touchdowns on two of them in 1981, when he also set the franchise record for average on kickoff returns at 29.7 yards per runback.

Bernie Nordlinger   An attorney who worked with team founder George Preston Marshall, Nordlinger drew up the corporate paperwork for the company that was formed when the Redskins moved to Washington in 1937.

Brig Owens   A standout safety for the Redskins from 1966 to 1977, Owens ranks second in the team record books with 36 interceptions and as of this writing holds the record for most career interception yards gained, with 686.

Bob Pelligrini   Pelligrini was a linebacker from the University of Maryland who played for the Redskins from 1962 to 1965.

Gene Pepper   Pepper came out of the University of Missouri and played guard on the Redskins offensive line from 1950 to 1953, protecting legendary quarterback Sammy Baugh in the last days of his career.

Dan Riley   The Redskins strength coach who was brought to Washington by Joe Gibbs in 1982 after building a revolutionary strength training program at Penn State, Riley is credited by a number of players for their success with the Redskins.

Jeff Rutledge   A career backup quarterback in the NFL, Rutledge came to Washington in 1990 and became valuable as the holder for kicks. He led the greatest comeback in franchise history when he passed for 363 yards in 1990 against the Lions, leading Washington back from a 35–10 deficit to a 41–38 win in overtime.

Mark Rypien   The quarterback who led one of the most high-powered offenses in franchise history in 1991, scoring a total of 485,

Rypien connected on 28 touchdowns on the way to the championship in Super Bowl XXVI, where he was named the league's Most Valuable Player.

Bert Sugar   A noted author and sports historian, Sugar grew up in Washington as a Redskins fan who worked at and attended many games at Griffith Stadium.

Diron Talbert   One of the "Ramskins" who came to Washington from the Los Angeles Rams when former Rams coach George Allen was hired by the Redskins in 1971, Talbert, the defensive tackle and a Texas native, helped fuel the rivalry with the Dallas Cowboys until he retired in 1980.

Charley Taylor   A member of the Pro Football Hall of Fame, Taylor broke in as a running back out of Arizona State in 1964 but soon became one of the most productive pass receivers in the history of the game and a favorite target of quarterback Sonny Jurgensen. An eight-time Pro Bowler, Taylor retired with 90 touchdown receptions and 649 catches overall for 9,130 yards.

Joe Tereshinski   An end out of Georgia, Tereshinski played for the Redskins from 1947 to 1954 alongside such great franchise stars as Bones Taylor and Sammy Baugh.

Joe Theismann   The quarterback who led the Redskins to a 27–17 victory over Miami in Super Bowl XVII, Theismann was named the Associated Press's NFL Most Valuable Player and the AP Offensive Player of the Year in 1983. He ranks third among Washington quarterbacks in career touchdown passes with 160.

Rusty Tillman   A linebacker who was one of the special teams players and whom George Allen coveted so much, Tillman played for Washington from 1970 to 1977.

Harry Ulinski   Ulinski played center for legendary quarterback Sammy Baugh from 1950 to 1951. After leaving to play in Canada in 1952, Ulinski came back at the urging of new coach Curly Lambeau to play for the Redskins from 1953 to 1956.

Rick Walker   "Doc" Walker was a tight end out of UCLA who came to the Redskins in 1980 and became a big part of two of the more popular units on the team: the Hogs, as a blocking tight end, and the Fun Bunch, the group of Redskins receivers whose end zone celebrations were eventually outlawed by the league.

Don Warren   A standout blocking tight end who was also a reliable pass catcher during his time with the Redskins from 1979 to 1992,

Warren caught 5 passes in Washington's 27–17 win over the Dolphins in Super Bowl XVII and was part of all three franchise Super Bowl champion teams.

Joe Washington   The running back with the small frame and the big heart, Washington was one of the players drafted by coach Joe Gibbs in 1981. Coming from the Baltimore Colts, he responded by gaining 918 yards rushing and 558 yards in pass receptions.

Introduction

If America is a melting pot, Washington, D.C., is the bubbling center of it. People from all parts of the country and beyond the borders, from all walks of life, move in and out of one of the most important cities on the face of the Earth. Presidents change, members of Congress change, and the people who work for them and the businesses and industries that revolve around those institutions change as well. Some of those people leave, and others find a way to stay, discovering that Washington is a place with so much to offer.

It is a city of politics, which divides people. It is also a transient city, which makes it difficult for people to connect. People form their own little communities, based on race, nationality, social standing, or other qualities, but there is little that weaves all these individual communities together to create the overall community of Washington.

One institution that does cut across all the divisions and finds its way through all those little communities is one that has been in Washington for nearly seventy years, bringing joy, anguish, and memories to those who pass through and those who stay: the Washington Redskins.

When the team arrived from Boston in 1937, they were embraced by fans, with thousands following the team on the road to their first National Football League (NFL) championship. They continued to embrace the players who have worn the Redskins uniform since then, through championship seasons and losing seasons, through the glory days and the dark days. They loved Sammy Baugh, Eddie LeBaron, Sonny Jurgensen, Billy Kilmer, Joe Theismann, Doug Williams, Mark Rypien, and nearly every player who has led the Redskins on the field—not just the quarterbacks, but the special teams players like Rusty Tillman and Otis Wonsley.

"The fans are great here," said defensive end Tony McGee, who spent only the last two years of his NFL career playing for the Redskins but has since made Washington his home and is a fixture in the community. "Once you are a Redskin, you are for life. They make you feel welcome here. I have been here twenty years since I retired. I made this my home. That tells you something. You might have thought I would go back to New England, where I played the longest in my career and had some of my best years. But I stayed here. The one thing that we have here that we have always had are the Washington fans. I don't know of any better."

The Redskins are the tie that binds the bicycle courier with the lawyer, the janitor with the lobbyist, the electrician with the elected official. Everyone in Washington is from somewhere else, and some are very rich and others are not. But come Monday morning from September through December, and, if lucky, through February, people from all walks of life talk about the touchdowns that were scored or the ones that weren't. They debate politics and other issues in Washington with a vitriolic tone, but the passion that takes place over arguments about the Washington Redskins is one that seems to actually connect the community rather than divide it. One of the traditions in Washington has been the repeated controversy over the years about who should play quarterback. It started with the debate of Sonny versus Billy, carried on when Theismann arrived, and continued with Williams and Jay Schroeder, and Rypien and Stan Humphries, and even recently with Mark Brunell and Patrick Ramsey. But come the day when the Redskins take the field, those fans will back whomever is behind center for the Washington Redskins, because he is a Redskin.

This loyalty has survived the controversy of owner George Preston Marshall, the larger-than-life presence of Edward Bennett Williams, the flamboyance of Jack Kent Cooke, and the heavy-handedness of Daniel Snyder. Whoever has owned the Redskins has always belonged to the Washington community; he has treated the Redskins so well that the team has become one of the most valuable sports franchises in the country.

Since 1937, there have been twelve presidents. There has been World War II, the Korean War, the Vietnam War, and now the war in Iraq. There have been scandals that have rocked the country and shook the very foundations of America. But in the end, in the nation's capital, these institutions have withstood all of that: the White House, Congress, the Supreme Court, and the Washington Redskins.

1

Finding a Home

George Preston Marshall thought he was in on the ground floor of the next great sports craze of the Roaring Twenties when he purchased a professional franchise in a new sports league called the American Basketball League (ABL). He was right, in one sense: basketball would someday capture the attention of the American sports public. But Marshall was ahead of his time, and he didn't have much patience to wait decades, let alone years, to reap the rewards of his sports venture.

He was already a successful Washington businessman, inheriting the Palace Laundry from his father and building it into a profitable business. But Marshall liked action and being in the spotlight. He was a showman by nature, and he wanted to expand into something that gave him a greater rush than cleaning clothes. He hoped the ABL would do that, but in the era of Babe Ruth, Bobby Jones, and Jack Dempsey, there was no such icon for roundball.

Marshall's basketball venture was not in vain, however. He made some important contacts with men of that era who had similar dreams. One man in particular who had a clearer vision of the future of American sports was George "Papa Bear" Halas. And Halas had a standard bearer to compete with the likes of a Ruth, Jones, and Dempsey: Red Grange, who would help launch the National Football League in the 1920s.

Halas, a former standout end and baseball player (he played with the New York Yankees in 1919), was hired in 1920 by the Staley Starch Company of Decatur, Illinois, to organize a company football team. That team, the Decatur Staleys, with Halas as player-coach, joined the new American Professional Football Association (APFA) that year. They moved to Chicago in 1921. The Staley company didn't renew the franchise in 1922, but Halas kept the team in operation and emerged as one of the leaders in the league. In January 1922, Halas suggested that the APFA should also be given a new name, the National Football League (NFL), and so it was named.

Four years later, Halas helped establish the league by signing one of the legends of college football—Red Grange, the three-time All-American from Illinois known as the "Galloping Ghost"—to play for the Bears. His presence broke league records, drawing 65,000 fans in New York and soon after 75,000 in Los Angeles. While baseball was still the national pastime, and would remain so for many years to come, the NFL was now on the sports landscape in America.

Halas and Joe Carr, the NFL president, were looking for owners to expand the league, and Halas looked to some of his cohorts in another of his sports enterprises, the ABL, where he operated the Chicago Bruins, for new partners. In 1932, Halas recruited Marshall, who owned the Washington Palace Five basketball team, to buy the bankrupt Duluth Eskimos franchise for $100. But the NFL was not interested in Washington, which was considered a southern city at the time. The midwestern and northeastern parts of the country were seen as fertile territory for professional football, where blue-collar, ethnic communities could be found, and Boston was available. That city was a hotbed for sports, with two baseball teams (the Red Sox and the Braves), professional hockey and soccer franchises, big-time college football, an active semipro football scene, and many fight and wrestling fans.

So Marshall, with three other investors—Jay O'Brien, a New York investment banker; Vincent Bendix, an auto supplier from South Bend, Indiana, and Larry Doyle, a New York stockbroker—bought the Eskimos and opened up shop in Boston for the 1932 season. They would play their home games at Braves Field, the home of the Boston Braves, a National League baseball team. The ballpark, built in 1915, was located about three miles west of downtown Boston and one mile west of the rival Red Sox field, Fenway Park. Trying to gain local recognition right away by connecting to the Braves, Marshall came up with a name for his new football team—the Boston Braves.

There was no fanfare with the arrival of the new NFL franchise in Boston. When the team was about to hold its first practice in nearby Lynn, the only mention of it in the September 7, 1932, edition of the *Boston Globe* was a short item at the bottom of one of the sports pages. And that amount of space was devoted to the problems the team was facing with its roster and finalizing a place to play:

> Members of the Braves professional football team arrived in Boston yesterday, and, with Head Coach Lud Wray in command, will have their first practice session today at Lynn Stadium. More than forty men will take the field to condition themselves and perfect team play. Though Ernest Pinkett, who was claimed by the New York Giants, did not report yesterday, his case has been definitely disposed of by the president of the league, who awarded him to Boston. Therefore he will play with Boston or be absent from organized professional football. President George Marshall of the Braves has been in Boston the past several days to prepare for the coming of the team.

Marshall hired Wray, a former player with Buffalo in the APFA and a coach at the University of Pennsylvania, as his first coach, and the *Globe* reported that on the first day of practice, "Routine training regulations have been established, and in addition to pep talks, Coach Wray has outlined the what's and what not's of their behavior program."

The following are the players who were at that first practice in Lynn—the first Redskins, or Braves, as was the case in that first season. Two of them, Turk Edwards and Cliff Battles, would go on to become Hall of Fame players:

Backs Reggie Rust, Oregon State; Henry Hughes, Honolulu; Jim Musick, Southern California; Jack Roberts and Marion Dickens, University of Georgia; Cliff Battles, West Virginia Wesleyan; Ken Goff, Rhode Island State; Meyers Clark, Ohio State; Oran Pape, University of Iowa; Fait "Chief" Elkins, ex-Chicago Cardinal and Frankford Yellow Jacket; Larry Dullaire, Salem High; and L. T. "Cowboy" Woodruff, University of Mississippi.

Ends   Paul Collins and Jim MacMurdo, Pittsburgh; George Kenneally, St. Bonaventure; Dale "Muddy" Waters, University of Florida; Dick Murphy, New York University; Jim Sofish, Keisterville, Pennsylvania; Fred Belber, University of North Dakota; Kermit Schmidt, Olympic Club of San Francisco; and Basil Wilkerson, Oklahoma University.

Tackles   Russell Peterson, University of Montana; Milton Rehnquist, Providence Steam Rollers; Hugh Rhead, University of Nebraska; Al Pierotti, Washington and Lee; C. W. Artman, Stanford; and Albert Glen "Turk" Edwards, Washington State.

Centers   Ken "Buck" Hammes, Oregon State; Lavon Zakarian, University of Maine; Andrews Anderson, Cambridge; Henry "Babe" Frank, Syracuse University; Tony Siano, Fordham University; and "Bank" Barber, Dartmouth.

Guards   Hilary Lee, University of Missouri; Jack Cox, Oregon State; Jim Wigmore, University of Maryland; and George Hurley, Washington State.

Utility men   C. C. Belden, Chicago, and W. A. Boyd, Louisiana.

Signing Edwards was a coup for Marshall and showed that he recognized the value of star power. Edwards came out of Washington State as an All-American tackle and the star of the Cougars' 1931 Rose Bowl team. He was highly sought after by other clubs in the league, but Marshall won out with the highest bid, paying Edwards $1,500 for that first season in Boston.

Edwards was one of Marshall's selling points to a new audience in Boston, and he would need every selling point he could find. These were not good times to make a buck in Boston. As the country grew during the post–Civil War era, new waterfronts and factories sprang up in other cities. The textile industries in the city were closing up shop, and the Great Depression was taking a severe toll.

In tough times, people turned to entertainment venues for relief from their woes, and sports offered that sort of relief. The problem in Boston, though, was the competition for the limited entertainment dollars that were being spent. It was a baseball town, with two major league franchises, and a big college football town. And football was hardly a pageant. Uniforms were not very colorful. These were still the times of the leather helmet—when a player did wear a helmet; it not did become a piece of required equipment in the league until 1943.

Marshall hoped to capture the early attention of football fans there by lining up exhibition games against local semipro clubs that were well established in the region. More than 3,000 fans came out to see the team's first exhibition contest against the Quincy Trojans; they won 25–0, behind 2 touchdowns by running back Jim Musick. But press reports indicated that Wray was not pleased with the effort on the field, and he put his team through a five-hour workout in their first practice following the game. One newspaper report stated, "After the workout, Coach Wray and his men were confident the Braves would be far better next Sunday against the Providence Steam Rollers."

The Steam Rollers, though, were a step up from semipro competition. The club had been in the NFL before dropping out after the 1931 season, and the Braves' confidence took a beating, as did the players, in a 9–6 loss to the Steam Rollers. Fortunately, not much of the Boston sporting public would hear about the embarrassing defeat. The arrival of the NFL remained a small novelty for the Boston media, and the loss was written up as a brief report. Ironically, the game was overshadowed by a preview of the first game of the season by Boston's pro soccer team. In New England in the 1930s, pro soccer received more attention and interest than did pro football.

The Braves had one more exhibition game before opening their first season. In front of about 1,500 fans, they beat the semipro team from Beverly 31–0 in Lynn Stadium. It was time for the NFL to make its official debut in Boston, on October 2 at Braves Field. Marshall took out newspaper advertisements proclaiming "Big League Football," with the game to be played "rain or shine." Ticket prices were $1.50 for box seats, $1.25 for reserved grandstand, $1 for grandstand, and $0.50 for bleacher seats, "plus 10 percent government tax." Marshall advertised that he would announce updates to the crowd of the World Series game between the New York Yankees and the Chicago Cubs. He also held a dinner for local sportswriters and dignitaries to promote the first game. All that work was for naught, though, as a disappointing crowd of about 6,000 showed up to watch the Braves lose to the Brooklyn Dodgers and quarterback Benny Friedman, 14–0. Things did not get much better after that. The Braves won their next game, 14–6, over the New York Giants, before a slightly larger crowd of 8,000. The team continued an up-and-down performance, however, posting a 4-4-2 record in the inaugural 1932 season, with low attendance at the box office. The franchise wound up losing about $46,000, and Marshall's three partners dropped out.

Pro football was trying to find its place, not just in Boston, but on the sports landscape in America, period, and it attracted a variety of fans. The crowd that showed up for pro football games was a mixture of hard-nosed gamblers, blue-collar workers, and socialites who wanted to be seen at the city's latest attraction. The socialites in Boston were drawn in particular by Marshall, who was a fashion plate, dressed to the hilt in expensive suits and overcoats. But neither the owner nor his team was enough of an attraction to be profitable. Still, the Washington showman believed that someday pro football would be successful in Boston, if he found the right formula. He was half-right; his franchise would be successful, but not in Boston.

The NFL would also undergo significant changes after the 1932 season that would eventually help Marshall's franchise be successful. The league was going through some tough times. Even with the addition of the Braves, it had fallen to just eight teams, the lowest in league history: the Braves, the Chicago Bears, the Portsmouth Spartans, the Green Bay Packers, the New York Giants, the Chicago Cardinals, the Staten Island Stapletons, and the Brooklyn Dodgers.

But one game would take place to generate interest in the league: the precursor to the Super Bowl. Back then, the league champion was determined by which team won the most games during the season. A team, though, could play anywhere between ten and twenty games over a season, and then the argument would be over who had the greater winning percentage.

In 1932, the Portsmouth Spartans tied the Chicago Bears for first place in the league, so their owners decided to hold a game for the NFL championship. The game was supposed to be held at the Bears' home, Wrigley Field. But blizzards and severe cold forced officials to move the December 11 game indoors to Chicago Stadium, thereby making this the first arena league football game as well.

Chicago Stadium was the home for the National Hockey League (NHL) Chicago Blackhawks. It was also used for boxing matches and other events. During the week before the football game, the circus had been there. The concrete floor was covered with several inches of dirt. Truckloads of dirt, wood shavings, and bark were piled on top of that base to provide more cushioning.

Because of the size of Chicago Stadium, some of the rules were changed. The field was only 80 yards long and 130 feet wide compared to the standard 100-yard-long, 160-foot-wide field. The sidelines were butted up against the stands. The goalposts were moved from the end lines to the goal lines. The ball was automatically moved back to the 20-yard line every time one team crossed midfield. And for the first time, all plays would start with the ball on or between the hash marks.

The league had been playing under collegiate rules—a forward pass from behind the line of scrimmage was not allowed—and it opted for new pro rules. The title game, which drew about 10,000 fans, had been decided on a dispute over this rule. With a scoreless tie going into the fourth quarter, Chicago's Carl Brumbaugh handed the ball off to Bronko Nagurski, who then threw it to Red Grange in the end zone for the score. The Spartans argued that Nagurski did not drop back the required 5 yards before passing to Grange, but the touchdown stood, and the Bears later added a safety for the 9–0 win. The game generated enough interest to convince team owners to hold a title contest every year.

The game also sparked league rule changes. The college football rules were abandoned, and the forward pass became legal anywhere from behind the line of scrimmage. Also, all plays would start with the ball on or between the hash marks.

Furthermore, the shape of the ball changed in 1933. Before that, the ball was rounder than the modern ball, making it difficult to throw a tight spiral to keep it on target over any distance. Passes were often thrown high into the air, more like a shot put.

Offenses also struggled because of poor field conditions in Boston and other northeastern and midwestern cities. Those places usually experienced lots of rain in October and November, and the soggy fields would get chewed up as a result. Complicating matters further, one ball was typically used for an entire game, and often that ball would be soaked because of the wet conditions. As a result, there were few games with high scores. When the Bears won the 1932 championship, they averaged just 11 points a game.

Marshall changed fields after 1932, moving from Braves Field to Fenway Park, home of the Red Sox. He also changed the franchise name to the Redskins. When Wray quit after one season to coach and become part owner of the Eagles, a new Philadelphia franchise, Marshall hired, of all people, William "Lone Star" Dietz, a full-blooded

American Indian, who had played with Jim Thorpe at Carlisle, to coach in 1933. The changes did not result in success, either on the field or at the gate, where the largest crowd the team drew was 26,000 in a 21–0 loss to the Bears in 1934. (They never drew more than 20,000 fans for any of their remaining home games during their tenure in Boston.) The Redskins continued to draw small crowds, received little attention in the local media, and under Dietz turned two more seasons of mediocrity: 5-5-2 in 1933 and 6-6 in 1934. Marshall tried another coaching change in 1935 by hiring Ernie Casey, a well-known local figure as the former head coach at Harvard, but the team only got worse, posting a 2-8-1 record and drawing just 5,000 fans for their final home game of the 1935 season. Marshall made another change, which was one of several he made during the following two seasons that brought success to his franchise.

The Redskins owner hired Ray Flaherty, the former All-Pro tight end for the New York Giants, to lead his team in the 1936 season, and Flaherty would prove to be one of the most successful coaches of his time, posting a 54-21-3 record and winning two world championships. Flaherty made an immediate impact by convincing Marshall to acquire two key All-Americans that year: end Wayne Milner from Notre Dame and tailback Riley Smith from Alabama, both of whom would liven up the Redskins offense, although not right away.

The Redskins lost the opener in Pittsburgh to the Steelers 10–0 but bounced back with two road wins over Philadelphia (26–3) and Brooklyn (14–3). When they came home to play the New York Giants, it was before another disappointing crowd of 14,133. Marshall had already started plans to move the franchise if there were not some signs of a box office turnaround in 1936, and now he had seen enough to realize it was just not going to work in Boston, a rabid sports town that did not make room for pro football. Major league pro football would not return to the city until the upstart American Football League came to Boston in 1960, and it was hardly considered major pro football at the time of its inception.

By the time the final game of the season was to take place against the Giants in New York—a game the Redskins needed to win to get to the NFL title game against the Green Bay Packers—the team's Boston offices had closed and the portable football stands at Fenway Park were taken down. Flaherty's team defeated the Giants 14–0 to post the franchise's best record to date—a 7-4 mark and a chance to win the

NFL championship. Ironically, the Redskins had the home-field advantage, which meant the game was supposed to be played in Boston. But Marshall and the league decided that their best chance to make money in the game was to play it on a neutral field—in New York, rather than Boston, at the Polo Grounds. "We'll make much more in New York than in Boston," Marshall told reporters. "We certainly don't owe Boston much after the shabby treatment we've received. Imagine losing $20,000 [the Redskins' 1936 losses] with a championship team."

Joe Carr, the NFL president, made the following statement about moving the title game to New York: "The decision to play the game in New York was reached following a canvas of the club owners involved and of the players of the two teams. Since the playoff game is largely one in which the players are rewarded for winning the division titles and their sole remuneration is from the players' pool made up from gate receipts of the playoff, it was decided that New York was the place in which the players would benefit to the greatest degree possible under existing conditions."

Carr was right—the game drew nearly 30,000 fans, who watched the Packers, led by Don Hutson, defeat the Redskins 21–6 to win the NFL championship. The reported gate receipts were $33,471, with $250 going to each Packer player and $180 to each Redskin player. The Boston press—the ones that noticed the Redskins were leaving town—did not criticize Marshall for his decision. "It's hard to feel resentment against a guy who has stayed in there trying for five years and spent $100,000 in vain pursuit of a championship," wrote Paul Craigue of the *Boston Globe*. "Marshall would have been satisfied with an even break financially, and he went through a long siege without cracking."

The siege had ended, and Marshall was going home to Washington, where his Palace Laundry was based. The Maryland Pro Football corporation was formed, and Marshall signed a lease with Clark Griffith, the owner of the Washington Senators, to play his team's games in Griffith Stadium. Marshall officially left Boston after a brief announcement on December 17, 1936. It was buried at the bottom of a page inside the *Globe* sports section. On February 13, 1937, the NFL officially approved the move to Washington, where the Redskins, and Marshall, would find the fame and fortune they had sought in Boston.

Marshall was determined to own a successful sports franchise, blending his showmanship with his competitiveness. He was very many other things that made people either love or hate him. He was charismatic, stubborn, visionary, blinded, and, as would be written about many times during the years of the franchise, hardly colorblind. The Redskins were often the target of newspaper attacks for refusing to integrate until finally, in 1961, in order for the team to play on federal land in the new D.C. Stadium, Marshall was forced by the U. S. Department of the Interior to bring in a black player.

To say the least, George Preston Marshall was a complicated man. He was born in Grafton, West Virginia, on October 13, 1897. He went to school at Randolph Macon College and inherited his father's laundry business in 1918. He used the money he made in the laundry to launch his venture into professional sports, first in basketball and then in pro football, where he was one of the pioneers of the league and, despite his critics, helped shape the success of the NFL until, due to ill health, he stepped down as the Redskins owner in 1963.

Bernie Nordlinger was Marshall's longtime attorney and was there at the start of the Washington Redskins. Perhaps more than anyone, he knew what this important and controversial figure in the history of the NFL was like.

Attorney Bernie Nordlinger   "I helped organize the Washington Redskins. I drew up the papers for Maryland Pro Football, Inc. Marshall left Boston, saying he wasn't going to play football in a place that gave more publicity to a girl's hockey team than to football. Back then, the league was all so new. It was amazing how little they paid the players, and the team had to hold out a third of what they paid the players, because if they gave it all to them, they were afraid the players wouldn't show up for the next game. Cliff Battles got $157.27 for one game, with $52.52 held back. Vic Carroll got $75, and they held back $25. Wayne Milner got $93.75, and they held back $31.25. Riley Smith got $150, and they held back $50, but they also gave him a $100 bonus. Coach Ray Flaherty got $416.78.

"Marshall and George Halas and Wellington Mara and Art Rooney, they were the men that made the NFL. Marshall made the Redskins enormously popular. He was the first owner to have a band and cheerleaders, and the first one to have a team song. He was responsible for changing the rules that required quarterbacks to be 5 or 10 yards behind the line of scrimmage when they passed. Marshall got the rule changed so that you could pass anytime up to the line of scrimmage. The entire movement of the game was different when they had to pass the ball 5 or 10 yards back. That was very important to the development of the game and the growth of the NFL.

"He saw the possibilities of the use of television in football. When it came along, Marshall learned more about television than anyone else in the game. He grasped the power of it very early. He was responsible for developing the idea of having an amendment to the federal antitrust laws to permit the league to sell television as a group, rather than individually. The league had a rule early on where each team sold its television rights individually—like baseball, so the New York Giants got more television money than, say, a smaller market like the Green Bay Packers. The big teams were getting richer and the little teams couldn't compete. So, at Marshall's urging, they adopted a rule that no team could telecast into another team's area while the game was going on. The government was seeking to get an injunction on the issue of limitation of territory, that it was a violation on its face. The court overruled that, and we won. That was important for the league. That created the revenue sharing that made the league so strong for years to come.

"Marshall made a lot of money from the Palace Laundry, but he lived high. All the big money he had came from football. In later years, the laundry became second fiddle for him. He got so much of his living from pro football. He was an extremely sagacious man in terms of money management.

"Marshall was a loud, dynamic, forceful, and arrogant man who many people thought was unpleasant. I would say he was an intensely loyal man, which kept people close to him. And very few people who stayed around Marshall left him, because he was so darned interesting. He was a volatile, wild man, in that sense. There were so many times I wanted to quit because he made me so angry. But there were so many other times when he made up for that."

Marshall did everything big, right or wrong, and he recognized the value of star power—a big name as an attraction. So while the move to Washington was pivotal to the future success of the Redskins, it was the personnel decision the owner made on the field in 1937 that would put the franchise on the right path. Marshall made Sammy Baugh the team's first-round draft choice for the inaugural season in Washington.

Hailing from Texas Christian University (TCU), Baugh had been the biggest name in college football as the best passer and punter in the game. Marshall built and promoted the team around Baugh, milking the image of the tall Texas cowboy coming to the nation's capital to lead the football team to glory. He convinced Baugh to wear a ten-gallon hat and cowboy boots when he arrived by plane in Washington to meet reporters.

Baugh was born on March 17, 1914, on a farm near Temple, Texas. When he was sixteen, his family moved to Sweetwater, Texas. According to legend, as a youth, Baugh hung an old automobile tire from a tree limb in his backyard. He would swing it in a long arc and back off 10, 15, or 20 yards, trying to throw a football through the tire as it swung back and forth. He did this for hours, sometimes while on the run. He became a high school quarterback star, and went on to TCU. As a junior, he led TCU to a 10-0 record before losing to Southern Methodist University by 20–14, and then he helped take the team to the Sugar Bowl and beat Louisiana State University 3–2 in a rain-soaked game. During his senior year, Baugh led his team to the first Cotton Bowl and a 16–6 win over Marquette. He had changed the face of college football, throwing the ball as many as forty times a game, and now he was about to do the same for pro football, although there were doubters because he was not particularly big. Sportswriter Grantland Rice warned Marshall, "Take my advice: if you sign him, insure his right arm for a million dollars. Those big pros will tear it off."

Baugh wasn't particularly convinced the NFL was right for him, either. He was a great all-around athlete and considered to be a baseball prospect, so much so that he was also negotiating to play for the St. Louis Cardinals. He balked at Marshall's initial offer and went to play baseball for the summer.

Quarterback Sammy Baugh "We talked contract, and I agreed that $5,000 sounded like a pretty reasonable figure, but I also had major league baseball scouts after me. I was a right fair third baseman and shortstop at TCU, and I really wanted to give professional baseball a try."

End Joe Tereshinski "He was a heck of a baseball player and almost didn't sign with the Redskins because of baseball, not from playing it, but because of an accident. Sam Breeden was the owner of the St.

Louis Cardinals, and he and his friend Tonto Coleman, who was the coach at Georgia Tech, went to see Sammy in Texas. Breeden was pulling this trailer, and the story goes that Sammy Baugh was in the trailer. Tonto and Breeden were driving down a hill, talking about what a good baseball player Sammy was, and they had to come to a sudden stop. The trailer came off the car and passed right by them, with Sammy Baugh in it. It was a good thing he wasn't killed."

Marshall was determined to make a big impact in his hometown with his new team and not to lose Baugh to baseball. With the help of Texas businessman Amon Carter, a friend of Marshall's and a TCU patron, he was able to reach a deal with Baugh, paying him $8,000, plus a $500 signing bonus, more than twice what the average NFL salary was at the time. "When I found out what the rest of the players were making, I felt badly about asking for so much money," Baugh told reporters.

He was worth it. "Sammy Baugh was a dynamic personality on the football field," Nordlinger said. "He was a great leader and an exciting ballplayer." Marshall instructed his staff to make sure Baugh looked like a cowboy when he was presented to reporters. "Get him a pair of cowboy boots and a ten-gallon hat, and make him look like he is from the wild, wild West," he said. But when Baugh was introduced to reporters upon his arrival to Washington and asked how he felt, he pointed to the boots Marshall had made him put on and said, "My feet hurt. We hardly ever wear things like this in Sweetwater."

On his first day of practice in Washington, the story that has been repeated over the years is that the quarterback put on quite a show. Coach Ray Flaherty was not pleased that his new player was not in camp earlier, and he made that clear when Baugh arrived in Washington. "Well, it's about time that fellow arrived," Flaherty said. "If he's going to play football for us, he'd better show up in a hurry or there won't be any place for him." When Baugh took the field, Flaherty asked sarcastically, "Do you want to participate?" To which Baugh replied, "Sure do. I'm in shape for most anything. I got two [college] All-Star Games under my belt already, which is more than you fellas. I'm ready to work. You don't have to worry about me."

That was clear after Baugh put on a nearly perfect exhibition of pass completions in front of about 3,000 fans that day. As the story goes, after practice Baugh went into Coach Flaherty's office to go over some plays. Flaherty drew an X on the blackboard and pointed to it as he told Baugh, "When the receiver reaches here, you hit him in the eye with the ball."

Baugh asked, "Which eye?"

Baugh would go on to become an NFL legend and a symbol of the rugged old Texas cowboy, so much so that Robert Duvall, after visiting Baugh at his ranch in Texas, used some of the old quarterback's style and personality to develop his legendary character Augustus McCrae for the miniseries *Lonesome Dove*.

Baugh was down home, but his story was Hollywood, and that was right up Marshall's alley. Marshall was a showman, and Baugh was a show, someone he could appreciate. Marshall traveled in show business circles, in large part because of his marriage to singer Corrine Griffith, who, in her own way, had her share of influence on the Redskins. She is credited with writing the lyrics for the famous Redskins' fight song "Hail to the Redskins" and setting the stage for the Redskins Marching Band. In her book *My Life with the Redskins*, Griffith said she got a call during the summer of 1937 from Barnee Breskin, the leader of the Shoreham Hotel orchestra. Breskin said that since the Redskins were going to be in Washington, he thought they should have a song. He had written one he called "Hail to the Redskins" and played the music for her. Impressed, she decided to write the lyrics.

Washington sports fans were ready to hail their team. The Redskins drew nearly 25,000 fans at Griffith Stadium for their first game, which was against the New York Giants. Baugh marched the team down the field the first time they had the ball, completing passes to Ernie Pinkett and Charley Malone and running the ball to set up a Riley Smith field goal, which put the Redskins on top 3–0. The Giants tied the game in the third quarter, but Smith gave Washington a 6–3 lead with another field goal. Then the Riley Smith show closed when he intercepted a Giants pass at the Washington 40-yard line and went 60 yards to score the clinching touchdown and a 13–3 victory. The game got a solid review from sportswriter Bill Dismer Jr. in the *Washington Evening Star*: "As for the near 25,000 crowd, methinks the patrons were more than satisfied with professional football's debut and believe that the pros, like the talkies, are here to stay."

Turk Edwards, who played in front of the apathy in Boston, welcomed all the attention they received in Washington. "We just can't get over it," Edwards told reporters. "The fans in Washington have been wonderful to us, and we'd like to let them know that every one of us appreciates their treatment from the bottom of his heart."

The Redskins compiled a 7-3 record and captured the hearts of Washington fans as they went into the final game of the season against the division-leading Giants in New York. It was a particularly important homecoming for Coach Flaherty, who played for the Giants in 1928 and again from 1931 to 1935, during which he became a standout receiver. It was an emotional game for both sides, particularly when Giants coach Steve Owen, after being asked by reporters to name an all-NFL team, did not select one Redskin.

A win over the Giants would put Washington in the NFL championship game for the second straight year. Nearly 12,000 fans boarded trains on that December 5 Sunday morning to travel to New York, and Marshall brought his band with him—about 150 members. They, along with Marshall, led the fans in an impromptu parade as they got off the trains in New York. "At the head of a 150-piece band and twelve thousand fans, George Marshall slipped unobtrusively into town," one newspaper report said of the Redskins' arrival that day.

They left triumphant. Washington opened up the game with a 14–0 lead in the first quarter on two scoring runs by Cliff Battles and made it 21–0 before the first half was over on a run by Max Krause. The Giants began to mount a third-quarter comeback on an interception return by Ward Cuff and another score by Tuffy Leemans, cutting the Redskins' lead to 21–14. But Baugh found Ed Justice on a 48-yard touchdown pass to open up the lead to 28–14, and then Washington added 21 unanswered points in the fourth quarter for a 49–14 win. Battles had rushed for 170 yards, and Baugh completed 11 of 15 passes for 1 touchdown pass. The delirious Redskins fans and the players rode the victory trains back to Washington, where more than 5,000 fans were waiting at Union Station to greet them. Marshall wanted to lead a parade with his band up Pennsylvania Avenue after getting off the train, but Washington police wouldn't allow him to do so without a permit. The Redskins owner still tried to muster an impromptu parade, but the police showed up again and arrested the band's drum major. Marshall went to the police station to bail him out.

Fan celebrations became part of the Redskins' legacy, but they became more of a pregame tradition than a postgame ritual. Tailgating takes place in every NFL city in America, but it really took hold in Washington, the most southern city in the league at the time. Football tailgating began as a southern tradition at college games.

More than 3,000 Washington fans celebrated not from the back of their cars, but on the Chicago-bound train to watch their team play in the NFL title game against the Bears and the man who brought Marshall into the NFL: George "Papa Bear" Halas.

Led by the legendary runner Bronco Nagurski, the Bears were more physically imposing than the Redskins. Nagurski was one of the most feared players in the league, averaging 4.4 yards per carry over his NFL career and spending his off seasons as a professional wrestler. The wily Bears coach did not fall into the same trap that Owen did in New York. When writers asked Halas which Redskins would be on his All-Pro team, the Bears coach named a Redskin to every position and said, "Please see that these selections get into the paper before Sunday."

A frigid day in Chicago kept the crowd down to about 15,000, but maybe 20 percent of them were hardy Redskins fans who made the trip from Washington. It was a hard day to move the ball offensively, given the Bears defense and the weather conditions (both teams wore sneakers because of the footing on the frozen Wrigley Field, an irony that would become apparent eight years later for Redskins fans). After the score was tied at 7–7 in the first quarter, Baugh was intercepted, and the Bears capitalized on the miscue to take a 14–7 lead on a 39-yard touchdown pass from Chicago quarterback Bernie Masterson to end Jack Manders. Things got even worse when Baugh twisted his knee and sat out much of the second quarter, as neither team scored, with the Bears carrying their 14–7 lead into the locker room at halftime.

The tough Texan quarterback, though, came out warmed up in the second half, and on one leg turned in the sort of performance that had made him one of the biggest stars in his new Washington home and an NFL legend. On the first play he ran from scrimmage in the third quarter, Baugh tied the game with a 55-yard touchdown pass to Wayne Milner. Chicago came back with another scoring pass from Masterson to Manders to take the lead again, 21–14, but Baugh was destined to play the hero role on this cold December day and quickly connected a 78-yard touchdown pass to Milner to tie the game at 21–21. And before the third quarter ended, Baugh gave the Redskins the lead by hooking up with Ed Justice on a 35-yard touchdown pass. As the fourth quarter began, the Redskins led 28–21 and were on the verge of winning the NFL championship in their first season in the nation's capital. Now it was up to the Redskins defense, and they came through by holding the Bears scoreless in those final fifteen minutes and, with a minute remaining, stopping the Bears from tying the game when Riley Smith stepped in front of a wide-open Ed Manske to intercept Masterson's pass and seal the win and the championship—as well as the legend of Sammy Baugh, who, on one leg, threw 3 touchdown passes and completed 17 of 34 passes for 352 yards, 4 more yards than the entire Bears offense managed.

There was a raucous scene on the field before the end of the game, though, when some Bears players slid on the field into the Redskins' bench. A brawl broke out, and, according to the account in Griffith's book, Marshall jumped out of the stands and into the fray. He got into a shouting match with Halas on the field, in the middle of a melee between Bears and Redskins players. But when the final gun sounded to end the game and anoint the Redskins as the new NFL champions, Marshall had very little to be upset about.

The year before, there was so little interest in George Marshall's professional football team in their Boston home that they had to go out of town to play in the NFL title game, which they lost. This year, after winning the NFL championship, they were the biggest thing in one of the most important cities in the world. Marshall didn't bask in the glory of victory too long to abandon his thrifty ways, however. Even though his team drew a total of 120,000 fans in Washington for the season, compared to 57,000 the year before in Boston, Marshall did not pay for his players to return to Washington for a victory celebration. Instead, the players went to their various homes.

Still, Coach Flaherty, while talking to reporters, went out of his way to praise the support of Washington fans they had received throughout the season. "It's not merely the contrast between Washington and Boston fans," he said. "It's the fact that the sentiment in Washington is a thing apart, something which couldn't have been imagined. Believe you me, this has been the happiest football season of my life. Even if we had lost yesterday, the memory of those Washington fans would have been sufficient to cheer me through the next nine months until we return."

The Redskins did not return to the championship game until 1940. They were expected to be the NFL champs in 1938, but they lost Cliff Battles, the league rushing leader in 1937, and finished the year with a 6-3-2 record. The club did, however, add two premium talents in the draft that year: running back Andy Farkas, from the University of Detroit, and quarterback Frank Filchock, from Indiana.

They came close in 1939, finishing with an 8-2-1 record, and for the third straight season, the road to the NFL championship for the Redskins went through New York and the Giants. More than 12,000 Washington fans made the trip to the Polo Grounds for a game that would live in Redskins lore. The Giants managed 3 field goals to lead 9-0 going into the fourth quarter when Washington climbed back into the game with a touchdown pass to Bob Masterson to close the gap to 9-7. With time running out, the Redskins moved the ball down to the Giants' 15-yard line—a seemingly easy field goal for Bo Russell and a Redskins win. It appeared that way to the Redskins and many others in the stadium when Russell kicked the ball. But referee Bill Halloran called the kick wide right, which sparked such an outcry from the Redskins that Marshall told reporters after the game that Halloran would never work an NFL game again—and he never did. A crowd of more than 8,000 Redskins fans greeted the team at Union Station after the loss to show both their support and anger, chanting, "We was robbed."

Still, Redskins fans had been treated to championship-level play ever since the team arrived in town in 1937, and despite falling short three straight years following that 1937 NFL title, interest in the team was higher than ever going into the 1940 season. The Redskins did nothing to dispel those hopes from opening day, when they defeated Brooklyn 24–17 at Griffith Stadium before a crowd of nearly 33,000. They reeled off seven straight wins before losing a close one, 16–14, to Brooklyn at Ebbets Field. They came back to beat their hated rivals, the Bears, at home by a score of 7–3, thanks to a goal-line stand by the Redskins defense at the end of a bitterly fought game that carried over into the newspapers the next day, as Marshall, full of himself after his win over Halas, gloated to reporters about the win. "The Bears are a team that folds under pressure against a good team," he said. "They are a team that must win by a big score. Don't ask me why they lose the close games, except that they do. If I were to guess why, it would probably be that there is not too much harmony on that team. Too many stars, and stars are inclined to beef at one another when the going gets tough."

The going was about to get tough for the Redskins, with Marshall sharing the blame for his postgame comments. In the next game, Washington lost to the Giants in New York, 21–7, but they clinched the Eastern Division title the following week with a 13–6 win at home over Philadelphia. This win set up a rematch of the game between the Bears and the Redskins, as Washington, with its record of 9-2, was given home-field advantage. By the time the game was over, the Redskins would have certainly preferred that this spectacle had taken place well out of the view of their fans. Chicago scored in the first minute of the game on a 68-yard run by Bill Osmanski, and it appeared that it would be a tightly played game when Washington nearly scored on the following possession. Max Krause ran back the Chicago kickoff 56 yards to the Bears' 40-yard line, and several plays later Baugh nearly connected with a touchdown pass to Charlie Malone, but the ball bounced off Malone's chest. It turns out that it was perhaps the most irrelevant drop of a touchdown pass in NFL history.

In 1940, the he Bears introduced a new wrinkle in the NFL: the T-formation, where the quarterback lines up directly behind the center, and the running backs are 4 or 5 yards behind the quarterback. Before the T-formation, offenses were generally limited to the single wing, invented by Glenn "Pop" Warner at Carlisle in 1912. The tailback took most of the snaps from the center and was a triple threat to run, pass, or kick. This formation was based on power because of the unbalanced line. There were double-team blocks and pulling blockers. The quarterback, also known as the blocking back, could line up behind either guard, or between them, or sometimes between the strong-side guard and the tackle. There was very little passing under the single wing.

Clark Shaughnessy, considered one of the offensive geniuses of college football, began working as a consultant for the Chicago Bears in 1939 and made some revolutionary changes to the T-formation, which was new to the NFL at the time. He introduced the hand-to-hand snap from center to quarterback. Previously, the quarterback stood a half-yard to a yard behind the center, and the snap was a short toss of the ball. The hand-to-hand snap speeded up the action, because the quarterback didn't have to wait to make sure he had control of the ball. Now he took the ball, came away from the center, and began running the offense more quickly. He also moved the offensive linemen away by a yard or so, which forced the defensive line to open up holes that the speeded-up offense could take advantage of with the running back hitting the hole at full speed.

This offense, fueled by Marshall's comments after the previous game with the Bears, went on a rampage. They scored 21 points in the first thirteen minutes of the game and took a 28–0 lead into the locker room at halftime. After the defense ran back 2 Redskins passes for touchdowns in the third quarter, Chicago led 48–0 going into the fourth quarter and then made Washington pay for every word Marshall had said about the Bears, scoring 25 points in the fourth quarter—11 touchdowns in a 73–0 record defeat. It was such a bizarre game that the teams ran out of balls, which kept going into the stands for the extra points, so they had to use practice balls near the end of the game. This is one noteworthy fact from that game: the head referee was Irv Kupcinet, better known in later years as "Kup," the famous Chicago newspaper columnist. Marshall's criticisms may not have been the deciding factor in a 73–0 game, but they were certainly a motivating factor.

Sammy Baugh   "There was a lot of stuff in the newspapers that Mr. Marshall had put in there about the Bears. I think any team would have beaten us that day. The team was mad at Mr. Marshall because he said some awful things about the Bears."

The next day the two NFL owners met, and there was tension in the room between Marshall and Halas. But Marshall reportedly walked up to Halas, put his arm around his old friend, and said jokingly, "George, you misunderstood me. I said the score would be 7–3, not 73." Regardless, the beating appeared to have left a hangover the following season, as the Redskins had their worst season under Flaherty, going 6-5. After losing the opener at home to the Giants before 35,000 by 17–10, the Redskins reeled off five straight victories. But injuries to backs Dick Todd and Wilbur Moore hurt the offense, and Washington lost its next four games before salvaging a winning season with a 20–14 season finale victory over Philadelphia at Griffith Stadium. The win, though, was overshadowed by events taking place at Pearl Harbor, when, on this day, December 7, 1941, during the Redskins game, military and government leaders began leaving the stadium after receiving word that the United States had been attacked by the Japanese.

It had been four years since the Redskins won an NFL championship, and while Washington fans had been treated to winning football since then, there was disappointment because of the perception that with the talent this team had during that time, they should have had more to show for it—more of a legacy. In 1942, the Redskins would put the finishing touches on that legacy.

Washington opened at home with a 28–14 win over Pittsburgh before 25,000 fans, but lost the following week at Griffith Stadium to the Giants by 14–7. It would be the last time Redskins fans or anyone else would see this team lose the rest of the season. After just getting by Philadelphia 14–10, Washington beat the Cleveland Rams 33–14 and went on to run the table, scoring 227 points and holding their opponents to 102 points, with 2 shutouts and just 13 points allowed in the final four wins of the season against the Chicago Cardinals, the Giants, Brooklyn, and Detroit. The Redskins would be in the NFL title game for the third time in six years, and playing the same team for the third time: the Bears, the team that had humiliated Washington in the championship game two years before. And Chicago, favored to win, appeared to have just as powerful a team as in 1940, with a perfect 11–0 mark and an offense that had put 376 points on the board, led by their own star quarterback, Sid Luckman.

With more than 36,000 fans at Griffith Stadium and the game being broadcast to a record 178 radio stations, it looked as if the Redskins would be overwhelmed early on, when Dick Todd fumbled the ball and Bears tackle Lee Artoe scooped it up and ran 50 yards to put Chicago on top 6–0 early in the second quarter. It was an unusual play that turned things around for the Redskins. Baugh, deep in his own territory, took the Bears defense by surprise when he quick-kicked a ball that wound up going down to the Bears' 15-yard line. Not long after that, Wilbur Moore intercepted a Luckman pass, and Baugh converted it into a touchdown when he hit Moore with a 39-yard touchdown pass, and, with the extra point, the Redskins took a 7–6 lead into the locker room at halftime. The Redskins would score again in the third quarter on a 1-yard plunge across the goal line by Andy Farkas, but it was the Washington defense that carried the day, making that 14–6 lead stand up against the powerful Chicago offense and delivering the Redskins their second NFL championship. It was a stunning upset, and the revenge for the 73–0 defeat at the hands of the Bears in 1940 was not lost on sports columnists.

New York Times **columnist Arthur Daley**   "By way of supplying a final madhouse touch to a football season that was noted for its lunacies and upsets, the Redskins soundly trounced the supposedly invincible Bears before an incredulous and deliriously happy gathering of 36,036 spectators in Griffith Stadium today to win the world professional championship. This was a team that was so much an underdog that the gamblers stopped giving 7–1 odds and handed out as much as 22 points. This also was largely the team that had been beaten 73–0 in the playoff two years ago. Yet it cracked into the mighty Bears with disregard of the Chicagoans' reputation and handled them as easily as if the Monsters were only P.S. 9."

It was a bittersweet win. Baugh recalled the quick-kick—where the offense lines up in a formation as if they are going to run an offensive play, but the player taking the snap surprises the defense by punting the ball—that turned the game for Washington, but he also remembered it was the last game he would play for Coach Flaherty, who left the team to join the U.S. Navy and serve in the war.

Sammy Baugh   "That kick turned out to be a big play. When I quick-kicked, I had the wind to my back, and that's why I did it. If the quarter had run out and we had to punt, we would have had to do it against the wind. . . . Ray Flaherty was one of the better coaches I ever played for. Everybody respected him as a coach."

A local favorite would replace Flaherty in the 1943 season: Arthur "Dutch" Bergman, a former coach at Catholic University in Washington who had been a scout for the Redskins in 1942. He picked up where Flaherty left off, with a 27–0 debut win over Brooklyn before 35,450 at Griffith Stadium, and the team went unbeaten in its first seven games, with a tie against the Philadelphia-Pittsburgh team that was combined during 1943. The Redskins lost their final three games of the regular season, however, including two straight season finale defeats by the Giants.

In between those two losses to the Giants was a blow that could have been far more devastating than a defeat on the field. On December 8, 1943, the front page of the *Washington News-Herald* had the banner headline PROBE REPORTS OF PRO FOOTBALL GAMBLING. The story that followed reported that the league was investigating rumors that players were closely associated with known gamblers and that a number of Redskins were part of the investigation after the Redskins' 27–14 loss to the "Steagles," the Philadelphia-Pittsburgh team.

"Reports that a betting coup had been effected, headed by one of Washington's three biggest gamblers, spread through the ranks of the underworld in New York, Chicago, Philadelphia and other major cities from coast to coast, following the second Washington-Phil-Pitt Steagle game," the newspaper report said. "All betting on National Professional League football games now has been curtailed and under no circumstances will bookmakers accept a bet. After the [November 21] game with the Bears and the second contest a week later with the Steagles, one Washington gambler [later revealed to be convicted bookmaker Pete Gianaris] is reported to have won over $150,000. The Times-Herald has learned that Owner Marshall's appeal to Major [Edward] Kelly [superintendent of Washington police] that he investigate was based not entirely upon suspicion of gambling, but that Marshall told Kelly he suspected some of his players of visiting night clubs and other places in the city where they should not be."

Accompanied by nearly the entire team, Marshall stormed the *News-Herald* offices and demanded that the editors provide proof of the allegations. Nothing ever emerged from the probe, and Washington, with its 6-3-1 record, turned its attention to a playoff for the Eastern Division title and a third straight game against the Giants. This time, playing at the Polo Grounds, Washington finally defeated the Giants and did so soundly by the score of 28–0, led by 3 touchdowns by Andy Farkas.

Again, they would face the Chicago Bears for the fourth time in the NFL title game, and Chicago evened it up with a 41–21 win over the Redskins in Chicago. Baugh missed most of the game when he was kicked in the head early on while trying to make a tackle. He had completed 8 passes in 12 attempts for 123 yards and 2 touchdowns during his limited time, and it might have been one heck of an offensive duel between Baugh and Luckman, who completed 15 of 26 passes for 286 yards and a record-setting 5 touchdown passes. After all, Baugh had enjoyed one of his best seasons that year, having thrown 23 touchdowns with 1,754 yards passing, plus leading the league on defense in interceptions, with 11, and leading the league in punting as well, with a 45.9-yard average.

Baugh and the Redskins had seemingly not missed a beat with the departure of Flaherty and the arrival of Dutch Bergman. But the Dutchman wanted out of coaching, so he took a job in broadcasting, leaving Marshall to find his third coach in three years. He selected Doug DeGroot, the head football coach at Rochester University.

DeGroot had his share of problems during the 1944 season as he tried to install the T-formation, with Baugh missing big chunks of playing time because he had to tend his cattle ranch, as the government was making heavy demands for beef during the war. Frank Filchock wound up with the majority of the playing time in 1944, posting a 6-3-1 record.

With the war ending, Baugh was able to devote his full attention to football in 1945, and he thrived under the T-formation once he mastered it, completing a record 70.3 percent of his passes and putting together an 8-2 record and the Redskins' fifth trip to the NFL title game. They traveled to Cleveland to play the Rams on December 16, 1945. It turned out to be more than a title game—it turned out to be the end of an era in Washington Redskins history.

The cold wind off Lake Erie blew into Municipal Stadium, making the conditions nearly impossible to play, with temperatures reportedly 8 degrees below zero. The field was frozen and slick, which made it difficult for the players to run. The Redskins were prepared for those conditions, having brought sneakers to use in case the footing was treacherous. The Rams, even though it was their home field, did not have any sneakers to use. So Rams coach Adam Walsh requested of DeGroot that Washington not use their sneakers, and to the surprise of everyone, including Walsh, DeGroot agreed. In return, DeGroot should have asked that Walsh take down the goalposts.

In the first quarter, the Redskins were down in their own end zone when Baugh, who had thrown 11 touchdown passes that season for 1,689 yards, went back to pass to Milner, but as he threw the ball, it bounced off one of the uprights. That was scored a safety for Cleveland, which now led 2–0. On a cold day like that one, every point would count. The weather only made things worse when Baugh hurt his ribs and had to leave the game later in the first quarter. His replacement, Frank Filchock, hit Steve Bagarus for a 38-yard touchdown pass in the second quarter, putting the Redskins ahead 7–2.

Cleveland came back near the end of the second quarter when Rams quarterback Bob Waterfield connected with Jim Benton on a 37-yard touchdown pass. And again, the goalposts came into play, when Waterfield's extra point kick hit the goalpost bar, and it could have gone either way. It barely made it over for the extra point for a 9–7 Rams lead. When the teams came out for the second half, the Rams hit again on another score to take a 15–7 lead on a 44-yard touchdown pass from Waterfield to Jim Gillette. The Redskins had come out seemingly a beaten team when they emerged from the locker room for the second half, and, as it turned out, for good reason. The tale of the destruction of the franchise from that date is one of legend, starting with Marshall's halftime confrontation with DeGroot, because of his refusal to use the sneakers. The Redskins played the second half without a head coach, because Marshall fired DeGroot at halftime.

Center Al DeMao "The field was a sheet of ice because it was so cold and bitter that day in Cleveland. We came in at halftime, and Marshall came into the locker room and told Coach DeGroot, 'Okay, Doug, let's get out the sneakers.' Doug said very meekly, 'Mr. Marshall, we made a gentleman's agreement that we wouldn't use the sneakers.' He was, in essence, fired right then and there. Marshall said, 'This is no gentleman's game. That's the last decision you will ever make as coach of the Redskins.'"

After the Rams scored to take the 15–7 lead, Washington seemed energized again, moving the ball down the field near the end of the third quarter on a 70-yard scoring drive, when Filchock tossed an 8-yard touchdown pass to Bob Seymour on the fourth down to bring Washington to within one point, 15–14. That would be the final score, as the Redskins failed on two fourth-quarter field goal attempts by Joe Aquirre, and Washington lost its third NFL title game. Since the Redskins had been there so many times in their short history in Washington, Redskins fans figured there would be a next year. There wasn't—at least not for another thirty-seven years.

2

Futility

After the Redskins moved to Washington, most of the buttons that the volatile George Marshall pushed worked, starting with signing Sammy Baugh. Even after losing such a treasured coach as Ray Flaherty, Marshall still managed to get back to the NFL championship game with two different coaches, even though his team lost both times. So when he turned over the reins of the club to a longtime Redskins favorite, legendary tackle Turk Edwards, it seemed like a natural fit and that the winning ways would continue. Edwards led the Redskins defense from the birth of the team in Boston in 1932 until he retired in 1940. His play during the early days of the league was recognized in 1969 when he was inducted into the Pro Football Hall of Fame.

He was not inducted as a coach, however. "Turk was a hell of a football player and a good line coach, but he never did make a good head coach," said center Al DeMao.

And if you weren't a good coach, working for Marshall would be tough. "Mr. Marshall was awfully tough on coaches," Baugh said. But Marshall was a little more patient with Edwards than he might have normally been, because Edwards was a franchise icon and Marshall was fond of him.

Part of the problem for Redskins coaches and Marshall was that deep down, the Redskins owner wanted to be the coach, like his friend and rival in Chicago, George Halas.

End Joe Tereshinski   "Turk was a great football player with a great
reputation, but he was probably too nice to be a head coach. Having
played with some of the guys on the team, it was hard for him to come
down on those guys. We had a good team, but we lost a lot of tough
games. . . . Mr. Marshall would have loved to have been the head
coach. I always firmly believed that his life would have been complete
if he could have coached the team for one season. He was always competing with George Halas, and it made Mr. Marshall jealous because
Halas would be on the field and Marshall would have to sit up in the
stands. He would call his general manager, Dick McCann, who sat
behind the Redskins bench, and tell him plays to give to the coach."

   Edwards was dealt a tough hand from the start because he lost two
key players: end Wayne Milner, who retired, and quarterback Frank
Filchock, who was traded to the New York Giants. One of his first
games was an exhibition contest against the team that had just beaten
Washington in the NFL title game: the Rams. This time, though, it
would not be in Cleveland. The Rams had moved during the off
season to Los Angeles and had a rematch of the NFL championship
game—a charity game to raise money for the Los Angeles Times Boys
Club. The game raised $96,711. The Redskins lost 14–6.
   Edwards's squad started out the regular season with a 14–14 tie
before a hometown crowd of 33,620, and the outcome of that game
would prove to be a prediction of the rest of the 1946 season—a tie, as
Washington finished with a 5-5-1 record. The final game of the year
was particularly embarrassing, a 31–0 beating by the Giants. And
1947 was even worse, a 4–8 mark. There were some bright spots for
Washington fans, though. They got to see all four wins at home. And
they were introduced to the franchise's newest star, an end named
Hugh "Bones" Taylor, one of thirteen rookies who joined the 1947
team. "Taylor had a long stride," DeMao said. "After he caught the
ball, you could see him open up and spread the distance between him
and the defender, running away from them. He was a good receiver."
   Tereshinski, who played end on the same squad with Taylor,
remembered how Taylor came to the Redskins. "Turk Edwards was
looking through a football guide," Tereshinski said. "At the time, they
had a football digest for the college players coming up, and he read
about Bones Taylor. He never saw him play, but he drafted him based
on what he read. . . . Bones was frail, about 6-foot-4 and 175 pounds.

He was a vegetarian and not much of a blocker. One thing I could do very well was block."

Tereshinski and others blocked very well on one particular day— "Sammy Baugh Day" at Griffith Stadium on November 23, 1947, which turned out to be a memorable event for what happened both on and off the field. What happened on the field was that Baugh had one of his finest days as a Redskin, completing 25 of 33 passes for 355 yards and 6 touchdowns, in a 45–21 upset win over the Chicago Cardinals, a team that had a record of 7-1 going into the game, with the league's top defense, compared to the 2-6 Redskins.

Quarterback Sammy Baugh "In 1947, we didn't have what I would call one of our better teams. But the team got together and they decided that on that day, I wasn't going to get my pants dirty at all. I wasn't even going to get knocked around. That was the easiest game I ever had. The Cardinals had the number-one team in the league. We weren't supposed to beat them, but we did. Our team really played a great game. I was proud of them."

The fans were proud of Baugh and what he meant to Washington, and Marshall held a ceremony that day to honor Baugh, including presenting him with a new car, a station wagon with the words "Slinging Sam—the Redskin Man" on the car. Baugh liked it so much he drove it that night.

Sammy Baugh "My sister and her husband were down from Philadelphia to see me that day, and after the game I was going to take them home. On the way up there, I remembered that I was supposed to go to some school back in Washington the next morning. I had intended to spend the night up there and then come back later. But I had this appearance the next morning, so I told them that I couldn't spend the night. I had to turn around and go back to Washington. At that time of the night there were hardly any cars on the highway. I saw this car coming toward me. It was coming across the middle of the road a little too much, I thought. I slowed down a little bit. I thought he would straighten the car out. But he kept coming toward me, so I moved over to the right a little bit. He kept coming toward me, so I had to do something. I went on the gravel. I thought he was going to hit me head on. When I hit that gravel, I slid right into a concrete bridge. It destroyed one side of the car. That guy didn't stop. He just kept going."

Another player also had his own day of sorts that year—Al DeMao—though it happened in Pittsburgh, when the Redskins were coming in to play the Steelers. The Washington center, who had played college football at Duquesne, was getting to start against the Steelers and made the most of it by having a strong game. He had a special conversation with Marshall the day after that Pittsburgh game.

Center Al DeMao   "The Monday after the game, I went into the team offices to get my money. They put it in bank envelopes every Monday, in cash. Marshall called me into his office and sat me down. He said, 'You played all right since you've been here, but yesterday you played great.' I told him that was the first time I started for the Redskins and that I was a real competitor. That gave me more incentive to play. And the fans gave me a watch up there. It was like DeMao Day. Marshall said, 'Was it that watch they gave you that made you play so well? Should I give you a watch every game? I'll give you a watch every game if you play like that.' I started every ball game after that."

The young team seemed to grow in 1948, improving to a 7-5 record, including a season finale 28–21 victory over their hated rivals, the Giants. But Marshall made a fateful personnel decision that would haunt the club for years. He had two young quarterbacks signed in camp that season, Harry Gilmer and Charley Connerly. Marshall decided he could not keep both, so he sold Connerly's rights to the rival New York Giants and kept Gilmer, whose career was plagued by injuries and would never reach its potential. Meanwhile, Connerly would be the star quarterback for the Giants for the next fourteen seasons.

Marshall had seen enough of Edwards as coach. He didn't fire him, because he was too fond of him and his place in Redskins history. So he moved him into the front office and sought to hire another coach he had his eye on. If Marshall had been successful, perhaps the fortunes of the Redskins and college football would have changed. Marshall had gotten to know Paul "Bear" Bryant when he was on the coaching staff at the University of Maryland. Bryant later became a successful head coach at Kentucky. Marshall offered him the Redskins job in 1949. But the story goes that the school would not let Bryant out of his contact, so the opportunity was missed. Bryant, of course, went on to become a college coaching legend at the University of Alabama, eventually setting the record for the most coaching victories, while the Redskins went on to become legendary losers—picking up right where Edwards left off with Marshall's choice to coach Washington: John Whelchel, a well-known retired admiral who had been the coach at the U.S. Naval Academy in nearby Annapolis. Whelchel was both a hard case and a strict disciplinarian who clashed with Marshall and lasted just seven games; he was fired after going 3-3-1. "Marshall was always looking for a big name, so he got Admiral Whelchel out of the navy," DeMao said. "But the admiral had been out of football for a while, and the game had changed a lot." Herman Ball, an assistant coach and scout, took over for the rest of the 1949 season and won just one game; the Redskins finished with a 4-7-1 mark.

Losing and Marshall's volatile nature was a bad mixture, and his frustration sometimes resulted in confrontations with players, such as the one Marshall had with linebacker Pete Stout following a loss to the Chicago Cardinals in 1950.

Joe Tereshinski   "The Cardinals had one particularly good pass receiver, and we had a lot of our defensive backs out with injuries. So they asked Pete Stout, who was a linebacker, to cover this end, even though he didn't have the speed to keep up. Stout had to cover him on some plays, and it was a mismatch. The guy caught 3 touchdowns in the first half. We were in the locker room at halftime, eating oranges, and everyone was downcast. Mr. Marshall came in, wearing his fur coat, and he was fuming. He got on all of us, and he really got on Pete Stout. He started cussing Stout out, and Pete, who was already mad at himself, got so furious that he jumped up and grabbed Mr. Marshall by the throat. Pete said, 'Mr. Marshall, I am playing out of position and doing the best that I can to cover this man. We've got guys hurt, and I was asked to play that position, and I am doing it to the best of my ability. My father never talked to me that way, and I won't let you.' He finally released Mr. Marshall, who by that point was turning red. Mr. Marshall jumped up on a foot locker in front of him and yelled to the team, 'Now that's the kind of fight I want to see from you fellows. Go out there and give me that kind of spirit and fight and I will be proud of you.'"

. . .

They didn't have much fight, though; in 1950–the worst Redskins season in fifteen years–they posted a 3-9 mark, with just one of those victories at home, even with the acquisition of running back Bill Dudley, who came to Washington in the twilight of his career and who would eventually be voted into the Hall of Fame. The 5-foot-10, 182-pound halfback ran, passed, punted, and placekicked. Nicknamed "Bullet Bill" even though he was never considered to be fast, Dudley was a first-round draft pick of the Pittsburgh Steelers in 1942. He demonstrated from the start that his relatively small size and lack of blazing speed wasn't a detriment. In the first game of his pro career, he ran for a 55-yard touchdown, and in his second game he scored on a kickoff return. He finished his rookie season as the league's leading rusher, with 696 yards, and earned all-league honors. His career was interrupted in 1943 and 1944, when he served with the U.S. Army Air Corps during World War II. He returned to the Steelers in 1945, and in 1946 he led the league in rushing, punt returns, interceptions, and lateral passes attempted, and was named the NFL's Most Valuable Player that year. He was traded to Detroit for the 1947 season and then came to Washington in 1950.

This disappointing season was a historic one, though, because it would be the first time an NFL team would broadcast their schedule of games on television. Marshall the showman saw the power of television and made a deal with American Oil to sponsor the telecasts. He also saw the value of sharing that television revenue and how it would benefit all the clubs, which proved to be the foundation for the success of the NFL for many years to come.

The season had some more excitement before it even began, because Redskins fans were looking forward to the sight of the team's newest star: the rookie running back from North Carolina, Charley "Choo-Choo" Justice, who, in four seasons at the school scored 64 touchdowns running and passing and set a school total-offense record of 4,883 yards that lasted until 1994. He finished second in the voting for the Heisman Trophy, which is given to the nation's best college football player, in 1948 and 1949. North Carolina went to the Sugar Bowl twice and to the Cotton Bowl during the Justice era. The Tar Heels lost all three games, going 32-9-2 while Justice played in Chapel Hill. His fame went beyond the football field, as his popularity inspired the song "All the Way, Choo Choo," which was recorded by bandleader Benny Goodman in 1949. The highlight of Justice's career may have come in the College All-Star Game of 1950 at Chicago's Soldier Field. The All-Stars walloped the Philadelphia Eagles, led by Steve Van Buren, 17–7. Justice, who was named the Most Valuable Player of the game, gained 133 yards individually, or 48 more than the Eagles posted as a team. He set up a touchdown on a 60-yard pass from one of his future teammates, quarterback Eddie LeBaron.

Marshall went after the popular running back because the Redskins had a strong following in North Carolina and throughout the South. The Redskins were the only NFL team south of the Mason-Dixon Line, and the owner milked those southern connections for all they were worth, often drafting less talented players just because they came from southern schools. It was this mentality of pleasing his southern audience that would hold back the franchise for many years to come. Choo-Choo Justice's tenure was cursed from the start, and he never fulfilled the expectations for him. He held out in a contract dispute and didn't report to the team until after the fifth game of the season. "Choo-Choo Justice was his own worst enemy," DeMao said. "He held out the first year, and the second year, after running for about 200 yards in the first half of an exhibition game, he broke his wrist on the last play of the half and never did recover from that. He was never the same player." Justice played in 1950 and again from 1952 to 1954 for Washington. He is widely believed to be the role model for Frank Deford's fictional novel about college football, *Everybody's All-American*, which was made into a feature film.

Marshall would embrace the notion that the Redskins were a regional southern team with each passing that year the District of Columbia went through changes. In 1950, the district reached its highest population—802,178, ranking it as the ninth largest city in the United States. But as the years passed, the population began declining, as people moved to the suburbs in Prince George's and Montgomery counties in neighboring Maryland, and across the Potomac River in Arlington and Fairfax counties. Yet many of these people found jobs in the district, as the federal government grew during the prosperity of the post–World War II era, and Washington was known as a federal city.

There was a connection for the city to the south as time went on but not the one Marshall wanted. More black Americans began leaving the South, and those in Virginia and North and South Carolina came to Washington, seeking to leave rural poverty behind and find a better life in cities such as Washington.

They would not be welcome at Redskins games, at least not by Marshall. After all, this was a team where the words "fight for Old Dixie" were lyrics in its team song. The Redskins did not employ any blacks during the twenty-four years they played at Griffith Stadium.

Marshall worked hard to market the team wherever he could to find new fans, because it was stuck in a rut on the field. He stayed with Herman Ball to start the 1951 season, but after three straight losses—the final blow a 45–0 beating by Cleveland—Ball was fired and replaced by another former Redskins player and fan favorite, former running back Dick Todd. He finished out the season with a 5-4 record, thanks in large part to the running of Rob Goode, who set a franchise record by rushing for 951 yards. But Todd wasn't cut out to be a head coach. "Dick Todd was a good guy, but he thought everyone should be as good as he was, which is a problem when you coach," said guard Gene Pepper, who remembered the scene in the locker room after Todd's final game as Redskins coach, a 20–10 loss to Pittsburgh in the final game of the season.

Guard Gene Pepper   "Marshall was madder than hell after that game. It was a cold, rainy day, and you couldn't make a dent in the field with your cleats, it was so cold. Orv Tuttle was the line coach, and he tried to play all these mental games with us. Slug [Casimir] Witucki was playing on the line that day, and he got hurt with about two minutes left. Now, it was so cold that I couldn't feel my toes. Orv said, 'Get in there. Slug is hurt.' I said, 'Orv, I don't care if Slug is dying.' If I had gone in there, I could have broken my toes. I had no feeling in them. Orv said, 'You get in there or I'm going to fine you.' I said, 'You can fine me in the locker room if you want, but I'm not going in there.' So the game is over and we get into the locker room. I'm massaging my toes, trying to get the feeling back. Orv comes over to me, punches me in the shoulder, and threatens me, as if I was going to lose my job. 'I don't know where you're going to be next year, but I know where I'm going to be.' I said, 'Whatever you say, Orv.'

"About that time, Marshall comes into the locker room, and he's mad. He blew the doors off the hinges. He was pretty good with the adjectives, and he fired a volley at the coaches about losing the game. He was so mad, I'm surprised he didn't have a heart attack. Finally, he said, 'The whole goddamn bunch of you are fired!' I tugged on Orv's shoulder and said, 'Hey, Orv, I don't know where you're going to be next year, but I know where I'm going to be.' Marshall left, but came back in and yelled, 'And you've got twenty-four hours to get out of town.' So I said, 'Orv, the Marshall just gave you twenty-four hours to get out of town.' He was stunned. He thought he had a job with that organization for life. That's how stupid he was. I played there for five years under five different head coaches."

One of the head coaches that Pepper played for was an NFL legend, former Green Bay Packers great Earl "Curly" Lambeau, in 1952. Todd started the 1952 season, but he got into a nasty argument with Marshall because he refused to play Baugh in an exhibition game and reportedly resigned at halftime during the game, which the Redskins lost. Lambeau was sitting beside Marshall in the stands, and the Redskins owner reportedly offered the legendary coach the job right then and there.

Lambeau had founded the Green Bay Packers in 1919 and was the team's first playing star and coach. He was the first pass-minded coach in the NFL and led the Packers to championships in 1929, 1930, and 1931. After signing future Hall of Fame receiver Don Hutson in 1935, the Packers won three more titles. Lambeau resigned from the team following the 1949 season and later coached the Chicago Cardinals for two losing seasons in 1950 and 1951, going 8-17, before going to Washington. For many years his 229 career victories ranked second only to George Halas's. It seemed like a brilliant move. Lambeau had the sort of star power and leadership that attracted Marshall, but that was one of the complexities about the Washington owner. He liked powerful people, as long as they didn't interfere with his power. So it was inevitable that Lambeau, who also had a volatile personality, and Marshall would clash—unfortunately, just at the time when the franchise appeared to turn it around in his second season.

Center Harry Ulinski "Curly was quite a character. He used to walk around with his cigarette holder. He was very dapper, very meticulous about the way he looked. We used to laugh about that long-stemmed cigarette holder. That was unusual for a man to use. You would see women using something like that. It was hard to picture him as a football player in uniform for the early Packers. He wasn't that big. He looked like an executive. I don't know why he came to Washington. He was good publicity for Marshall, who needed a big-name coach. Marshall was feared by all of his coaches except Curly. They were from the same era, and Curly would not take any guff from him."

Ulinski had played for the Redskins before Lambeau arrived but left to play in Canada. Lambeau, though, convinced him to return to Washington after one season away from the NFL.

Harry Ulinski   "I was there in 1950 and 1951 and left because of Dick Todd. Todd was frustrated with the losing in 1951, and after one particular loss, he was picking apart the players. I played under Bear Bryant at Kentucky, and I could take a lot of guff because Bryant was a rough coach. But what Todd was doing, taking apart players in front of the team, hit me the wrong way. I told him to go someplace. It had built up in me. I heard all these comments he was making about players, and by the time he got to me, I exploded. Dick Todd was a great athlete, but as a coach he tried that college rah-rah stuff on a bunch of veterans, many of whom were in World War II, and they weren't going to take it. His comments were belittling. I played the rest of the season but left after that to play in Canada with a friend of mine. After playing for Ottawa for a year, I got a call from Curly Lambeau, asking if I would be interested in coming back. He said he watched me on some Redskins films and wanted me to come back."

Before that, in his first year with the Redskins, Lambeau had a minicrisis on his hands before the season even began: one of the earliest efforts by the players at organizing themselves into some sort of union. Marshall handled the crisis as only the Redskins owner could.

Al DeMao   "We had six exhibition games scheduled. We didn't get a cent for exhibition games then. Then Marshall threw in an extra exhibition game on us. So one day after lunch we had a players' meeting, and since we knew some of the other teams were giving their players $50 a game, we wanted that, too. We nominated Sammy Baugh, Bill Dudley, and me to meet with Mr. Marshall about this. Sam was the spokesman. He said, 'We're here as a committee.' That was all he got out of his mouth. Mr. Marshall hit the ceiling, saying he didn't recognize any organizations or unions. He walked out of the meeting.

[General manager] Dick McCann brought him back in. Sam went on, asking for any kind of money. We were agreeable to anything we could get out of him. But Mr. Marshall said no, and said he would meet with all the players before the afternoon practice. He got us all in a circle on the field before practice and told everyone the same thing he told us. He pointed to the gate and said, 'If you don't like it, there's the gate. Feel free to go.' I don't know what he would have done if we didn't go on with practice. But no one made a move to leave, and we started practicing, and we were back to where we had been."

There were benefits, though, to playing those exhibition games, particularly since the team often began by playing in Los Angeles as they headed east after breaking training camp at Occidental College. Movie stars could often be seen at the Los Angeles games, and the players noticed.

Gene Pepper   "Once we played the Rams in an exhibition game in Los Angeles. We beat them 17–10, but the big deal of the day was Marilyn Monroe, who was the halftime guest. So we didn't go into the locker room at halftime right away because we all wanted to see Marilyn Monroe. She came out wearing a big skirt like the one she wore in that movie, and she was twirling around in it. You couldn't tell from the stands, but we could see from where we were that she didn't have a stitch of clothes on under that skirt. On the field, you could see her bare ass when she spun around. That was the highlight of the game for us.

"After the game we were coming out of the locker room and walking up the ramp in the Coliseum. Bob Waterfield, the Rams quarterback was there, and Jane Russell was waiting for him. We were all talking about the game, and Jane was trying to get Bob's attention. He said to her, 'Oh Jane, be quiet a minute, would you please?' One of the players said, 'Did you hear what he said to her? He can't talk to her that way. That's Jane Russell.' And I said, 'No, that was his wife.'"

The stars, though, did not seem aligned with Lambeau's squad that season. Goode had left to serve in the army in Korea, Baugh broke his hand, and the team was led by a small (5-foot-9, 170-pound) but exciting rookie quarterback named Eddie LeBaron out of the College of the Pacific. LeBaron had been drafted in 1948 by Washington but had to finish a two-year commitment to the U.S. Marines before

he could report for football. It truly was a commitment—he was injured
during his tour of duty in Korea when a mortar shell exploded; before
he left Korea, he had earned the Bronze Star and two Purple Hearts.
While LeBaron was serving his country, his team went just 4-8 in
Lambeau's first season. They opened the next season with a 23–7 win
in Chicago over the Cardinals and followed that with an unsuccessful
homecoming for Lambeau, a 38–20 defeat at the hands of the Packers
in Green Bay. When Lambeau made his debut before the hometown
fans in Washington, it was also a failure—a 17–8 loss to the team they
had beat two games earlier, the Cardinals. After they beat Pittsburgh
on the road, 28–24, the Redskins lost their next six games in a row
before finally coming away with a 27–17 win over the Giants in New
York. Dick Alban, a rookie defensive back, remembered how hard-
nosed a coach Lambeau was:

Back Dick Alban   "The week before the Giants game, I got hurt
when we lost to Cleveland. I tackled a guy and jammed my neck. I
went to the hospital and they gave me some treatments. They hung
me in some kind of contraption by my neck, and I had to stay in that
all week. I got out of the hospital by the end of the week, and Curly
said, 'Dick, you come along with us to New York. You're not going to
play or anything, but it's good to have you with the team.' So I made
the trip with the team to New York. When we get to the visitor's locker
room, I notice my gear is hanging in the locker. Curly said, 'Dick,
you're not going to play today, but it's good for you to dress and be
with the team on the sidelines.' So I got my uniform on and went out
on the field. I tried to do some running, but I could hardly run at all.
My neck was still very stiff and jammed. I felt terrible. We had lines of
players who would go out and try to catch passes in warm-ups, and I
kept staying at the end of the line and never went out to field a ball. At
the time, the roster limit in the league was thirty-three players, but we
went up to New York with only about twenty-eight players, because of
various injuries. I was on the bench, and the guy who was playing in
place of me got knocked out in the second quarter. I got up and put
my helmet on to go in the game, and Curly said, 'No, Dick, stop; wait
a minute.' He turned around and looked up and down the bench,
turned back to me, and asked, 'How do you feel?' I went into the
game thinking to myself, 'I'm going to get killed.' I moved to tackle

some guy and we both went down. I got up and didn't hurt myself. I played the rest of the game and was okay."

In the season finale, Lambeau and the Redskins gave the home fans a 27–21 victory over Philadelphia. It was an emotional day for everyone at Griffith Stadium, because it was Sammy Baugh's last game and the end of an era.

Al DeMao   "Sammy would still have all the passing records in football, if he had the receivers they had today. Sam never had that luxury. We had outstanding players, but they had to play both ways. Bones Taylor was probably the best end Sammy had to throw to, but someone like Sonny Jurgensen had Charley Taylor, Bobby Mitchell, and Jerry Smith to throw to. If Sam had those kind of receivers, there's no telling what kind of records he would have set.

"Sammy was as cool as they come, but when he would come up behind me at center and put his hands under me to get the ball, his hands would be shaking. I don't think he was nervous. It was just a habit he picked up. I could feel his hands quivering.

"He could punt nearly as accurately as he could pass. I saw him put on a show once in a clinic for some high school coaches before we played an exhibition game in Denver. I'm snapping the ball back to him, and he put four punts right in the hands of four fellows lined up across the field, about 50 or 60 yards away. They were automatic, and those guys didn't have to move a step to catch the ball. He was known for his coffin-corner kicks."

Joe Tereshinski   "My locker was next to Sammy Baugh's for six years. He was a tremendous guy. The first time I saw him, I walked into Griffith Stadium when he was punting the ball down the field to Dick Todd. Dick was 50 yards away and never had to move to field these punts, not at all. I never saw such accuracy in a punter. Then he backed Dick up 5 yards and hit him again, and another 5 yards, and maybe Dick had to move a yard either way to catch the ball. On broken-pass plays in practice, when the routes weren't run correctly, Sam would punt the ball down to the players. He was a coach on the field. He would call pass patterns and tell receivers where to go, changing them right on the field."

. . .

Dick Alban   "I was a rookie in Sammy Baugh's last season in foot-ball. When we got back to Washington after training camp and after playing the exhibition games across the country on the way back from the West Coast, I didn't have any place to stay. I had one suitcase full of stuff, and that was it. Sammy said to me, 'Come stay with me until your wife gets here and you get an apartment.' Here he was, the biggest star in football, and I was a rookie defensive back that no one knew about, and he was willing to help me. We went to the Shoreham Hotel and went in the back entrance. I wondered why we didn't go in the front door. We walked up two flights of stairs, down the hall, and into a suite of rooms that was huge. There had to be seven or eight rooms in that suite. Outside, in the front of the building, there was a big sign that said 'Condemned.' The hotel was closed. But Sammy still stayed there. He was friends with the manager of the hotel. You wouldn't think that a veteran and a star like that would help a rookie. But that was Sammy."

The 1953 season, despite the departure of Baugh, seemed more promising, as the Redskins started with a 24–13 win in Chicago over the Cardinals. After tying the Eagles 21–21 in Philadelphia, the Red-skins won their home opener before 26,241 fans at Griffith Stadium, a hard-fought 13–9 victory over the rival New York Giants. Backup quarterback Jack Scarbath threw a 38-yard scoring pass to Bones Tay-lor to open up a 7–0 lead in the first quarter, and the Redskins defense held the Giants to 104 yards rushing, compared to 215 yards on the ground, led by Justice, who would have his best season for the Red-skins in 1953, averaging 5.4 yards per carry and rushing for 616 yards on 115 attempts. But after opening the first three games undefeated, the Redskins lost their next three games. They managed to salvage the season, however, by winning four of their final six games, finishing with a 6-5-1 record, their first winning campaign since 1948. The sea-son ended with some hope for the future. That hope didn't last long.

Washington began the 1954 season without two of its key players: LeBaron and defensive end Gene Brito, both of whom left for more money in the Canadian Football League. More important, the Red-skins started the season without the legendary coach who Marshall and Washington fans hoped would return the franchise to glory. Curly Lambeau never made it out of the exhibition season. He was fired by Marshall over a couple of bottles of beer.

Gene Pepper   "We had played an exhibition game in Sacramento, and it was really hot. We all lost a lot of water weight—some guys ten to fifteen pounds. The sweat had been running in our shoes. After the game we were in the Senator Hotel, and Bones Taylor came in with a brown bag under his arm, walked toward the elevator, and went up to his room. One of the coaches saw this and went to George Marshall, who didn't want us drinking, and told him. George went to Curly and said, 'Do you know these boys are drinking beer? What are you going to do about it?' Curly answered, 'George, it's no problem. We lost a lot of weight out there today. It was hot. Let them drink a beer.' But George raised hell and Curly wasn't about to take that. He was an equal to George—both of them were legends in the game. He didn't have to take a step back from Marshall. He did Marshall a favor by coming to Washington to coach. It got pretty nasty in the hotel lobby between George and Curly, and at one point Curly grabbed George and put him up against the wall and said, 'You can't talk to me like that, you son of a bitch! I don't have to take that from you. If these guys want to drink beer, they can drink beer.' I was watching the whole thing and I said to myself, 'Oh, shit, another new coach.' I knew Curly was gone. George hated drinking."

For those players who were not in the lobby when the argument occurred, such as Dick Alban, this was how they found out Curly Lambeau was not the Redskins coach anymore:

Dick Alban   "We had a lot of hope that things were turning around with Curly after the 1953 season. But we showed up for practice one day and the assistant coach was the head coach. He said Curly was gone, and we just went through practice."

Bill Dudley, who had left the Redskins to be the backfield coach at Yale in 1952, came back as a player-coach in Washington in 1953 for Lambeau's second season there. He believed the legendary coach was probably not as diligent a coach as he had been in Green Bay.

. . .

Running back Bill Dudley   "I think when people retire and then come back, like Curly did, they don't pay as much attention to the details as they did when they were winning the first time. For example, we had a big tackle on our team that year, and he was great as long as someone was on his tail, but if that didn't happen, he tended to loaf a lot. When that guy was pointed out by myself and some of the other coaches, Curly got a little miffed, because this guy had played for him at Green Bay."

Like so many Redskins players, Dudley had some difficult financial dealings with George Preston Marshall.

Bill Dudley   "When I went back to be a coach in 1953, Marshall said, 'Bill, why don't you play some?' I said, 'Mr. Marshall, if you want me to play, you're going to have to pay me more money.' I was getting $5,000 as an assistant coach, and I said I would need another $1,500 to play. He said, 'We will talk about it.' I said, 'You're the owner. If you don't think I deserve it, don't give it to me. If you think I deserve it, give it to me.' He said, 'I don't like it, but all right.' At the time, they used to hold back 25 percent of your check until the end of the season. I went in to pick up my check, and it was $1,500 short of what I expected. I went to see Mr. Marshall, and he told me to come into his office. His desk was set up high so he was always looking down on you. We talked about the season and he asked me, 'Are you getting ready to go home?' I said, 'Yes, sir, but I thought my check was a bit short.' I reminded him of our talk at the start of the season, and he asked me, 'Do you think you deserve it?' I said, 'If I didn't, I wouldn't be here.' So he told his secretary to give it to me. If I hadn't gone in there, I don't think he would have given it to me."

There were few dealings with Marshall that were not difficult, as witnessed by the six coaches Marshall went through since Ray Flaherty left after the 1943 season. Now, after firing Lambeau before the 1954 regular season began, he quickly had to hire one. He went after Joe Kuharich, who had replaced Lambeau in Chicago. A former player for the Cardinals, Kuharich went into coaching in 1947, after serving four years in the U.S. Navy, as the line coach for the University of San Francisco. He replaced Lambeau as the head coach for the Cardinals, but was let go after his team went 4-8 in 1952. He spent the 1953 season scouting for several clubs and was available when Marshall desperately needed a coach in Washington. His late arrival—and the defection of LeBaron and Brito to Canada—showed in the Redskins start of the season, losing their five games, and losing big—41–7 to San Francisco, 37–7 to Pittsburgh, 51–21 to the Giants, 49–21 to Philadelphia, and 24–7 to the Giants again. The Redskins finished the season with a 3-9 record; the fans were grateful that the three Washington victories—against Baltimore, Pittsburgh, and the Cardinals—came at home. The dissatisfaction by the hometown fans showed at the box office, however. In the season finale—a 37–20 victory over the Cardinals—only 18,107 fans showed up at Griffith Stadium, the third smallest crowd in Redskins history in Washington. Quarterbacks Jack Scarbath and rookie Al Dorow combined to throw 15 touchdowns and 30 interceptions, and Choo-Choo Justice, in his final season, ran for just 254 yards.

But the players were confident that Kuharich had the ability to coach a winning football team.

Joe Tereshinski "Joe Kuharich was a very loyal coach and very knowledgeable and dedicated. He worked hard and respected his players, and they respected him back. You could trust him. He was a man, and the team got behind him."

Given a full training camp to prepare in 1955, and the return of LeBaron and Brito (though Bones Taylor retired), Kuharich managed to turn in the Redskins' best season since they last went to the NFL title game in 1945. The Redskins stayed even in their first six games, posting a 3-3 mark, but went on a tear to close out the season, winning six of their last seven games and finishing with an 8-4 mark, which was good for second in the Eastern Conference. They were led by three consistent runners: Vic Janowicz (a former Heisman Trophy winner who played baseball for the Pirates before coming over to Washington; he also kicked and scored a club record of 88 points, second in the league behind Doak Walker), Bert Zagers, and Leo Elter, who combined for 1,153 yards and gave Redskins fans hope for the future, particularly in the final game of the season at home against Pittsburgh.

Washington led 7–0 in the first quarter, but Pittsburgh came back to score 14 in the second and opened the third quarter with a drive that led to a 9-yard field goal and a 17–7 lead. But LeBaron, who came into the game to replace Dorow, the starter, sparked a comeback that resulted in an 11-yard scoring pass to Ralph Thomas to close the Pittsburgh lead to 17–14 at the end of the third quarter, and then led two fourth-quarter scoring drives that ended with a 5-yard touchdown pass to Dale Atkeson and a 1-yard dive by Janowicz for a 28–14 win.

It seemed as if the franchise had put losing behind them and were about to embark on another string of winning seasons. But they were dealt a devastating blow in 1956, when Janowicz, while at training camp at Occidental College in California, was in a career-ending automobile accident. LeBaron and Dorow also struggled with injuries, but still, with a 6-6 record and a third-place finish in the conference (and wins over two undefeated teams, the Detroit Lions and the Chicago Cardinals), Kuharich's team had played well enough to remain optimistic about the franchise, particularly with the addition of two new players: running back Dick James, a rookie out of Oregon who averaged nearly 5 yards a carry, and placekicker Sam Baker, who set a team record with 17 field goals. Off the field, Baker was one of the leaders of the practical joke squad that would often dominate the locker room, particularly to break the monotony of training camp.

Running back Dick James   "Chuck Drazenovich, a tough linebacker who came from coal-mining country in Pennsylvania, was always bragging about his clothes and how much his suits cost. One time at training camp at Occidental College, Sam Baker, who was his roommate, took one of Drazenovich's best suits and ran it up the flagpole. There it was, fluttering at the top of the flagpole as everyone came out the dining room after eating. A few weeks later, Drazenovich got Sam back. We were in Washington, getting ready at Griffith Stadium to go up to New York to play. We were going to take a bus. Drazenovich got out of the shower before Baker and took Baker's dress shoes and put them on a ledge on the cinderblock wall. Sam couldn't find them, but when he finally did, they fell behind a hole in the wall and he couldn't get them. So there was Sam, wearing his Redskins blazer and a tie, going into a fancy restaurant we stopped at on the way up, and wearing sneakers. We had a lot of fun playing the game."

. . .

But the team regressed after that, going 5-6-1 in 1957 (the year the "Three Lollipops"—the nickname for the trio of rookie running backs, Don Bosseler, Ed Sutton, and Jim Podeley—led the rushing game and became fan favorites), despite having an array of brilliant NFL minds on the roster. Don Shula, who went on to become the winningest coach in NFL history and led the Miami Dolphins to two Super Bowl championships, was a cornerback on that 1957 squad. Joe Walton, who went on to become a successful offensive coordinator and a head coach for the New York Jets, was an end on that team. There was also defensive back Norm Hecker, who later became the head coach of the Atlanta Falcons; Dick Stanfel, a guard who became an assistant coach for a number of NFL teams; defensive tackle Ed Khayat, who went on to coach the Philadelphia Eagles; and linebacker LaVern "Torgy" Torgeson, who became the defensive line coach for the Redskins.

Washington didn't fare much better in 1958, going 4-7-1, and Kuharich, perhaps noting that he was already operating on borrowed time—he had the second-longest tenure of any coach in franchise history—took advantage of a great opportunity when he was offered the head coaching job at Notre Dame, even though he had just signed a five-year contract with Marshall.

The Redskins owner was ready for a change as well, after exhibiting record patience by sticking with the same coach for five seasons. Marshall promoted backfield coach Mike Nixon, who would lead the club to the worst two-season stretch in franchise history, going 3-9 in 1959 and 1-9-2 in 1960—the last year the Redskins played in Griffith Stadium. They lost the final game at the old ballpark, a 38–28 defeat to Philadelphia before a crowd of just 20,558. In that presidential election year, the only victory for the Redskins came in the second week of the season, a 26–14 victory over the expansion Dallas Cowboys.

The seeds for the legendary Redskins-Cowboys rivalry had already been planted when bandleader Barnee Breeskin, who wrote "Hail to the Redskins," got into a fight with Marshall (no surprise—everyone who knew the volatile Redskins owner had a feud with him at one time or another) and sold the rights to the song to Texas oilman Clint Murchison, who was trying to establish a Dallas expansion team but ran into opposition from Marshall, who considered the South—all of the South, including Texas—his territory. Murchison used the song rights to force Marshall to go along with the expansion, and then sold the rights back to the angry Washington owner.

There was a new coach in 1961—Bill McPeak, the offensive backfield coach—and a new stadium, a state-of-the-art dual-use facility. D.C. Stadium (changed to Robert F. Kennedy Stadium in 1969 to honor the memory of the slain New York senator and presidential candidate) at East Capitol and Twenty-second streets was the first of the so-called "cookie-cutter" facilities that would follow in places like Philadelphia (Veterans Stadium), Cincinnati (Riverfront Stadium), St. Louis (Busch Stadium), and Pittsburgh (Three Rivers Stadium). It was the first of the generation of stadiums built with both baseball and football in mind, an indication of how far pro football had come in the sports landscape of the country. The $20 million stadium had a football seating capacity of 55,672, and, unlike Redskins games at Griffith Stadium, there would soon be black faces in the seats, at the concession stands, and on the field for Redskins games, despite Marshall's objections. This was not Washington 1950. The face of the city was changing, as the black population continued to grow and with it the anger over the southern attitudes that were still found in the city.

There was one other major change that happened with the franchise, though fans didn't realize it at the time. On January 11, 1961, Milton King, a Redskins stockholder, sold some stock to Jack Kent Cooke, a Canadian minor league baseball owner and communications magnate. On the field, though, little else changed for Washington football fans, as the team managed to win just one game again over the entire schedule, posting a 1-12-1 record—again the only win coming against the Cowboys, this one in the final game of the season, which meant that the Redskins went from October 9 to December 17, 1961, without a victory. But the fireworks that surrounded that one 1961 win were memorable.

Dick James had a career day by scoring 4 touchdowns and rushing for 146 yards. He should have scored 5 touchdowns, but was prevented from doing so by Redskins quarterback Norm Snead.

Dick James   "I was a yard and a half from the fifth touchdown. I came into the huddle and said to Norm Snead, 'Let's take it in.' So

Snead sneaks it in himself. When I asked him after why he didn't give the ball to me, since I already had 4 touchdowns, he said to me, 'I thought you said sneak it in.'"

Snead may have been distracted by what had happened on the field at halftime at D.C. Stadium: an invasion of chickens let loose on the field, when Marshall traditionally had Santa Claus arrive by helicopter for that final December game. The "fowl play" was the work of Murchison, and the ringleader of the chicken caper was a Washington native, a law school graduate who was earning his pay in those days working as a stringer for Washington investigative reporters Drew Pearson and Jack Anderson. He eventually became one of the best-known sports authors and historians of his time: Bert Sugar.

Author Bert Sugar "I had gone to Redskins games since the time I was a little kid. Marshall had a rule that anyone who could walk under the turnstile–a kid–could get in free. I duck-walked under that turnstile until I was seventeen years old, pointing behind me, saying, 'He's got them,' and running like hell. On this day, I was in Pearson's office on K Street, and they shared their office with a public relations man named Irv Davidoff, whose client was Clint Murchison. Clint was always trying to get under George Preston Marshall's skin. For some reason, they had a running joke, dating back to the days when Marshall, a showman, put on the Dallas exposition shows that involved chickens. Davidoff came to me and said, 'I've got $100 and chickens. Can you get four people to sneak these chickens into the stadium and release them at halftime on the field? I can get you the tickets.' I got some people and we got them into the stadium and let them go on the field. They were running all over the place, and we were running back to our seats. People were running all over the field trying to catch them, and they looked like chickens with their heads cut off."

In 1962, there was something else on the field that Redskins fans had never seen before: black football players in Redskins uniforms. Over the years, Marshall had come under heavy criticism for his refusal to sign black players–his supporters say because of his fears of alienating his southern fan base and his detractors say because of his personal prejudices. Whatever the reasons for being the last NFL team to integrate, Marshall had to relent when the U.S. Department of the

Interior, which controlled the federal land that the new stadium sat on, pressured him to add black players. For a city that was going through tremendous changes—from a provincial southern town to a city with a growing black power and identity—the presence of black football players was a long-awaited victory for the black community in Washington—a victory in a battle that the community fought for many years with Marshall, from lobbying him to eliminate "Dixie" from the Redskins' fight song to his eventual surrender to the times by being forced to have black Washington Redskins players. As a result of this, black workers began getting jobs at the stadium, and black fans slowly began to show up at games.

Even that act by Marshall the showman had an unintentional twist of drama to it, though it turned out to be a tragic one. Marshall had the first pick in the NFL draft that year because of the Redskins' dismal 1961 record, and he used it to pick Heisman Trophy winner Ernie Davis, the black running back from Syracuse. The Washington owner quickly traded Davis to the Cleveland Browns for another black flanker/running back, Bobbie Mitchell. Marshall had unintentionally made a deal that would, tragically, benefit only his team. Soon after the draft, Davis was diagnosed with leukemia and died before ever playing for the Browns, while Mitchell continued his Hall of Fame career with Washington. Three other black players joined Mitchell that season: another halfback, Leroy Jackson, guard John Nisby, and defensive back Ron Hatcher.

The additional talent, along with Norm Snead's improvement at quarterback, guaranteed at least some improvement over the previous year, and that was what they got—some improvement, finishing the season with a 5-7-2 mark.

The Redskins' rivals, the Cowboys, had improved as well, under Coach Tom Landry and led by a young, brash quarterback named Don Meredith. The two teams met in the season opener, and in a wild battle at the Cotton Bowl in Dallas, they played each other to a 35–35 tie. Mitchell made an impressive Redskins debut, scoring 3 touchdowns—a 6-yard touchdown catch, a 92-yard kickoff return, and an 81-yard touchdown reception. But the game came down to a missed Dallas opportunity at the hands of two former Redskins. Eddie LeBaron, playing quarterback at the end of the game, put the Cowboys in position by connecting on a 34-yard pass to Frank

Clark, putting the ball on the Washington 34-yard line. But former Redskins kicker Sam Baker missed the field goal, and the game ended in a tie.

It was a promising start for the Redskins, as they went on a three-game winning streak, then tied the Cardinals in St. Louis 17–17 and won again, 22–21, against the Eagles, leaving them undefeated after five games. Then the Redskins played another season—their version of Mr. Hyde, a totally different squad that lost seven of its final eight games, including an embarrassing 38–10 defeat to the Cowboys before a hometown crowd of 49,888 at D.C. Stadium. But the debut of black players was a resounding success, in terms of what they brought to the team—Mitchell had an outstanding receiving year, catching 72 balls for 1,384 yards, and 11 touchdowns, an average of 19 yards per catch. Both he and Nisby made the Pro Bowl. Their seasons only served to illustrate how much damage Marshall inflicted on the franchise for his refusal to bring in black players until being forced to do so.

Mitchell didn't chose to fight this battle, but he was up to the task, as difficult as it was. And it was difficult.

Running back/end Bobby Mitchell   "When I found out about the trade, I thought, 'I'm going to Washington, of all places?' When I went to a kickoff luncheon there, everybody stood up, and I thought they [the Redskins band] were going to play the national anthem. Then I heard, 'I wish I was in the land of cotton [Dixie].' But in the black community, I was a shining light, the player they had waited for all those years. I couldn't make any mistakes on the field. I had to be perfect every game. I had upset the apple cart, you see, when all I wanted to be was a great football player. . . . I wasn't accepted by a lot of the white guys on the team. The fans would yell, 'Run, nigger, run.' I was spat on in Duke Ziebert's [restaurant]. I wanted to punch someone. But I found out quickly that how I handled myself made a world of difference. A lot of bad things happened to me, but as long as the black kids saw me stay within myself and not lash out, they would stay within themselves and not lash out. I wished I could have played one day without any problems. I went to the stadium with a trunk on my back. It never ended. When you've got to play like that and still make All-Pro, I'm proud of that."

. . .

This was the 1960s, the decade of change, and change was coming quickly for the Redskins everywhere except in the win-loss column. So far, they had integrated the team, moved into a new stadium, and added a new investor to the franchise, and, in 1963, they moved their training camp from their longtime site at Occidental College in California to Dickinson College, a small college located in Carlisle in Pennsylvania Dutch country, which was about a two-hour drive from Washington. It didn't bring them any closer to victory, though. Snead, who had thrown 22 touchdown passes in 1962, slumped miserably in 1963, tossing just 13 scoring passes while giving up 27 interceptions. The team took a step back as well, finishing with a 3-11 record. Mitchell still managed to be a diamond in the rough, catching 69 passes for 1,436 yards, a 21-yard-per-catch average, with 7 touchdowns, including a record-setting 99-yard touchdown pass from backup quarterback George Izo in the season opening 37–14 defeat to Cleveland.

Still, the players managed to make the most of the bad times, and they valued the friendships they made while losing, week in and week out.

Linebacker Bob Pellegrini "We had a great time. I played for the Eagles when they won a championship, but I had a lot more fun playing for the Redskins. We didn't have the greatest talent, but we played hard and got along with each other. Abe Gibron was coaching the offensive line, and we used to have weigh-ins on Thursday. Fran O'Brien would fill up with all kinds of laxatives on Wednesday night. He would look withdrawn and pale, but he would be grinning at Gibron during the weigh-in. By the time the game came around on Sunday, Fran had his strength back."

Remarkably, after three dismal seasons, McPeak was not fired. That was because the fight was going out of George Preston Marshall. His health was failing, and he could not continue to run the franchise. So at the end of the 1963 season, Marshall stepped down and turned over the operation of the club to three of his board members: Milton King, Leo De Orsey, and famous Washington trial lawyer Edward Bennett Williams. They made two moves that would shake the world of the NFL and change the face of the team for years to come.

3

Sonny and Sam

S onny Jurgensen enjoyed a good joke as much as anyone—probably more than most. He was a fun-loving young quarterback with a blessed arm, playing for the Philadelphia Eagles, just four years removed from their championship season, in a town that was very passionate about its teams and athletes. Born in Wilmington, North Carolina, Jurgensen starred at Duke University before joining the Eagles in 1957. He was a backup to Norm Van Brocklin for four seasons, including 1960, when the Eagles won the league title. He took over as Philadelphia's starter in 1961, after Van Brocklin retired, and had a sensational year, passing for a record 3,723 yards and tying the NFL record with 32 touchdown passes. But he was slowed by injuries in 1963, throwing 11 touchdowns and 13 interceptions in limited playing time.

Still, Jurgensen figured that he was the future of the franchise and that he would become one of those athletes that a town falls in love with. He would, but not in the town where he thought it would happen. So when Jurgensen was told on April Fools' Day in 1964 that he had been traded to the Washington Redskins in exchange for quarterback Norm Snead, he thought it was a joke.

Quarterback Sonny Jurgensen "I had just had a lengthy meeting in Philadelphia about what we were going to do. I left the office with the understanding that I was going to be around there. I went to have some lunch, and some people told me they heard I was traded to the Redskins. I said, 'Don't tell me that. I just left the coaches.' It was April Fools' Day, and I thought they were just kidding me. But that wasn't the case. It was a shock, especially after having that meeting. But in retrospect, it was the best thing that ever happened to me. I was from the South, and what little pro football we saw down there was the Washington Redskins."

The Redskins were not done yet. Nine days later, they dealt away popular running back Dick James, defensive end Andy Stynchula, and a number-five draft pick in 1965 to the New York Giants for one of the biggest stars of the game, the man who put the spotlight on defense: linebacker Sam Huff.

James figured he was on the way out.

Running back Dick James "I got into the doghouse with [Redskins coach Bill] McPeak after a sportswriter was in the dressing room following a game, going around and asking players what they thought about reports in the paper that McPeak was on his way out. Other players pumped him up, but I told it like I thought it was. He was not a head coach. He was an assistant coach, probably a good one. I said, 'I get paid to play football. I love the Washington Redskins and the fans. There are none better. But I get paid to play football and do the very best I can, and I will play the best I can regardless of who the head coach is.' A week later, I wasn't starting. The coaches would go to McPeak for talks before practice, and Johnny Sample would laugh and say, 'It's time for your weekly meeting.' A few months later, I was traded. I didn't want to leave Washington. [Sportswriter] Mo Siegel once wrote after a game, 'The boo birds were out again at D.C. Stadium, and, to a man, everyone was booed, with one exception. That was Dickie James, and nobody, but nobody, boos Dickie James in D.C. Stadium.' That's the way I felt about the fans there, too. I played the best that I could. It wasn't for any coach, and it wasn't for anyone in particular other than myself and to give people what they came to see. But I wasn't surprised to be traded."

But if Jurgensen was surprised at being traded, Huff was stunned and crestfallen. He was one of New York's biggest stars. Coming out of the coal mine region of West Virginia, Huff had appeared on the cover of *Time* magazine at the age of twenty-four and received tremendous attention when he was the subject of the television documentary *The Violent World of Sam Huff*. He became the symbol of the new glamour era for defensive football, and his battles against running backs Jim Brown and Jim Taylor became the stuff of NFL legend and lore. The last thing Huff imagined was that he would be shipped out.

Linebacker Sam Huff   "It came as a shock to me. I was twenty-nine years old and felt like I was on top of the world. We had just finished playing in the league championship game in January, and we lost 14–10. We had seven turnovers, but we had still kept the other team to just 14 points. I was feeling pretty good about myself. I was working for the J. P. Stevens Company in New York, doing a lot of things, like radio and television. And all of a sudden the rug is pulled out from under you. You're traded to the Redskins, a team you competed against and beat on a regular basis. I was depressed. I realized as an athlete you have very little say in what goes on in your life. You're a performer. These moves were made by people in the front office. My only salvation was that I asked myself, Do I want to get out of the game, or do I want to play? I came to the realization that I was a football player and that I had been traded to the Redskins. If I wanted to play, I had to play in Washington."

Edward Bennett Williams brought two stars to Washington and was starting to rebuild a franchise that had been running on fumes. He would do so through the draft as well. Another talented player arrived in Washington that year who, like Jurgensen and Huff, would be one of the cornerstones for the revival of the franchise: Charley Taylor, a rookie running back and soon-to-be-converted receiver out of Arizona State. Also, center Len Hauss, the anchor of the offensive line, would make his debut in that 1964 season.

Hauss started as center in 1964, beginning one of the most remarkable runs the NFL had ever seen—a string of consecutive game starts that ended when Hauss retired in 1977—196 straight starts.

Center Len Hauss   "You've got to be lucky to some degree to play that many games. But you also have to have a work ethic that is a little bit different. I came up thinking that I was supposed to play every down of every game. When I watched Cal Ripken break Lou Gehrig's record [2,130 consecutive games] on television, I almost stood up at home to honor it. I had a lump in my throat, because I could imagine what type of guy he may be. For someone to be able to do what this guy did, he must have a work ethic, a mentality like I had: that you are supposed to play. That's your job, and you're supposed to do your job. You've got to figure that there had to be some flu and viruses in there somewhere that would keep people from performing over that period, but you go ahead and perform, because that's your job.

"I had five knee operations during my career, and I was able to put all of them off until after the season. You can play with cartilage or joint damage, and I did whatever it took to do the job. But there were times when I had injured my back, and my knees were bothering me or one thing or another that made it very difficult to play. One of the closer friends I had was Dave Crossan, who was the backup center to me. He told me one day, 'Playing backup to you is the hardest job there is.' Some weeks he would take all the snaps, and then come Saturday, I would be ready to play. He said, 'What makes it so hard is that I would be doing all the practicing and I knew you would wind up playing that week.' There were a few times when I was ill with something other than a football injury, when I stayed up all night and couldn't keep anything down. But I expected to play. There was no option."

The Redskins veterans got an early look at Hauss's determination during training camp.

Sam Huff "Nobody knew who Len Hauss was when he was a rookie. During training camp that year, we were running the nut-cracker drills, where you put two blocking dummies down and it is one on one. The offensive lineman has to block the defensive lineman, and the quarterback hands the ball to a back. It's almost like a split T-play, where the back has to break on the lineman's block, in between the two dummies. You have lines of defensive guys and lines of offensive guys, and they run these plays pretty fast. I was the middle linebacker, so my guy was the offensive center. So number 56 comes up there, and I don't know who he is. He's some rookie from Georgia. On the snap of the ball, I popped him and knocked the stuffing out of him. I'm feeling pretty good about that play, and I get back into the defensive line. Hauss goes back into the offensive line. My turn comes up again, and he's there again. I didn't think much about it. He went on a different count, snapped the ball, and boom, knocked the daylights out of me. I said, 'What's his name? I think he's going to be around here for a while.' He was a great center. He had heart, and he didn't quit."

The new arrivals certainly made games more enjoyable for Redskins fans to watch, but the changes didn't translate to winning, at least not a winning record. The expectations of a high-powered offense led by Jurgensen failed to materialize in the start of the 1964 season; they averaged less than 15 points a game while losing their first four, including a 27–17 defeat to Cleveland before 47,577 at D.C. Stadium. Then, a match-up at home with 49,000 people in the stands featured two traded quarterbacks against their former teams: Jurgensen against Philadelphia and Snead against Washington. Jurgensen threw 5 touchdown passes against his old team, connecting with Mitchell twice—a 29-yarder and a 9-yard scoring pass—and 2 long touchdowns with the rookie Taylor—a 66-yarder and a 74-yard touchdown connection. The Redskins led 21–0 after the first half, and the offense outgained Philadelphia's by an astounding 302 yards to just 2 yards for the Eagles. When the show was over, the Redskins had their first win of the season, 35–20, and the offense was on its way.

After losing the first four games, the Redskins went 6-4 the rest of the season and averaged 25 points a game in those final ten games. Still, they finished with a 6-8 record—now nine years and counting without a winning record—and a 15-38-3 record under four straight losing seasons with McPeak as the head coach. And even with the winning record over their final ten games and the emergence of the explosive offense, the season did not end on a hopeful note. The Redskins lost their final two games—14–7 to the Steelers in the final home game that year, and a 45–17 beating from their rivals up the road in Baltimore, in a match-up between the two great quarterbacks, Jurgensen and Johnny Unitas.

It was the season finale that was most disturbing, indicative of the personality of this Redskins team—playing well enough to tantalize their fans, but inevitably not sustaining that level of play long enough to consistently win. Washington led the Colts—the Western Conference champions—in the first quarter, when Vince Promuto recovered a Baltimore fumble at the Colts' 26-yard line and fullback Percy Atkins went around the end for 17 yards to give the Redskins a 7–0 lead.

Baltimore added a 25-yard field goal by Lou Michaels to make the score 7–3 as the first quarter ended. The Colts added a second-quarter touchdown, while the Redskins kept pace with a Jim Martin field goal, and it was a 10–10 game at halftime. The Redskins appeared to be ready to give the game away at the start of the second half when Charley Taylor fumbled, setting up a Baltimore drive that ended in a 7-yard touchdown run. Jurgensen took the team down the field and appeared ready to tie it up, but he was intercepted in the end zone by Jerry Logan. Still, despite the turnovers, the Redskins were right there in the game against the heavily favored Colts. Washington safety Tom Walters intercepted a Unitas pass at the Baltimore 36-yard line and ran it back to the 2-yard line. Jurgensen took the ball around the end to tie the score again, 17–17. But the Colts quickly took back the lead when they drove down the field and Unitas connected on a 22-yard touchdown pass to John Mackey, making it a 24–17 game.

That was as good as the Redskins would often be against a quality opponent—three-quarters good. Baltimore exploded for 21 unanswered fourth-quarter points, and Redskins fans left the stadium feeling that despite all the bells and whistles that had been added to the team, the bottom line was still a losing one.

So did Edward Bennett Williams, who desperately wanted to replace the coach and bring some star power to the franchise with a big name, but De Orsey was president of the team and running the show, so McPeak stayed for another season. Not surprisingly, it ended as a carbon-copy of the 1964 season, as the Redskins finished with another 6-8 record.

On a brighter side, the Redskins sent seven players to the Pro Bowl. Rookie safety Paul Krause, who would go on to star for the Minnesota Vikings, was All-NFL, as was Bobby Mitchell. Jurgensen threw 24 touchdowns and just 13 interceptions. Rookie Charley Taylor ran for 755 yards and caught 53 passes for 814 yards and 5 touchdowns. Mitchell caught 60 passes for 904 yards and 10 touchdowns. Krause had intercepted a remarkable 12 passes.

The star of this show was the quarterback—a charismatic, fun-loving figure with a golden arm and a pot belly.

Len Hauss "Sonny had style. One time the Washington Touchdown Club had chosen Sonny as its Most Valuable Player, and Tom Jones, the singer, was chosen as the Most Valuable Performer. We were all at this function, Sonny, myself, Tom Jones, and some other people standing around, talking. One of the Washington reporters walked up to Sonny and asked him, 'What does if feel like to be in the presence of a real star?' Sonny responded, 'Why don't you ask him?' referring to Jones, who at the time was probably the biggest entertainer in the business.

"Sonny was an interesting guy. History has shown he was one of the best quarterbacks to ever play the game. He probably had one of the best arms in football at the time. He was extremely smart and very much a leader. Coaches allowed him to run the show, and that worked for Sonny, who was a take-charge guy. He had an excellent football mind."

Sonny Jurgensen   "I didn't have a good tailor for my uniform, so I always had this little roll in front of me. Fans liked it. They could sit at home and say to their wives, 'I want to watch football,' and maybe the wife would say, 'You're just sitting around here drinking beer. Get in shape.' The guy could point to the television and say, 'Wait a minute. Look at that guy. If he can play, I can play.' Fans knew that I enjoyed life, but I played hard, and they knew that, too."

Fans in Washington saw the best of that play from Jurgensen in one of the greatest comebacks in franchise history that 1965 season, against the team that was most satisfying to do so against: the Dallas Cowboys, a team on the rise that was led by Meredith and by emerging stars such as Bob Hayes and Don Perkins. Playing at home on November 28, 1965, before a crowd of more than 50,000, the Redskins opened the game by giving the hometown fans the same sort of disappointing performance they had been nearly numbed by over the year. In the first half, Taylor fumbled twice and Jurgensen threw two interceptions and fumbled, followed by a blocked field goal attempt that Dallas safety Mike Gaechter ran 60 yards for a touchdown to give the Cowboys a 21–0 lead. Before the first half ended, Jurgensen managed to connect with Taylor on a 26-yard touchdown, but the Redskins missed the extra point, so Dallas led 21–6 at halftime. The Cowboys added a 29-yard field goal early in the third quarter to extend their lead to 24–6, with Washington's hopes of climbing back into the game stuck deep in its own territory, when Jurgensen had to start at the 10-yard line because of a clipping penalty on the kickoff following the field goal.

Then the fun started. Jurgensen drove the team down the field. He hit Angelo Coia on a 21-yard pass, and Taylor took off on a 16-yard run. Jurgensen found Mitchell for 22 yards and Coia again for 14 yards. On the twelfth play of the 90-yard drive, Jurgensen ran it in from the 1-yard line, and kicker Bob Jencks connected this time on the point after to cut the Dallas lead to 24–13. In the fourth quarter, Jurgensen began another move for the Dallas end zone. He connected with Jerry Smith on three straight passes and then with Taylor on a 21-yarder. Running back Danny Lewis bounced over the goal line for a 2-yard touchdown, and now the score was just 24–20 Dallas.

But the storybook comeback that would cement Jurgensen's place forever in the hearts of Redskins fans appeared to have ended when Cowboys linebacker Dave Edwards intercepted a Jurgensen pass, and Meredith converted it into a 53-yard touchdown to Frank Clarke, extending the Cowboys' lead to 31–20 with just six minutes remaining. Jurgensen, though, was on fire. He quickly moved the team down the field and scored again on a 10-yard pass to Mitchell, and, with 1:41 left in the game, Washington got the ball back with one final chance to overtake the Cowboys' 31–27 lead. Jurgensen would not be denied. He found Smith for 22 yards and then Mitchell for 35 yards, and it was first and goal on the Cowboys' 5-yard line with just over a minute left. Jurgensen completed the masterpiece with a corner scoring pass to Coia, and, after being behind for nearly fifty-nine minutes, the Redskins now led 34–31. RFK Stadium shook with the cheers of frenzied fans and the Cowboys-Redskins rivalry moved to another level. Dallas had one more chance, quickly moving the ball into position for a 44-yard field goal attempt. But defensive back Lonnie Sanders blocked the attempt, and the win was in the books.

Sonny Jurgensen   "We were able to have games like that because we were a quick-striking team. We had that capability. We laid it on the line, and people liked that. We fought hard, and that is what people wanted to see. The kind of offense we had, you may have stopped us three or four times, but then we were going to hit you on and on. In that Dallas game, we just kept plugging away."

The Cowboys-Redskins rivalry started between the two owners, Murchinson and Marshall, but it grew in intensity with the arrival in

Washington of a number of players from Texas, and games like the Redskins' 1965 comeback.

Receiver Charley Taylor "The Redskins-Cowboys rivalry was down to the bone, down to the marrow. I'm from Grand Prairie, just outside of Dallas, and my mom would get threatening phone calls when we played the Cowboys. It was an intense series, because about half of our ball club was from Texas, so it was like a homecoming, with all the family and friends at the stadium. All the guys from Texas had to produce because we had to live down there in the off season."

But the victory hardly spurred Washington on to finish the remainder of the season strong, as the Redskins turned in their usual three-quarter game performance in Cleveland against the Browns. The Redskins defense against the Browns and their legendary back, Jim Brown, kept the Browns scoreless in the first quarter, while the Redskins put together a scoring drive that ended with a 2-yard touchdown run by Charley Taylor. Bob Jencks missed the extra point, and Washington led 6–0. The Browns came back to score on a 7-yard touchdown pass from Frank Ryan to Gary Collins, but the Redskins took back the lead by a 6-yard touchdown pass from Jurgensen to Pat Richter and a 20-yard field goal by Jencks to take a 16–7 lead into the locker room at the end of the second quarter.

In one of those legendary battles between Huff and Brown, the defense held tough in the third quarter, allowing just a Cleveland field goal. But the collapse occurred right on schedule in the fourth quarter. Browns linebacker Vince Costello intercepted a Jurgensen pass, and Ryan hit Tom Hutchinson on a 14-yard touchdown pass. Lou Groza's extra point gave Cleveland a 17–16 lead. In the closing minutes of the fourth quarter, Jurgensen fumbled at his own 20-yard line, and several plays later Brown took it in from the 5-yard line for a 24–16 Cleveland victory.

The Redskins didn't even mount a three-quarter effort against the Giants the next week at home, losing 27–10 for their eighth loss of the season. If it wasn't for the hapless Pittsburgh Steelers, whom the Redskins pounded on in the last game of the season for a 35–14 victory, they would have failed to at least match the previous season's mediocrity. The similar record failed to show the step back the Redskins had taken, but the individual performances certainly reflected it. In 1965, just three Redskins made the Pro Bowl: Krause, Taylor, and Joe Rutgens. Jurgensen threw only 15 touchdown passes and had 16 intercepted. Taylor rushed for 403 yards.

Bill McPeak's tenure finally ended as head coach. Leo De Orsey died in 1965 and was replaced by the fiery, star-struck Williams, who would not put up with losing every year, and particularly losing with a coach with no profile. So Williams convinced one of the greatest players who ever took the field in the NFL to leave his coaching job at the U.S. Coast Guard Academy and sign a ten-year, $300,000 contract to coach the Redskins. Otto Graham was one of the best passers in league history. Over ten seasons, from 1946 to 1955, he led the Cleveland Browns to seven world championships in the All-American Football Conference and the NFL. He passed for 23,584 yards and 174 touchdowns, with a career win-loss regular season record of 105-17-4. He was a winner, and after an undefeated season coaching the Coast Guard team, he seemed like an inspired choice to coach the Redskins.

So much for inspiration.

Sam Huff   "A lot of times, great players are not great coaches. Otto Graham had a great staff–Mike McCormick and Ray Renfro–but he wasn't a great coach. He would spend a lot of time during the week working on trick plays, rather than fundamentals. And he wanted Sonny to change the way he threw. It was just one thing after another, and it doesn't take much for a coach to lose the respect of the players. Otto loved to play tennis. He loved to play golf. He wore hush puppies and athletic socks. The dedication just didn't seem to be there. He didn't pay attention to a lot of little things, and it just didn't click."

One example of Graham's misjudgment was his decision to take a chance on Joe Don Looney, a talented but troubled running back. The 6-foot-4, 230-pound Looney was a natural, who, when he was properly motivated, could play the game with ease. But ever since he was drafted out of Oklahoma by the Baltimore Colts, Looney had never found that proper motivation–not with the New York Giants, who drafted him and then traded him to Baltimore in 1964, and not with the Detroit Lions in 1965. So three games into the 1966 season, the Lions convinced an intrigued Otto Graham to deal for Looney, who had rushed for 356 on 114 carries and caught 12 passes for 109 yards the year before in Detroit. That would be the highlight of Looney's on-field NFL accomplishments. Off the field, though, Looney became a legend and part of Redskins lore because of his unpredictable personality.

Sam Huff "Joe Don Looney was potential talent that nobody could tap. Actually, Otto called Sonny and myself down to his office and said to us, 'We need a running back, and we have a chance to get Joe Don Looney.' Sonny and I agreed that this was a bad idea and told him, 'No, Otto, we have enough problems holding the players together here without him. Not one of those teams could control him. And he's going to come here.' The next morning, Joe Don was in a Redskins practice uniform.

"Looney and I had the craziest fight you would ever see on a football field. It happened during practice in his second season here. The first year, the Redskins offered me a bonus if I would room with Joe Don. Sonny and I had been roommates, but they offered me more money if I would room with Looney and keep him out of trouble. I did, but it was one of the toughest things I ever did. I didn't trust him. I didn't know if he was going to try to beat me up or what. I never slept much that year before a game.

"I kept him out of trouble that first year. In the second year, it was a little different. We were getting ready in practice for the opening game against Philadelphia. It was a hot, miserable day, and Otto made us wear pads all the time in practice. We were practicing at the old practice field, not at RFK, but where parking lot number five is now, there used to be a practice field. Looney is running the Philadelphia plays for our defense. They run a toss to the fullback, and he runs around the end. I go in pursuit, and kind of take it easy. Joe Don lowers his shoulder and hits me in the chest, running over me. Then he taunts me with the ball. Hey, this is just practice. I'm trying to save myself for the Philadelphia Eagles. I'm on the ground, and he sticks the ball in my face and says, 'How do you like that, big guy? I knocked the hell out of you.' I looked at him and said, 'You crazy so and so. You picked on the wrong guy. You're going to get yours.'

"So on the next play, he comes out of the huddle. I know what the play is, and Looney says to me, 'All right, big guy, here I come again.' I'm gritting my teeth. I'm going to nail that guy. So [center] Len Hauss blocked one way, and I stepped up to the middle. When Looney got the ball, I came off the ground with my fist and hit him dead on the chin as hard as I could. I knocked his helmet off, and the ball went flying. His knees buckled, but he didn't go down. I gave him my best shot. Then we got into a hell of a fight. They couldn't get us apart. So Otto makes one of his brilliant statements, saying, 'I don't think you guys should room together this week.'

"Looney was nuts, and he was a disruption for the team. One time in Cleveland our fullback got knocked out, and Otto told Joe Don to get in there. He said, 'No, I'm not warmed up yet.' He wouldn't go in the game."

Sonny Jurgensen   "Looney used to put weights on his dog's paws. He had a huge dog. He told us, 'When I take them off, he's really going to be fast.'"

Looney was out of Washington after the 1967 season, having appeared in just four games; he carried the ball eleven times that year. He was out of football after 1968. His name resurfaced years later as part of a religious sect in India, and he died not long after that. Looney was part of the circus off the field, but the Redskins offense was like a three-ring circus on the field, with the big numbers they put on the scoreboard, and it drew the fans, as the team enjoyed its first fully sold-out season in 1966.

Charley Taylor   "I don't think there was anybody in the league that could compete with us offensively. It was just that we couldn't stop anybody defensively. We had some great defensive players, but we had some holes that we just couldn't shore up. But we were unstoppable offensively. We had a guy with a great arm and no fear at quarterback, but we would lose games 35–33, scores like that."

There was one particularly memorable game at D.C. Stadium when that offense was literally unstoppable, the zenith of this talent's offensive performances. And for Huff, it couldn't have come against a more deserving opponent—the team that betrayed him, the New York Giants, on November 27, 1966. After three straight losses—37–10 at Baltimore, 31–30 to Dallas at home, and 14–3 to the Browns in Cleveland—the Redskins were facing Huff's former team for the second time that year, having lost their first game in New York, 13–10.

This one would not be as close. Huff felt the Giants had collapsed over the season, and on film now appeared to be one of the worst defensive teams he had ever seen.

Sam Huff "I knew we were going to beat them because they were just awful. Kyle Rote, who was playing for the Giants at the time and was a good friend of mine, was doing a radio show and had me on as a guest. He asked me, 'What do you think about today's game?' And I said, 'This is one of the worst teams the Giants have ever fielded. They're terrible on offense and terrible on defense. We will score 60 points.'"

They scored better than that, setting a league record for the most points scored in a game in a 72–41 victory. Safety Brig Owens intercepted a pass from Giants quarterback Tom Kennedy to open the game and set up a 5-yard touchdown pass from Jurgensen to running back A. D. Whitfield. Remarkably, the extra point by Charlie Gogolak was blocked. Needless to say, it was not a key moment in the game. Whitfield followed up the next time Washington got the ball by taking off on a 63-yard run to put Washington ahead 13–0 at the end of the first quarter, with Gogolak making the extra point this time. The defense scored the next touchdown early in the second quarter when linebacker Chris Hanburger forced a Kennedy fumble, which Owens picked up and ran 62 yards for a score, giving Washington a 20–0 lead. The Giants finally got on the board with a touchdown, but Whitfield and Looney, on a 9-yard run, both reached the end zone. New York scored again, and it was a 34–14 game at the half.

The second half was nearly a carbon copy of the first. Joe Morrison scored for the Giants first with a 41-yard touchdown reception from Gary Wood. Taylor scored on a 32-yard pass from Jurgensen. The Giants answered back with their own touchdown completion, from Wood to Homer Jones, but Taylor took another pass from Jurgensen and this time went 74 yards to the end zone. At the end of three quarters, the score was 48–28, and now Washington was ready to break the game wide open to its record conclusion. Ricky Harris ran back a punt 52 yards for a touchdown. Owens, having a career day among players having career days, intercepted another pass and took it all the way back 60 yards for his second defensive touchdown of the game. With the game clearly out of control, Graham put Bobby Mitchell in at running back, and Mitchell made the most of the appearance in his old position, taking off 45 yards for the tenth and final touchdown for Washington that day—a historic day in the NFL—with a total of 113 points scored, 72 by the Redskins.

Charley Taylor   "It should have been 79. I dropped a sure touchdown. I felt this guy on my shoulder as I dropped the ball, and after the ball had fallen to the ground, I looked over and it was the official running along with me. It sort of distracted me."

Actually, it should have been 69–41:

Sam Huff   "The score was 69–41 with about twenty seconds left to go. Our offense was on the field, and it was fourth down. Otto Graham was the coach, but he didn't yell for the field goal team. It was me. I said, 'Field goal,' and Charlie Gogolak goes in and kicks a field goal with twenty seconds remaining on the clock to make the score 72–41. That was a revenge game for me. I'll never forget looking across the field at the guy who changed my life and traded me. I thought, 'Justice is done.'"

The Redskins had enough left over the following week to continue their offensive juggernaut and to get revenge for a disappointing 31–30 loss to the Dallas Cowboys three weeks earlier. The Cowboys were emerging as one of the powers in the league, coming into Washington with a 5-2-1 record. Among those attending the game that day for the first time at D.C. Stadium was Jack Kent Cooke, an ambitious Canadian media magnate who was one of the newest minority investors in the Washington Redskins and who watched his team fail to protect a 30–28 lead with less than two minutes remaining in the game, with Dallas taking over on the Redskins' own 3-yard line. Don Meredith, though, turned in his own version of a miracle comeback that Jurgensen had accomplished the year before. He hit Pete Gent with several long passes to move the ball to the Redskins' 33-yard line, and then Washington linebacker John Reger got a personal foul call when he hit Meredith while the quarterback was running out of bounds, putting the ball on the Washington 20-yard line. Danny Villanueva easily hit the game-winning field goal with fifteen seconds left, giving the Cowboys a 31–30 victory. Now, in Dallas, on December 11, 1966, the Redskins would redeem themselves.

Neither team scored in the first quarter, but the Cowboys got on the board when fullback Don Perkins ran 20 yards off right tackle for a 7–0 Dallas lead early in the second quarter. The Redskins took advantage of a Meredith fumble recovered by linebacker Ron Snidow, and Charlie Gogolak hit a 43-yard field goal to make it a 7–3 game. The Redskins defense was holding fast, and Jurgensen led a drive down the field, with the big play a 34-yard reception by Jerry Smith, down to the Dallas 5-yard line. Looney fumbled the ball, and Cowboys linebacker Lee Roy Jordan picked it up and ran it back to their 33-yard line. But two holding penalties and a sack by Ron Snidow put the ball back near the Cowboys' goal line, and defensive end Carl Kammerer blocked the Dallas punt, and Reger fell on the ball for a Washington touchdown and a 10–7 lead. Dallas nearly tied the game as the second quarter ended, when Meredith moved the ball from Dallas's own 37-yard line to the Washington 37-yard line on three plays. But the Cowboys quarterback got knocked out of the game on a brutal hit by Huff, and a 42-yard field goal attempt by Villanueva failed. Washington took its 10–7 lead into the locker room at halftime.

But there was more to the hit that knocked Meredith out of the game than simply a blitz by Huff. There was a behind-the-scenes drama that showed that some things ran deeper than the Cowboys-Redskins rivalry—such as a dislike for Pete Gent. The Cowboys receiver, who would eventually leave the game and write one of the most important sports novels of his generation—*North Dallas Forty*—had his own television show in Dallas, and Huff remembered watching it in the hotel room before the Cowboys game. He didn't like what he heard, so he concocted a payback scheme with Meredith before the game started.

Sam Huff "This guy, Pete Gent, is giving a scouting report on the Redskins on his television show, and he gets to me. He says, 'Number 70 in the middle for eleven or twelve years now, is no longer the great star that he was. He should have retired a few years ago.' Sonny and I roomed together, and I turned to him and said, 'Who is this guy?' I nearly tore up the television because I was so mad. I wondered how I would get a shot at this guy the next day. He was a wide receiver, so he wouldn't come across the middle. I couldn't sleep all night. I was determined to get a shot at this guy.

"I figured the only way I could get Gent was to make a deal with

Meredith. We go out to the middle of the field for the coin flip. Chuck Howley, who was a teammate of mine from West Virginia, and Meredith are the captains of the Cowboys, and Sonny and I are the Redskins captains. I said to Meredith, 'I need a favor. Pete Gent doesn't think I can play this game. Bring that guy across the middle on a pass pattern. I want to hang him out to dry. I'll show him who can play this game.' Don said, 'Okay. I told him to keep his mouth shut.' I said, 'Just bring him across the middle. I'll kill him.' Well, we didn't develop a signal for when he was going to bring Gent across the middle. And we're leading in the game, and I forget about Pete Gent by now. So I am calling the defense and tell Chris Hanburger we are going to double blitz. I said, 'I'll go up the middle and you go in from the outside. We're going to get Meredith.' I go up the middle, and nobody blocks me. Meredith still has the ball, and I hit him in the chest. He goes down, and he's unconscious. This turned out to be the very play that he had Gent go across the middle on. This was the guy who was helping me try to get Gent, the guy I made a deal with, and I knock him out."

Huff's knockout nearly cost the Redskins the game. Rookie quarterback Craig Morton came in the game and led the Cowboys to a 10-point third quarter, moving the team into position for a 26-yard field goal by Villanueva and then connecting on a 23-yard touchdown pass to Bob Hayes, leaving the score tied at 17–17 after three quarters, as Washington scored an 11-yard pass from Jurgensen to Mitchell. Dallas appeared to be ready to run away with the game at the start of the fourth quarter when Dan Reeves took off for a 67-yard touchdown jaunt. But Jurgensen came back with 53-yard pass to Taylor and then scored on an 11-yarder to Smith, tying the score again at 24–24. Morton came back and drove the Cowboys down the field from their own 28-yard line, finishing it with a 6-yard scoring run by Don Perkins, and Dallas led 31–24. This was going to be a game, though, where the team that ran out of time lost. Jurgensen struck back with a 65-yard touchdown pass to Taylor with a little more than three minutes left in the game to tie it at 31–31. This time, the Redskins defense held, and when Washington got the ball back, Jurgensen led the offense to field goal range, with the big play being a 30-yard run by A. D. Whitefield, who played ball at North Texas State and was a former Cowboy.

Gogolak came on the field with eight seconds left, and from 29 yards, gave Washington the 34–31 win.

But there were days like the season finale at home against Philadelphia in 1966, a 37–28 defeat. It was the typical Redskins game: two touchdown passes from Jurgensen to Jerry Smith, and two more from Jurgensen to Charley Taylor. But the Redskins quarterback also fumbled and threw an interception, with both turnovers leading to Philadelphia scores, and the Washington defense could not stop Eagles backup quarterback King Hill. The Redskins had a one-game improvement to show for Otto Graham's first season as head coach, finishing with a 7-7 record. Jurgensen's numbers again indicated the fireworks display Redskins fans were treated to. He finished with 3,209 yards passing, having completed 254 passes in 436 attempts, with 28 touchdowns and 19 interceptions. Charley Taylor finished with 262 yards rushing and an outstanding 72 receptions for 1,119 yards and 12 touchdowns. With Mitchell's 905 yards in receiving and 9 touchdowns, and rookie Jerry Smith's 686 yards and 6 touchdowns, the Redskins receiving corps turned in one of the best seasons any trio ever had in the history of the league. The following season, they turned in the best ever—and still it didn't add up to winning, right from the very first game of the 1967 season.

At Philadelphia's Franklin Field, rookie John Love started the season on a positive note by running back the opening game kickoff 96 yards for a touchdown. The Redskins were on top for the first eighteen seconds of the season. It didn't last long. Behind the passing of Snead and the running of Tom Woodeschick, the Eagles took a 14–10 lead after the first quarter and came away with a 35–24 win.

Playing on the road the following week against the NFL's newest team, the expansion New Orleans Saints, the Redskins got an easy 30–10 win over the Saints and their quarterback, Billy Kilmer. A rookie fullback named Ray McDonald led the Redskins running attack with 98 yards and 3 touchdowns.

For the second year in a row, the Redskins were sold out for the season, and the team gave their fans what they were looking for in the home opener against the rejuvenated Giants and their scrambling quarterback, Fran Tarkenton, and it was John Love again who energized the 50,000-plus crowd and his team by scoring 20 points in a remarkably versatile afternoon. With Charlie Gogolak sidelined, Love filled in as the kicker and had a 30-yard field goal. He also caught a 14-yard touchdown pass from Jurgensen and recovered a fumble in the most unusual fashion by jumping on a ball in the end zone that Giants defensive back Les Murdock had just intercepted from Jurgensen before dropping it at the Giants' 2-yard line. Love also had 5 extra points, and fans went home talking about the Love fest that had taken place at D.C. Stadium.

Unfortunately, it was not the winter of Love in Washington. The Redskins would not win again for six more weeks. They lost to Dallas at home, 17–14, then settled for two ties on the road against Atlanta and Los Angeles, followed by two more home losses to Baltimore and St. Louis. They came back to beat San Francisco 31–28 and had a big win against Dallas 27–20. But they would win just one more game that year, a 15–10 victory over the Steelers in Pittsburgh. In the season finale and before disappointed Redskins fans, the team suffered an embarrassing 30–14 defeat at the hands of the expansion Saints. A symbol of the loss—and of the Washington season in 1967—came when the hero of the franchise early in the year, John Love, fumbled a punt in the end zone and the Saints nailed him for a safety.

This ended perhaps one of the most frustrating seasons in a long list of frustrating seasons, because, despite having league-leading offensive numbers, the Redskins finished with a 5-6-3 record. Jurgensen led the league in passing by completing 288 passes in 508 attempts for 3,747 yards, 31 touchdowns, and 16 interceptions. Three of the top four receivers in the league were from Washington: Taylor caught 70 passes for 990 yards and 9 touchdowns, Smith had 67 catches for 849 yards and 12 touchdowns, and Mitchell pulled down 60 passes for 866 yards and 6 touchdowns. All three averaged between 13 and 14 yards per catch. The Redskins sent five players to the Pro Bowl: Jurgensen, Hanburger, Hauss, Smith, and Taylor.

The frustrations and anger in the city were far greater than what was happening on the football field for the Redskins. The year 1968 was the year of rage in America, fueled by the assassinations of Robert F. Kennedy and Dr. Martin Luther King, the demonstrations in Chicago at the Democratic National Convention, and the rising tide against the Vietnam War.

There were riots in many cities across the country when Dr. King was killed, but Washington was ground zero when he was shot in Memphis on April 4. People took to the streets of the city, smashing windows, setting fires, and battling police. The violence continued for several days. President Lyndon B. Johnson ordered more than 13,600 federal troops to help the District of Columbia police. U.S. Marines mounted machine guns on the steps of the Capitol, and U.S. Army troops from the Third Infantry guarded the White House. At one point, on April 5, rioting reached within two blocks of the White House before the rioters retreated. The occupation of Washington was the largest of any American city since the Civil War, and by the time things had calmed down by Sunday, April 8, a dozen people had been killed and 1,097 injured, and over 6,100 arrests had been made. More than 1,200 buildings were burned, including over 900 stores, and damages were estimated at $27 million. The riots destroyed the city's economy, sending more residents out to the suburbs and increasing crime in the burned-out neighborhoods.

The Redskins could not offer much of a diversion from the city's woes in 1969. Their plight had its own particular depression. No one was happy about this dichotomy of production and losing—not the players, and certainly not Edward Bennett Williams. He was trying to replace Graham but was unable to land the candidate he felt would serve both of his purposes: a star coach with a winning resume. The players had lost respect for Graham, and the coach was a source of ridicule. That was evident even to a rookie punter out of Richmond named Mike Bragg in the 1968 season.

Punter Mike Bragg "Otto had a habit of slapping his clipboard. One of the players would take up a pool, and everyone put in a dollar. The bet was how many times Otto would slap his clipboard in practice that day. He did it out of habit, for emphasis. When it got near the end of practice, and everyone had been counting the clipboard slaps, there were some players going out of their way to prevent him from slapping the clipboard, and others who were dropping passes and fumbling to make him hit the clipboard, depending on what number they had in the pool."

Players sought out those sort of diversions to take away from the frustration, and those diversions were usually in high gear during training camp in Carlisle. The Redskins had made Dickinson College their new training home in 1963, and, a year later, when Jurgensen arrived, the legacy of the hunt for good times in the small college town began, particularly when Graham, who had the reputation of being a disciplinarian, was there. It was a losing battle for the coach.

Sonny Jurgensen   "We had a curfew, but I used to go out anyway. One night I was in one of our watering holes called the Walnut Bottom. I was playing shuffleboard with a young man, and I got a call at the bar saying they had double-checked on bed check and I had to come back in. When Otto was there, you had to go to the coach's room and let him know when you got back in, and you were fined accordingly. I knocked on Otto's door, and he is in his pajamas. He said, 'What do you want?' I said, 'I was told to come here because I was out after bed check.' He said, 'What did you do that for? Who were you with?' Right next to me, standing behind the door, was the young man I had been out playing shuffleboard with: Otto's son, Dewey. I said, 'I was with your boy, Dewey.' Otto was so mad. He kicked Dewey out of training camp. What happened was that when I was leaving that night and Dewey was just sitting outside, I asked him, 'You want to go?' He said, 'Sure,' and he went out with me. There were a lot of nights of getting caught out.

"One night at the same place I was with some other players, and some assistant coaches walked in. I dove right through a window into a wood pile. Len Hauss must have been invisible, because he walked right by them and they didn't even see him. I asked, 'Why don't you get caught?' He said, 'It must be your red hair.'

"We were months away from playing in a game. We were just breaking up the boredom of training camp."

In this atmosphere of bonding and boredom, players never knew when they might next be the target of their teammates' efforts to bond and break up the boredom.

Linebacker Chris Hanburger   "The upper floors of the dorms at Dickinson College had recessed windows, and pigeons used to flock there. I had gone into one of the rooms and left the window open during the day. So I went back up there at night, when the pigeons were roosting. I grabbed one and went back down to the second floor and quietly opened up Len Hauss and Dave Crossan's room. I had a pass key. I put the pigeon in there and closed the door. They woke up with a pigeon cooing and walking around the room."

Unfortunately, the laughs would soon end once the games began. The Redskins opened the 1968 season on the road for their first three games, and when they finally arrived home at D.C. Stadium, they had a 1-2 record, having lost two straight after winning the season opener in Chicago against the Bears. Again, one of the losses came against the Saints, one year removed from being an expansion team. The Saints offense scored 37 points, including the first 100-yard game in the history of the young franchise (Don McCall, 127 yards), while Washington managed to put up just 17 points. They took another beating the following week at Yankee Stadium, losing 48–21. Still, there was a sold-out crowd waiting for them in week four at home, and the Redskins gave their fans a 17–14 win, although they nearly blew a 17–0 lead after three quarters. And the next week, Washington won again at home, 16–13, against the Steelers. They now had a 3-2 record, and there was hope, particularly since the defense had held teams to 14 points or less in their last two games.

But now the offense was struggling, with Jurgensen suffering a series of physical problems, from the flu to broken ribs. In their third straight home game, Washington lost to the Giants 13–10, and Jurgensen completed only 7 of 25 passes for just 73 yards. The wheels came off after the Giants game. The Redskins won just two more games the rest of the year—16–10 in Philadelphia and the season finale at home against Detroit by the score of 14–3. And even the last game victory had a pall over it, with Redskins rookie defensive back Jim "Yazoo" Smith suffering a broken neck that ended his career.

There were no records set in this 5-9 season. Jurgensen threw for just 1,980 yards and 17 touchdowns. Only Hanburger and Hauss went to the Pro Bowl. Both Taylor and Smith caught 22 fewer passes than the year before, and Mitchell, in his final season as a Redskin, saw little playing time, as Pat Richter was the third option. There would be changes, but no one could have predicted that those changes would turn around thirty-three years of mediocrity and kick off an era of success that would raise the level of passion for Washington Redskins football from a hometown team to a hometown obsession—a religiouslike passion.

4

A Block of Granite

Vince Lombardi walked into the Chandelier Room of the Sheraton Carlton Hotel in downtown Washington to face a room full of reporters. They were on hand to record the historic moment when the greatest coach alive would take over one of the most storied but futile franchises in the NFL.

"It is not true that I can walk across the Potomac—even when it is frozen," Lombardi said jokingly, but accurately capturing the reaction to his arrival in the nation's capital as the new coach of the Washington Redskins.

Lombardi's move to Washington to coach the Redskins was treated like a biblical event. After all, Redskins fans had been looking for someone to lead them to the Promised Land since 1945, the last time Washington had played in an NFL championship game. Since then, the franchise had just three winning seasons, the last one coming in 1955, and had gone through nine head coaches, the latest failure being former NFL great Otto Graham, who was fired after the 1968 season—after three years and a 17-22-3 record.

Linebacker Sam Huff   "When Lombardi got here, it was like, 'God has arrived.' He was in charge of every room he walked into. He was like no one we had seen before in Washington."

. . .

Redskins owner Edward Bennett Williams, who became team president in 1965 after buying into the club three years earlier, didn't have the stomach for losing, and he had an eye for big names.

That was why he hired Otto Graham, the former Cleveland Browns star quarterback who had been coaching at the U.S. Coast Guard Academy and did not have any particular hunger for coaching in the NFL. Williams's ten-year, $300,000 offer to Graham made him hungry enough to take the job, but it was a bad fit from the start.

That was why, after the team's losses under Otto Graham, Williams took no such chances this time. He went out and hired not just a coach, but a savior, and Lombardi, who had led the Green Bay Packers to five NFL championships and an overall record of 141-39-4 during his tenure, did not disappoint at that historic February 7, 1969, press conference, as he handed down some of his commandments about winning:

> I will demand a commitment to excellence and to victory. That is what life is all about. . . .
>
> Hard-nosed football means what the mental approach of a player should be. They had better be physically tough when they start pulling on their football pants. . . .
>
> The first requisite for a team is defense. Go back through football and you will see that the team with the best defense wins.

Actually, if you go back through football history, you will see that the team with Vincent Lombardi coaching it usually wins.

Lombardi was born in Brooklyn, New York, on June 11, 1913. He attended St. Francis Prep in Brooklyn—originally studying to be a priest—and Fordham University, where, at 5-foot-8 and 165 pounds, he was one of the heralded Seven Blocks of Granite on the Fordham line. He graduated magna cum laude with a business degree in 1937 and spent the next two years working at a finance company, going to law school at night, and playing semipro football for the Wilmington Clippers in Delaware.

He never had a losing season as a coach in a career that started in 1939 at St. Cecelia High School in Englewood, New Jersey. In 1947,

Lombardi was a freshman coach at Fordham, and two years later he joined the staff of Red Blaik at West Point. He was hired by New York Giants coach Jim Lee Howell to be part of his staff in 1954. Lombardi was in charge of the offense, while another future NFL head coach, Tom Landry, led the defense.

Five years later Lombardi took over as head coach and general manager of the Packers. He took a team that had a 1-10-1 record the previous season and led them to a third-place finish in the Western Conference, with a 7-5 record. He never finished lower than second place with the Packers after that. He took Green Bay to the NFL title game in 1960 but lost to the Philadelphia Eagles 17–13. Lombardi brought the Packers back in 1961 and won the NFL title with a 37–0 win over the Giants. He won the championship again in 1962. He won three more NFL championships from 1965 to 1967 and also led the Packers to the first two Super Bowl wins over the American Football League.

Green Bay Packers quarterback Bart Starr "Lombardi's era coincided with a huge boom in the NFL's popularity. That helped make him the legend he became, but it also worked the other way. His mystique and the Packers' great success helped build the game's image as well."

But the physical and mental demands of the job had weighed on him over the years, and after the 1967 season Lombardi retired from coaching, moving upstairs to the Packers front office and a less stressful lifestyle. He didn't find the solace he sought, though. His wife, Marie, had long wanted out of Green Bay to go back east. The Packers organization was struggling, with Lombardi's successor, Phil Bengston, going 4-5-1 in 1968. And being a coach wasn't just a job that Lombardi once held. It was who he was.

Former Packer and team broadcaster Tony Candadeo "He just had to go back to coaching again. He felt lost up in that press box. He was the type of general who couldn't fight a war from his desk."

The word spread throughout football that Lombardi was looking to return to coaching. His name came up as a candidate for coaching the Eagles, the Patriots, and the Redskins. But there was never really any competition. Williams was not going to be denied his coach, particularly after the Redskins had failed to bring Lombardi to Washington several times before. Leo De Orsey, one of the former investors, tried unsuccessfully to get Lombardi to come to Washington in 1963. Williams had tried to lure Lombardi to Washington. A year after Williams took over controlling interest from George Preston Marshall, he tried to hire Lombardi. He also tried to hire Paul Brown, Bud Wilkinson, and Ara Parseghian before finally hiring Graham in 1966. But Lombardi was the man he had always wanted.

Williams needed a coach he considered on par with his own larger-than-life presence. As a trial lawyer, Williams had become one of the most powerful men in one of the most powerful cities in the world. He had become one of the country's most prominent attorneys, representing such clients as Mafia boss Frank Costello, Senator Joe McCarthy, and Teamsters Union president Jimmy Hoffa. He was also the lawyer for the *Washington Post* and would later press the battle for the paper to publish the Pentagon Papers and go to war with the Nixon White House. He became wealthy as a lawyer, charging a reported $1,000 an hour, and his wealth allowed him to buy into sports franchises such as the Redskins and later the Baltimore Orioles. He liked the stage that sports presented, and he enjoyed rubbing elbows with successful and powerful men—like Vince Lombardi.

Former Redskins general counsel and law partner of Williams, Larry Lucchino "Lombardi was [Williams's] kind of guy, his kind of man's man. It was a great achievement for him to talk Lombardi into coming to Washington. The big inducement was a piece of the ownership in the club."

That was the dealmaker for Lombardi—a piece of the team. Lombardi still had five years remaining on his contract with the Packers, but he was able to get out of it because he was becoming a shareholder with the Redskins. Per NFL policy, coaches and front-office personnel could be released from their contracts if they moved up to higher positions, and he was about to move up, thanks to Williams's offer: a $110,000 annual salary and the purchase of fifty shares of stock valued at $500,000. When Lombardi handed in his letter of resignation to Green Bay, he cited the ownership stake as the reason for moving on:

My decision was based on a number of factors. One was the equity position with the Washington Redskins, and I do not believe I need to go into the advantages of a capital gain position under today's tax law. The other factor was really altruistic in that I need a challenge and I have found the satisfaction of a challenge is not in maintaining a position but rather in attaining it. I can no more walk away from this challenge than I could have walked away from the one ten years ago. I am the same man today that I was ten years ago.

Of course, Lombardi also wrote about his drive to win. It was Lombardi-speak, part of his language: "Each of us, if we would grow, must be committed to excellence and to victory, even though we know complete victory cannot be attained, it must be pursued with all one's might. The championships, the money, the color; all of these things linger only in the memory. It is the spirit, the will to excel, the will to win; these are the things that endure."

Lombardi was criticized in Green Bay for leaving the organization—at least as much as Lombardi could be criticized. He was this small Wisconsin city's pride and joy, and there were some hurt feelings when he left. The *Green Bay Press-Gazette* gave him a lukewarm good-bye in an editorial, even taking him to task for not being more involved in civic affairs. And *Wisconsin State Journal* sports editor Glenn Miller wrote that Lombardi betrayed Packer fans: "It is true that our hero has treated us rather shabbily at the end. Vince Lombardi has gone off, without asking us about it, and made himself a deal in a foreign land to the east. He has cast us aside, rather roughly at that. It is probably true that our former idol has been crafty, calculating, even a little deceitful with us."

There was nothing lukewarm about his welcome to Washington. Before making the formal announcement at his press conference, Lombardi did the obligatory lunch at Duke Ziebert's Restaurant—Williams's favorite hangout and the most popular place in town among the city's power brokers. That gave all the news crews a chance to rush over from the morning press conference with President Richard M. Nixon at the White House to the Sheraton Carlton to cover the big news of the day.

"I want to announce that Vincent Lombardi will be the executive vice president and coach of the Redskins," Williams said, addressing the roomful of reporters. "This is the proudest moment of my life."

This was also the golden era of Washington sports. Lombardi would be coaching the Redskins. Hall-of-Fame slugger Ted Williams was managing the Washington Senators. And the flamboyant Lefty Driesell had taken over the basketball program at the University of Maryland in nearby College Park, declaring that he would turn the school into the UCLA of the East. Washington had gone from a sleepy sports town to a place filled with star power on par with the political power that defined the city. All this took place while the country and the nation's capital were being torn apart over Vietnam. It was a volatile time for the city, but Washington was center stage and Lombardi was now getting top billing.

Art Buchwald stated in the *Washington Post*, "Lombardi's hiring is the biggest news to hit Washington since Secretary of State Seward bought Alaska for two cents an acre." John McKelway said in the *Washington Star*, "Everything is going to be all right. Tough and talented, tireless and terrible-tempered, Lombardi is considered by many to be the greatest man alive today . . . so get ready. We are on the brink of a new era, a new beginning, a virtual renaissance."

Lombardi knew it was a big stage, and he embraced his place on it: "Why did I choose Washington among offers from other cities? Because it is the capital of the world. And I have some plans to make it the football capital . . . if the president is a pro football fan. He ought to be out to our games here in his home city."

Lombardi took on all questions, from his reasons for coming back to coaching to his expectations of the 5–9 team he was inheriting:

> My wife wants me back in coaching. She told me I was a damn fool to get out of it. She is a fan as well as a wife. Besides, I miss the rapport with the players. . . . I would like to have a winner in my first year, if possible. But we have got to have the right people. We will have to be fortunate with injuries. There will have to be a charisma between the teaching and the receiving. . . . I will try to make trades. It is not as easy as it was in 1959, when I began in Green Bay. Only two teams participated in the draft then. Now twenty-six teams do. Nobody wants to give up good players. . . . I know this—they [the Redskins] have a great quarterback [Sonny Jurgensen] and great receivers [Charley Taylor, Bobby Mitchell, and Jerry Smith].

The Redskins had great offensive players, but they needed help on defense, and an old favorite would return for the 1969 season. Linebacker Sam Huff had retired after the 1967 season, but happened to run into Lombardi on an airplane when negotiations were taking place for him to come to Washington.

Sam Huff   "I had retired after the 1967 season. I couldn't take it anymore, what I saw happen to that football team. I didn't want to be a part of that. I wound up on a flight with Lombardi. I said to him, 'I'd still like to play.' Lombardi asked me if I really thought I could still play, and I told him yes.

"He said, 'I need you to play for me.'

"So we struck a deal for me to be a player-coach. At the time, I wanted to be a coach. It was hard work, but it was quite an experience for me, to sit in meetings with Lombardi and see the man in action and learn all about him."

That was the kind of authority that Lombardi had—bringing retired players back before he even got the job. Once he did get the job, it was clear that he was in charge. The first time he met with the team as a group, he told them, "Gentlemen, there is just one thing that I want you to understand. If you do anything to embarrass me or the organization, in any way, you will answer to me and me alone."

Lombardi's demand for authority, though, raised questions about how he might get along with Williams, who, though he adored Lombardi, was not the kind of owner who was happy being out of the loop. Though Williams loved Lombardi and shared many things with him—including attending daily Catholic mass—they were very different men. Williams was the ultimate dealmaker, a man who loved the art of compromise and negotiation. He knew his coach was nothing like that. "Vince saw everything as black and white," Williams later said. "He saw a dichotomy between right and wrong. He didn't see gray areas."

During his introductory press conference, Lombardi was asked about who would be the final decision maker in the franchise. He replied, "Well, I have been given his office."

When asked if he would let Williams meet with the players, Lombardi said, "No, that won't be necessary."

Williams smiled up on the dais and said, "I just asked Vince if I could have my same season tickets."

But there was a moment when the two of them butted heads, although it turned out to be a one-sided affair. Williams liked the notion of schmoozing with players, but there would be none of that with Lombardi as coach. A few weeks after taking the job, Williams mentioned to Lombardi that Jurgensen had come to the owner's office to talk to him. Lombardi was enraged. "Wait a minute!" he yelled, "I want you to remember one damn thing. If you ever talk to the ballplayers or disrupt anything I'm trying to do here, you can find yourself a new coach! I'm the one who is the coach. I don't want you to talk to anyone!"

Williams was not used to being spoken to in that manner. He was a man who went toe-to-toe with the most powerful people in the country. But he so wanted the Redskins to be a winning franchise that he swallowed his pride and embraced Lombardi's iron hand.

Larry Lucchino "They were only together for a year, but it was as if he and Williams had been together for much longer, the way Williams spoke about Lombardi. He talked about him in the most reverential terms."

There was one other relationship the press was curious about: Lombardi and Jurgensen. The Redskins quarterback was a legendary carouser and was known for both his slight paunch hanging over his uniform and his rifle arm. Someone asked Lombardi to compare Jurgensen to Bart Starr, his great quarterback in Green Bay. "Sonny is a great passer," he said. "Starr is a good passer and does a lot of other things well. Sonny will, too, I hope."

And when he was asked about Jurgensen's quoted fondness for "Scotch and broads," Lombardi said, "I will have no preconceived notions about anybody. They will all be fresh faces to me. Everything about the past is in the past as far as I am concerned. . . . There are fifteen times more bars in Green Bay than there are in Washington, despite the difference in size. But I believe in as few rules as possible."

Lombardi believed in developing close relationships with his quarterbacks, and he treated them differently from his other players. He had one with Starr in Green Bay and he wanted to do the same thing with Jurgensen. He would meet with his quarterbacks for film sessions three mornings a week, apart from the team film meetings, of which there were many. It was important for Lombardi to be close to his quarterbacks, because they called the plays on the field, and he wanted them to think like he would think, to do what he would do.

He met with Jurgensen shortly after being hired and told him, "I've heard a lot of things about you as a person and as a player, and I'm sure you've heard a lot of things about me. Well, that's got nothing to do with our relationship. I just ask one thing of you: I want you to be yourself. Don't emulate anyone else. Don't try to be someone you're not. Just be yourself."

Jurgensen not only went along with Lombardi's style, he embraced it.

Quarterback Sonny Jurgensen   "It was easy to see why Green Bay had been so successful. He had simple concepts that were easy to understand and great preparation. He told me, 'I'm going to be tougher on you than anyone else, because you're the leader of this team.' And he was hard on me, but that was good, because it set an example for the rest of the players. They could see if he was hard on me, what would he be like with them. So everybody played hard.

"In our first practice, he told me I was throwing the ball too quickly. I said, 'I've had to throw the ball very quickly to get rid of it.' He said, 'We'll give you the best pass protection you've ever had.' And he did. We had a good year offensively, and after the year he congratulated me for the season I had in front of the other coaches. He said, 'I appreciate how hard you've worked, and the kind of year you had. Next year, you'll complete 70 percent of your passes because you didn't really know the system that well this year.' And if he had been there, I would have completed 70 percent of my passes.

"Bart Starr told me that Lombardi was all about intense preparation, and it was true. You were never surprised on the field, and he always gave you a chance to win."

The great preparation that was Lombardi's trademark took up most of his time after he got started on the job. Before meeting any of the players, Lombardi watched two years' worth of films of Redskins games, over and over, from morning to night. He studied each player and every defense and offense they faced. "On each play in every game I'd run the projector back and forth three or four times with seven or eight people in mind, and then I'd run it back again to see what the three or four others were doing," he once wrote.

He was stunned by the lack of preparation he saw. "They were making up plays in the huddle," Lombardi observed.

Lombardi took extensive notes and, on a yellow pad, charted each play for both offense and defense. Then he organized everything in an orderly and easily accessible filing system. He graded and wrote a report on every player, and then made judgments whether a player should stay or go. He also brought highlight reels from Green Bay to show the Redskins how it can be done when it is done according to Lombardi's standards.

Safety Brig Owens   "We had a lot of talent on the Redskins already, but what Lombardi brought was a sense of organization to the club, hard work, and a no-nonsense approach to the game."

The work, though, would get to Lombardi. Shortly after he arrived, he had a urinary tract infection, and he struggled with stomach problems that bothered him throughout his adult life. But he didn't let on to his players that he was anything less than the Lombardi they had heard of—and feared—from his private meetings with them, to the first time they took the field for a four-day minicamp on June 16 at Georgetown University, to training camp nearly a month later at Dickinson College in Carlisle, Pennsylvania.

Brig Owens   "There was a lot of fear when Lombardi got here. He was a legendary coach. When a coach of that status comes in, you know there is going to be some housecleaning, so you worry about whether or not you're going to have a job. And he turned out to be everything that I expected.

"If you were afraid of him, you couldn't play for him. He had his way of testing everybody. He felt if you could withstand his pressure, the games would be easy. And he was right. He was a master motivator. He said that consistency is the truest measure of performance. You can have good and bad days, but it is how you rebound and take the setbacks in stride and keep moving forward. Don't take anything for granted. Lombardi preached that."

. . .

Training camp began on July 9 in Carlisle, and it was a star-studded affair, with Washington elite such as columnist Art Buchwald and *Washington Post* editor Ben Bradlee joining Williams to observe. They saw a training camp that the Redskins had never seen before. Three rookies left camp in the first week. Second-year running back Bob Brunett walked out after becoming the target of Lombardi's abuse. And the coach had no patience for public relations. Once after a practice, with his wife coming toward him on the field, Lombardi told the writers, "Marie will answer your questions today," and he went into the clubhouse.

Then there was the first team meeting that took place in training camp, where players learned about "Lombardi time," with running back Ray McDonald the victim of the lesson. McDonald a big, highly touted back from Idaho, was the Redskins' first-round draft choice in 1967. But he was a huge disappointment during his rookie year, and he became a symbol of frustration of Redskins fans for the organization's ineptness, so much so that Lombardi went out of his way during the press conference when he was introduced to Redskins fans to defend Washington's decision to draft McDonald. Lombardi said he, too, would have drafted McDonald in 1967, as the Redskins did.

Later, during minicamp, Lombardi would make McDonald a project. He was 6-foot-4, 250 pounds, with huge potential, and Lombardi told backfield coach George Dickson to work with McDonald. McDonald never fulfilled his potential, but he did serve a purpose for Lombardi.

Cornerback Pat Fischer "His training camps were very tough. In his first meeting with us, we became acquainted with 'Lombardi time.' Ray McDonald came in late for a meeting. There were two swinging doors in the back of the auditorium at Dickinson College. McDonald came through those doors after Lombardi had been speaking for about four or five minutes. Right then and there, Lombardi announced that this player had been released.

"When he realized it was McDonald, he told him to pack up his equipment and report to a semipro team we had a relationship with in Virginia Beach. He never did come back to the team. You can imagine the impact that had. We didn't have anyone come late to meetings after that."

· · ·

Linebacker Chris Hanburger—an eighteenth-round draft choice in 1965 out of the University of North Carolina—was one of the few standout defensive players on those struggling Redskins defensive teams from 1965 to 1968. He welcomed the chance to play for a coach who valued defense like Lombardi did, although, like many of his teammates, he went into it with some fear.

Linebacker Chris Hanburger "It was great to play for Lombardi. I think most of us had a certain amount of fear, and certainly respect, for Lombardi. We really didn't know what he would be like, other than what we had seen and read, and that was enough to put a little fear in you. But he was a wonderful human being. He had a good sense of humor and could communicate with the players well. And things were well organized with him. It was a pleasure to play for him. I think the minute everyone knew he was coming here they scrambled to get into the best shape of their lives. I think he laid the foundation for the Redskins that took place in later years, especially for the players who stayed here. I enjoyed being around him.

"He told us in one of the meetings, before practice started, that we had to go around one of the fields at training camp three times. I used to go out there and walk around the field three times. He had a golf cart, and he would ride around before practice and make different stops. He didn't know all our names yet, so he stopped by me and said, 'Mister, why are you walking around the field?' I said, 'Coach, you said we had to go around the field. You didn't say how, but if you want me to jog, then I'll jog.' I was laughing when I said it, and he had a big grin on his face, shook his head, and said, 'Boy, have I mellowed.' I got a big kick out of that. It showed how human he really was."

Punter Mike Bragg said the change in approach from Graham to Lombardi was dramatic. Lombardi may have shown that he was human, but his training camp seemed anything but human.

Punter Mike Bragg "Otto was a nice guy, a great athlete in his own right, but oftentimes the greatest athletes don't make the greatest coaches. But when Lombardi came, it was completely different. Things were so tough. I was in the army then, in the reserves, and I had gone off to do my six months' active duty. I was at Fort Polk, Louisiana, and when I came back, I was about three weeks late for training camp. When I got there, everybody told me how bad it was. Lombardi came up to me the first day I got back and said something very nice to me. And I was in great shape. I had been sleeping on the ground, doing ten-mile road marches, and training, because I was in an infantry military police training program. When I came out of that, I was pretty damn tough. Half the guys who I was in basic training and advanced infantry training with were bound for Vietnam. I was in the reserves, so I came back. But it was a tough training camp, and it seemed to go on forever.

"We broke camp at Carlisle and came back to Washington and stayed at the Washingtonian Hotel in Gaithersburg, Maryland, and practiced at Gaithersburg High School. The bus would pull up at night, and a few people would get on and a few people would get off. Lombardi was looking at everybody, and he was looking for something special he could see in a person, a special mental toughness. You had to be mentally tough. You definitely had to be physically tough, but everyone had to be mentally tough. I don't care if you were a scout on the road; he demanded it."

If there was one particular example of Lombardi's coaching skill—his attention to detail—it was his handling of rookie running back Larry Brown. The promising young back had been struggling, and Lombardi was determined to find out why. It was Lombardi who saw in Brown what other coaches did not, after all the years Brown spent playing football at the youth, high school, and college levels.

Running back Larry Brown "We were sitting in a meeting at RFK Stadium before the season began. I was asked why I was late getting off on the snap count, compared to the rest of the time. When you slowed the film down, it was noticeable that I was late getting off the ball. I explained that I was having some difficulty in recognizing the defenses, which created the hesitation in my movement. He accepted that, at least I thought he did. Shortly after that, I was sitting in the locker room at RFK when I was approached by two men wearing white coats. They were doctors on a mission, under orders from Lombardi, to give me a hearing examination. When I saw them I said to myself, 'What did I do wrong?' All I could think of was they were from a mental institution. I realized then that my explanation didn't hold a whole lot of water, since he had decided that I needed a hearing exam.

"No one had ever asked me about my hearing before. I played four years of college football and no one ever addressed it with me. I thought I had covered it up pretty well. When I got in trouble on the field in college, I would look at the football and watch when it moved. I was out of sync for a second or two, but I caught up quickly. I had never talked about it, so no one had any reason to suspect it was a problem until Lombardi. I thought it was pretty shrewd for him to pick that up. It said a lot about the type of person he was and his knowledge of the game and players.

"He got permission from the league to have a hearing aid in my helmet. The day they hooked it up inside my helmet, Lombardi asked me to put the helmet on and to go to one side of the locker room, and he went to another side of the locker room. He said, 'Larry, can you hear me?'

"I said to him, 'Coach, I never had any trouble hearing you.'"

Lombardi brought a sense of discipline to the Redskins, harnessing the talent on offense and making more demands on defense. He did this through his repetitive practices—going over plays and techniques countless times, until the execution was second nature. He started the season focusing on fundamental principles. Throughout the exhibition season, Lombardi devoted the games to changing the philosophy of the high-powered but undisciplined offense, concentrating on Lombardi-style drives and a stronger defense.

Sonny Jurgensen   "Before Lombardi, we were struggling every week. It was always second and eight."

Not everyone appreciated Lombardi's hard-driving style, though they endured it.

Center Len Hauss   "Lombardi was a big influence on the franchise. His reputation preceded him. He was an impact-type of person, and he made an impact on the organization. But for me, I really didn't appreciate his style of coaching. That year under Lombardi was the toughest of my career. I'm not saying he wasn't a great coach. Of course he was. He was a great man. If he had been a writer, he would have been one of the best writers. If he had been a car salesman, he would have been the best at that, too. But I didn't particularly care for his methods.

"One day after practice at Carlisle, Sonny and I were out talking, and he said, 'Isn't this great? Lombardi is the greatest coach I've ever seen. He kicks you in the butt and makes you give one hundred percent. That's what we need.'

"I said, 'Sonny, you need that, but he's kicking me in the butt, and I'm already giving one hundred ten percent anyway. I don't need that.' I thought I was already giving everything I had. That was my nature. I didn't need that butt-kicking. But Sonny thought that was great, and that's fine. Sonny had a great year under Lombardi."

Hauss, though, was just the sort of player that Lombardi appreciated—as was someone who would later become a historic figure in the American sports landscape, a tough running back from Detroit named Dave Kopay, who, in 1977, would make history by later revealing that he was gay and writing the book *The Dave Kopay Story.*

Running back Dave Kopay   "I had always had good games against Lombardi's team, and when he brought me to Washington, I had just come off a knee operation. Detroit really messed me up. I tore my cartilage in training camp, and they never told me that it was torn. They just kept treating it during the week, draining it on Friday, I'd play a little bit on Sunday, they'd drain it again on Monday. I would get through the week, and it would happen all over again. Then at the end of the season they operated on me. Even though I was hurt, they traded a second- and fourth-round draft choice for me, which was kind of unheard of, since I had been a rookie free agent for the 49ers. Yet, I never fulfilled their ideal, and I got badmouthed for not playing like I should be playing. But I wasn't playing like that because I was hurt. I struggled through the whole year because I was hurt. It was horrible. And that was when I was really fighting the whole thing about coming out and wondering what the hell was going on. When I got to Washington, Lombardi treated me with respect. He would yell at me like he would anybody, 'What the hell are you doing there, mister? You're really something.'"

Kopay was not the only gay player on the Redskins. Years later it was revealed that All-Pro tight end Jerry Smith was also gay, and though a number of players were aware of it, it only became public knowledge after Smith died of AIDS in 1987.

Dave Kopay   "Lombardi was around people who were gay. I don't think he knew that I was gay. I sometimes wonder if he knew Jerry was. When I went to Washington, I met Jerry and fell in love with him. He was much more mature in terms of his being out than I was. I was just coming out, and he had been out for a while. In dealing with the gay culture, I hardly had any experiences at all, and Jerry was flying off to France and doing all kinds of things. I felt accepted in Washington, because as I got to be there with Jerry, and Walter Rock, who was straight and an old teammate from San Francisco, he made me feel comfortable as well. It made it easier for me to be accepted as one of the guys, because Walter knew me, so I was okay among the guys. And Jerry was so highly respected by everybody, with his friendship, too, I was very accepted and felt very good with the Redskins. They made me feel good about myself, and it eventually allowed me to speak out. When Jerry was still playing, and I spoke out, he was very supportive of me. A lot of our mutual friends thought I was outing him, but I wasn't outing him. I never directed anything to him. In fact, I directed everything away from him. If it wasn't for those people who gave me the courage to be myself . . . even Lombardi, in a way, who brought me there, it gave me a sense of well-being that I was okay. It was because of my time with the Redskins. The town was also a welcoming, open kind of place."

Kopay wrote about a gay Redskin in his book, but he didn't reveal that it was Jerry Smith. He used the fictional name "Bill Stiles":

Even before coming to the Redskins, I had heard talk about certain players there who were homosexual, but because of my own fears of being discovered, I never asked their names and apparently blocked them out if I ever did hear. The result was that I had no idea who they were when I first joined the Redskins. One was Bill Stiles (fictional name), an all-pro respected by his teammates on the field and personally liked by most of them, too. For myself, I admired the way Stiles played and his casual manner with his teammates.

Kopay wrote that he later went to bed with Stiles after a night out at a gay bar in Baltimore:

A while later Stiles and I had been in a party, and were so drunk we got lost on our way back to a friend's house outside Washington, where we both were staying. I took off my clothes and fell asleep as soon as I closed my eyes. I woke up with Stiles lying on top of me, kissing me all over. I had never felt anything like this. I was in a kind of ecstasy lying there in the arms of this person I shared so much with.

Kopay wrote that after this, he was disappointed that he was rejected by Stiles and that they never spoke of it again.

Dave Kopay   "That player in the book was Jerry. He wasn't really interested in a relationship. He was interested in a roll in the hay. Okay, I got what I wanted, like a man with a one-night stand with a woman. We got together a couple of times, but it was not very satisfying and it was frustrating. But even fighting that battle made me grow up a bit. It did make it more difficult for what I should have been focusing on on the field. I didn't want to name him when I wrote the book."

These were changing times, both in society and on the football field—particularly for the Redskins franchise. The club didn't have a "great" year under Lombardi. But they had a winning year, the first one since 1955, and, more important, the team gained credibility and respect, both among themselves and throughout the NFL.

The Lombardi regime got off to the right start on September 21 with a 26–20 win at New Orleans, with Jurgensen throwing two touchdown passes to Taylor and Smith. They defeated a future Redskin in the process, Saints quarterback Billy Kilmer. In the final minute of the game, the Saints drove to midfield, but with two seconds left, Pat Fischer knocked down a long pass to Saints receiver Al Dodd, and Lombardi had his first Redskins victory.

Mike Bragg   "He entered the locker room after the game and came over to me, just the second time he ever spoke to me, and said, 'You did a great job out there today.' He was very emotional, hugging everyone because it was his first game and first win as a Redskin. But the next day at practice, all that emotion was out the window. He had seen the film and was shining the light on everybody. He was running the film back and forth, saying to people, 'What the hell are you doing here? What are you doing here? Look at you.' He would run it back and forth, back and forth. So the elation of winning the first game was gone. It was back to work. You had twenty-four hours to enjoy it. When we came back, it was like it never happened. We got used to it, and it was a great year for us."

Washington lost to Cleveland 27–23 on the road, in a game that Washington had led, 23–20, with five minutes to play. The Browns scored to take the lead with less than two minutes remaining, and the Redskins took the kickoff and nearly marched down the field to win the game on a series of passes from Jurgensen, but the time ran out with Washington on the Browns' 23-yard line. After the game, Lombardi told reporters, "I told the team when we started that if we lost, I wanted it to be only because they ran out of time, not out of desire or condition. They saw what I meant against the Browns."

Then, in their third straight road game, they tied the 49ers at San Francisco 17–17, pulling out the tie when Jurgensen threw a 1-yard touchdown pass to Smith with twenty-five seconds left in the game.

With a record of 1-1-1, Redskins fans finally got to see Lombardi at home, in the newly named Robert F. Kennedy Stadium, after the late New York senator. Washington defeated St. Louis 33–17, with Jurgensen completing 19 of 34 passes for 239 yards and 2 touchdowns. It was a strong defensive performance for the Redskins, holding Cardinals quarterback Jim Hart to just 13 completions and intercepting 5 passes.

They followed that with a 20–14 victory over the New York Giants, behind an 86-yard punt return by Ricky Harris after the Giants took a 14–0 lead in the first half. The city was now in a Redskins frenzy, which created a very strange atmosphere and quite a contrast to the political turmoil that brought 250,000 people to Washington for the October 15 moratorium against the Vietnam War. Lombardi, who was considered a hero by political conservatives for his disciplinarian style and military demeanor—though Lombardi never served in the military—was not pleased by the displays on the street. So he engineered a halftime show at the Giants game called

"The Flag Story," a patriotic display that brought a letter of appreciation from President Nixon.

Lombardi was a hero to the Republican Party, and there were
rumors the year before that he was being considered as a vice presidential candidate to run with Nixon—until party officials learned that the
coach was actually a registered Democrat. Lombardi would also
become a symbol of the country's ills to the antiestablishment youth
except in Washington, where he was royalty, no matter what his political leanings were. And they were most definitely conservative, according to the description of Lombardi's politics and personality by his
friend and boss, Edward Bennett Williams. "He was very, very conservative, very right wing, and very hard line," Williams said. "He was
very impatient and intolerant of the kids and their revolutionary ideas.
He really felt a certain hostility to the tremendous forces of change."

The Redskins won their third straight game with a 14–7 victory
over the Steelers in Pittsburgh, then they went to Baltimore to take a
severe 41–17 beating from the Colts. The Redskins offense nearly
matched the Colts in total yards, with Washington amassing 357 yards
and the Colts 359 yards. Jurgensen threw 3 interceptions, and the
Colts blocked a punt as well.

With a 4-2-1 record, the Redskins returned home to play Philadelphia, tying the Eagles 28–28. It should have been a Redskins win, but
rookie defensive back Mike Bass was called for pass interference with
a little more than a minute remaining, putting the ball on the 1-yard
line, which led to the Eagles' touchdown to tie the game. Lombardi
was livid that a similar call wasn't made on the Eagles with seconds left
on a Redskins drive, and after the game he told reporters that it was
"one of our most disappointing games."

Mike Bragg   "We were having trouble all year with punt snaps. John
Didion, I think, hit me in the hands with a perfect snap from center,
and I dropped it. I was lucky because it hit the ground flat and
bounced right back up into my hands. I looked up, though, and
nobody was rushing me. So I took off and ran 40 yards with it. It was
right before the first half. I came to the sideline, thinking, 'Damn, that's
the biggest play we had in the whole first half.' Lombardi came over
and started screaming at me. He said, 'All you've got to do is catch
the ball and punt it.' He was mad. I wasn't supposed to be running the
ball. He was screaming and hollering at me."

Washington lost its next home game, going down to the Dallas Cowboys 41–28, in a game attended by President Nixon–the first president ever to see a regular season NFL game in person, as he watched Jurgensen throw three touchdowns in defeat. Nixon was an avid football fan, but his relationship with the Redskins grew much closer under George Allen, whom Nixon had known for twenty years.

Lombardi was frustrated by his team's inconsistency. "We're a team that plays in spurts," he said. "But they're playing with everything they got and once in a while they put it all together for a long drive. You can't give more than the best you've got. But obviously we can be outclassed."

They came back to beat the Atlanta Falcons before the hometown fans by 27–20, but lost to the Los Angeles Rams 24–13. Redskins fans got a glimpse of the future in this game, as the Rams won in typical George Allen fashion, with the Rams blocking a punt and intercepting a pass.

Playing the Eagles in Philadelphia this time, the Redskins came out on top 34–29, and came home to defeat the Saints for the second time 17–14. They lost their last game of the season 20–10 to the Cowboys in Dallas, in what turned out to be the last game Vince Lombardi would coach.

The team finished with a 7-5-2 record. Jurgensen led the league in passing with 3,102 yards, 274 completions, and 22 touchdowns. Taylor caught 71 passes for 883 yards, and Brown rushed for 888 yards. Six Redskins went to the Pro Bowl: Jurgensen, Brown, Smith, Fischer, Hauss, and Hanburger. Lombardi said he was disappointed, even though it was the same record he had in his first year at Green Bay. "I thought we could have had a better win-loss record," he said. "I hope we can find some better people. That's what we're going to have to do–find them."

But he would not get the chance to search for his kind of players. Lombardi had shown signs of fatigue during his first year back in coaching, and after the season his health began to deteriorate. He was suffering from internal bleeding and general weakness, though the official word was that he had "flu-like symptoms." He went to see team doctor George Resta, who sent Lombardi to Georgetown University Hospital. He was first officially diagnosed with a stomach virus, but doctors were looking for something more. They found it on June 27, 1970, when, while performing exploratory surgery, they found a tumor in his colon and operated to remove it.

Lombardi got out of the hospital on July 10, but his line coach, Bill Austin, was now running the team on an interim basis. Lombardi was driven to Baltimore to watch a rookie scrimmage against the Colts rookies at Memorial Stadium. He was gaunt and had difficulty speaking, as he sat in the press box during the game. But he went into the Redskins' locker room before the game and talked to the rookies: "You're my people; I've selected you. You're going to wear this uniform with pride. You're now a member of the Washington Redskins, and there's a lot of responsibility that goes along with that. Don't you ever forget it."

Lombardi went back into the hospital for more surgery on July 27. Doctors had now diagnosed the tumor as malignant. He had more surgery, and it was determined that the cancer had spread through his body. While this was going on, the NFL was embroiled in its first players' strike. The new union—a merger of the NFL and the American Football League Players Association—was led by Baltimore Colts tight end John Mackey, who refused to deal with management as the union had in the past, which typically was simply to accept what was offered. Mackey led the players out on strike during training camp over more money for pensions and other issues.

A number of players kept working out on a practice field at Georgetown University. Lombardi had a view of those workouts from his hospital room. Players came to see him every day.

Sonny Jurgensen   "One day he asked me who was leading the team when we did laps. I told him it was me. He looked at me with his big grin and said, 'Don't you lie to me, Jurgensen,' and we both started laughing."

Chris Hanburger   "A lot of us were working out in Georgetown. He came to one of our sessions. He was driven there. He looked like he wanted to yell and holler at us, but I don't think he had the strength to do it. That was the last I saw him. I remember having a lot of sorrow in my heart for the man."

Lombardi's condition and how quickly he seemed to fail caught some players by surprise.

Larry Brown   "We discovered he had a problem, and then he was gone, just like that. There wasn't much time in between. He knew this problem existed long before we did, and to me that is just another layer of the toughness that he displayed."

Though he was confined to a hospital bed, Lombardi wound up playing a role in the dispute between owners and players—an ugly role that he was likely unaware of: his condition was used by management to pressure the union to stop their walkout.

Baltimore Colts tight end John Mackey   "I was in Duke Ziebert's with my teammate and union confidant, Bill Curry, having dinner with Sergeant Shriver, the former head of the Peace Corps. He was trying to get the Players Association into working for Democratic candidates. In walks Edward Bennett Williams. He saw me and yelled across the room, 'It's your fault.'

"I didn't recognize him. I said, 'What do you mean it's my fault?'

"'The problem we're having with the players and the owners is your fault!' Williams said.

"I turned to Shriver and said, 'Sergeant, I don't even know this man. I don't mind taking criticism, but I'd like to know where it's coming from.'

"Shriver said, 'John, meet Edward Bennett Williams.'

"I had heard so much about Williams and admired him so much that I asked him for his autograph. He gave it to me and went off to another part of the restaurant and had dinner, but later he came over and asked me if he could talk to me. We went to the bar and sat down.

"'You know, there's only one thing in life that I've ever wanted, and now that I have it, nothing means anything,' he said.

"'What are you talking about?' I asked.

"'I always wanted to be in business with Vince Lombardi, and now that we're in business together, he's dying,' Williams said, his voice breaking up as he started to cry.

"I couldn't believe what was going on. I found myself crying along with him. But while I'm sure Williams was genuinely upset about the prospects of Lombardi dying, he turned out to be the opening act in a full-court press by the owners to use Lombardi's deathbed as a bargaining chip.

"Not long after seeing Williams, I went to a meeting with NFL commissioner Pete Rozelle and we wound up at Ed Sabol's house in

Philadelphia. Rozelle gets a phone call and leaves the room. He comes back with tears in his eyes and says, 'Vince is dying. You know what that means? If he dies before you sign the contract, the public is going to believe you killed him. You've got to sign it because he is the Kennedy of football. If you don't sign before he dies, everything is going to stop and we're going to lose the whole season.'"

They didn't lose the season. The union signed a new contract on August 1 and came back to camp. But Lombardi would never leave the hospital. He was dying, and his former players from Green Bay– Jimmy Taylor, Jerry Kramer, Fuzzy Thurston, and Willie Davis, among others, made the trip to Washington to say good-bye.

The end came at 7:12 A.M. on September 3. Vince Lombardi, at the age of fifty-seven, had died from colon cancer. President Nixon interrupted a state dinner for the president of Mexico in San Diego to speak about Lombardi.

The funeral was held at St. Patrick's Cathedral in New York City. Terence Cardinal Cooke, a friend of Lombardi's, officiated the memorial service. Among his pallbearers were Williams, Starr, Davis, Paul Hornung, and Giants owner Wellington Mara, who was a class-mate of Lombardi's at Fordham. The entire Redskins team flew to New York to be among three thousand mourners at the funeral. Two days earlier, they played an exhibition game against the Miami Dolphins in Tampa.

Williams eulogized Lombardi: "He had a covenant with greatness. He was committed to excellence in everything he attempted. . . . Our country has lost one of its great men. The world of sports has lost its first citizen. The Redskins have lost their leader. I personally have lost a friend."

Receiver Charley Taylor "Lombardi would get the most out of every athlete he had. He knew their limits. He knew how far to push them. He had a great feel for his talent and his people. He taught us how to win."

Sam Huff "Lombardi was the one who turned not just the football team around, but the whole city. When he died, it was like your father passing away."

The league also lost one of its legends. Three days after Lombardi's death, Rozelle renamed the Super Bowl Trophy the Vince Lombardi Trophy. Lombardi was inducted into the Pro Football Hall of Fame in 1971. But while the Redskins may have lost their leader after just one season—only fourteen games—he was there long enough to have a lasting legacy on the franchise.

Quarterback Sonny Jurgensen   "He was a great leader. Nobody came close to him. It was unfair to have him around all the time. What an advantage you had. He turned the franchise around."

The Redskins enjoyed success later under George Allen and then Joe Gibbs, but it was Lombardi who started them on that path after so many years of losing. He didn't walk across the Potomac. He just paved the road to victory.

5

Every Time You Win, You're Reborn

Edward Bennett Williams was a man struck by stars. The Redskins owner brought Vince Lombardi to Washington, and, after one losing season under Lombardi's successor, Bill Austin—a 6–8 record and a fourth-place finish in the National Football Conference (NFC) Eastern Division—Williams was determined to bring in another big name. Thanks to Los Angeles Rams owner Dan Reeves, he got his star when Reeves fired his high-profile head coach George Allen, despite a record of 49-17-4 during his tenure with the Rams. Reeves didn't like the way Allen operated: aggressively and secretly.

Williams could live with that, if Allen finished the job that Lombardi had started—taking the Washington Redskins to an NFL championship. Jack Kent Cooke, still a minority owner of the Redskins who also owned the Forum in Los Angeles, was a fan of Allen's and tried to have him hired in Washington the first time Reeves fired Allen in 1968, before Williams convinced Lombardi to take the job and before Reeves changed his mind and brought Allen back to coach the Rams again.

When Cooke and Williams got the chance to hire Allen again, this time they sealed the deal, and Williams made it clear why they did when he made the announcement of the Redskins new coach. "We have had a losing syndrome for fifteen years with one exception," Williams told reporters. "I think we have an obligation to get the best possible coach and personnel. I think we have taken a dramatic step in signing George Allen."

Williams said he would have made the coaching change even if he could not get Allen. Austin was gone, regardless. "I was terribly disappointed with our 1970 season, particularly the fourth quarter of our loss to the Giants in New York and the debacle in Dallas. But it was the most distasteful thing in my adult life— not renewing Austin's contract. I have a high regard for him. I admire him. But I know he has another job in the NFL, which it is up to him to talk about."

But he had his sights set on Allen. Williams told reporters that he had been in deep negotiations with Allen's high-profile Hollywood attorney, Ed Hookstratten, for a week before closing the deal. "I regard him as the best football coach in the world," said Williams, who couldn't imagine himself hiring anyone but the best. "I am delighted. Many other teams have coveted his services. I am saying unequivocally, unqualifiedly, and unambiguously that he is the last coach I will ever hire."

Allen, who was forty-nine at the time he was hired, had been sought after by several other teams, but Williams closed the deal by giving Allen a long-term contract and assuring him that he would have all the authority that Lombardi had in picking players and assembling a team. That would later come back to jokingly haunt Williams, who would be quoted as saying, "I gave George an unlimited budget and he exceeded it."

Allen tended to exceed limits because he was so driven to be the perfect football coach and was so obsessed with the details of football that he was often oblivious to life around him. Born near Detroit on April 29, 1922, he grew up as a football, basketball, and track star in high school. He enlisted in the U.S. Navy during World War II and went to school at Michigan after the war. His first coaching job was at Morningside College in Sioux City, Iowa. In 1951, he took the coaching job at Whittier College, where he spent the next six years. He made his NFL debut with the Rams in 1957, and a year later he was hired by the Chicago Bears as a defensive assistant. Under George Halas, Allen flourished, and in 1963 he was awarded the game ball following the NFL championship game in which his defense recorded five turnovers. That led to the head coaching job in Los Angeles, and then, to Washington.

At the press conference introducing Allen, the coach gave reporters a pretty honest look at the future of the Redskins under Allen's leadership. "I intend to concentrate on defense, where I will spend a majority of my time," he said.

When he was asked if he planned to make trades, Allen said. "I hope to. I plan to win in 1971. I have never believed in long-range programs of six, seven, or eight years."

He certainly wasn't lying. The benchmark of Allen's tenure as the Redskins coach was marked by one trade after another of draft choices in exchange for veterans—many of them defensive players.

George Allen made it clear to everyone the philosophy that has so identified his time as the Redskins coach: "The future is now."

His emphasis on defense would be a complete reversal of the Otto Graham days of the 1960s, when the Redskins had one of the league's most explosive offenses and more porous defenses. Under Lombardi, they reached a balance. Under Allen, it tipped far to the defensive side and would eventually result in a rift between the coach and the star quarterback he was inheriting, Sonny Jurgensen, who had thrived under Lombardi's discipline but was not Allen's kind of conservative quarterback.

Allen had nothing but praise for Jurgensen in his first Redskins press conference. Allen evaded a direct comparison of Jurgensen with Roman Gabriel of the Rams, but did say, "Sonny is one of the greatest passers in modern football with his accuracy and quick release. One of his disadvantages is that he never had the benefit of a great defense. . . . Sonny can have just as good a year next season as John Brodie of the 49ers had this year."

But he didn't have a Brodie year, or a Jurgensen year, or any kind of year, and there is a question about whether or not Allen really wanted Jurgensen to have that kind of year. He was not Allen's kind of quarterback. A broken-down quarterback named Billy Kilmer, who was wallowing in New Orleans, was, however, and Allen brought him to Washington to run what would be the exact opposite of the explosive Redskin offenses that Jurgensen had led.

What is interesting is that personality-wise, Kilmer and Jurgensen were very similar—mavericks who liked to lead on the field and have fun off of it. But Kilmer did not have the physical skills that Jurgensen did, and the skills he did have were diminished by a serious car accident that had broken both his legs a few years earlier. But he had a tremendous will to win, and that, combined with his limited skills, made him the perfect quarterback for Allen's conservative offensive style. Kilmer wasn't the starting quarterback when he arrived in Washington, but when Jurgensen broke a bone in his left shoulder while trying to tackle Dick Anderson, who had intercepted a pass, during an exhibition game against Miami going into the 1971 season, Kilmer became the Redskins starter. This began what would be perhaps the greatest quarterback rivalry, at least among fans, that the NFL had seen in recent years. As time went on, the greatest debate in Washington wasn't a political one; it was Sonny vs. Billy.

Needless to say, when Allen arrived, Jurgensen soon realized it was not the second coming of Lombardi, at least not for him, and a drastic shift in the personality of the team was about to take place.

Quarterback Sonny Jurgensen   "When Allen came in, it was strictly defense. He was the Buddy Ryan of his era. He didn't care about offense. His idea of offense was don't make any mistakes offensively and we'll win defensively. That didn't sit well with me, and it was frustrating. We had all this talent. We could score. But it became 3 yards and a cloud of dust. We clashed over the system. It was a power struggle from the get-go. Believe me, he was a heck of a defensive coach. He brought in the 'Ramskins,' all those players, and made them a good defense, and that was fine. But he didn't do anything with the offense."

It was a big adjustment for the entire offense, not just Jurgensen.

Center Len Hauss   "I was one of those guys who thought at the time that they put a little too much emphasis on the defense. One time, during a meeting, I said, 'Way to go offense. We're here to do things right. The number-one thing on our team is defense. The number-two thing is special teams. The number-three thing is the hot dog vendor, and number four is offense.' That's kind of the way George looked at it. When George came here, there was already the nucleus, to some degree, of a pretty good football team. Sonny was there, and there were several of us on the offensive line who would be starters on the Super Bowl team who were there before Allen got there. We had a pretty good team, offensively."

Regardless, there were a few offensive players who benefited from Allen's conservative approach, such as those who carried the ball.

. . .

Running back Larry Brown   "What if you were George Allen, and you had the same personnel that he had, what would you have done? Hand it off to Larry Brown. When you didn't have the ball in your hands, you didn't have a chance to demonstrate your capabilities. It worked to my benefit, because if you don't carry the ball, it's likely you won't be around long. But the more you carry it, the more punishment you take."

Some would say Larry Brown took too much punishment carrying the ball for Allen, and it cut short his career. In Allen's first season, Brown carried the ball 253 times, more than he had in either of his two previous seasons. The following year, it was even more—285 carries, followed by 273 in 1973. His totals dramatically dropped each year after that, until he was done in 1976—probably prematurely.

Allen tried to squeeze every drop of football out of a player, taking on veterans after other teams had given up on them, for one reason or another, which brought a host of new players to the Redskins shortly after Allen arrived, including the group Jurgensen referred to as the "Ramskins"—the transplanting of the Los Angeles Rams defense to Washington. Allen dealt away the Redskins' seven draft picks for a group of veterans that included linebackers Jack Pardee, Maxie Baughan, and Myron Pottios; defensive tackle Diron Talbert; defensive back Richie Petitbon; guard John Wilbur; and special teams player Jeff Jordan. He didn't stop with the Rams, though. He traded for defensive ends Verlon Biggs from New York and Ron McDole from Buffalo, and brought in receiver Roy Jefferson from Baltimore.

George Allen loved veterans, and he loved players with leadership skills who might have been too outspoken for other coaches. He went out of his way to trade for player union representatives, because he considered them to be leadership material.

Safety Brig Owens   "George enjoyed a challenge. He felt that he could change a person who had problems. He always felt a person needed a second chance. This was during the time when if a player became a player rep, he was either blackballed or traded. At one time, we had about seven or eight former player reps on the team. George would pick them up because they were leaders. With all these leaders on the team, he didn't have to do a whole lot to get players to perform. George enjoyed having leaders around him."

The players already in Washington didn't know quite what to make of the new arrivals.

Punter Mike Bragg "The guys that he brought in from the Rams, the Jets, the Bills, and all the other teams, he knew they were proven veterans, and they probably had done something in a game against him, if they didn't play with him on the Rams or the Bears. When Richie [Petibon, who was thirty-three at the time] came to training camp that year, everyone was wondering, 'How the heck can he still play? Look at him.' But he intercepted three passes in the first game. Where the ball was, Richie was. Richie was a riverboat gambler. He loved the element of chance. He was a smart, physical player. I saw him play when I was ten years old, when Tulane came up and beat Navy in Norfolk, Virginia. Tulane upset Navy, which was number two in the country at the time. Richie was the quarterback at Tulane."

Pat Fischer had been in the league for four seasons when Allen arrived, so while he was no rookie, he was still much younger than the new teammates he would be playing alongside on defense.

Cornerback Pat Fischer "We didn't know what to expect, but it was reassuring for the older players who were there, because many times when you have a change in coaching, there is usually a movement to go with youth, something that is quite different from the philosophy that George Allen had. It was all new, but a lot of these guys were players that I already knew. So it was a comfortable feeling because you felt that if you played well for George, you were going to be all right."

All these veterans and leaders were the perfect mix for the group that became known as the "Over the Hill Gang"—a team of discarded players considered past their prime who were united in their quest for winning and their quirkiness.

Pat Fischer "The Over the Hill Gang gave us an identity, and it also stimulated us. We're too old? If we had been with any other team, we probably would not have been on a team."

. . .

George Allen may have liked old players, but he got a chance to practice in a brand-new facility constructed by Williams for his team in northern Virginia, not far from Dulles Airport. Redskin Park—the first one—became the headquarters for the team and Allen's fortress, pride, and joy. He wanted everything perfect and in order at Redskin Park.

Defensive tackle Diron Talbert   "We finished training camp at Carlisle and then came down to stay at the Dulles Marriott. George brought in two buses to take the team over to see the new place for the first time. He didn't want any of us to drive over on our own. He wanted the team to see it together. He said, 'I'm going to take you over.' He wanted to hear everyone say, 'Ooh, aah.' It was really nice. When we got there, we went down to see the football fields. There were two grass fields and a turf field. George said, 'One of these grass fields has some holes in it. I want everybody to get on the goal line.' We still had a bunch of players who had not been cut yet, so there were a lot of players there. We got on the goal line and stretched across the field, taking up every space. He had the trainers give us a bunch of tongue depressors and long cotton swabs. George said, 'We're going to walk down this field, and every time you feel a hole, stick one of these sticks or swabs in the ground.' Well, he was talking to the craziest group in the world. By the time we got to the 50-yard line, we ran out of tongue depressors and sticks. So they went and got some more, and when we got to the other end of the field, there must have been 2,000 of those things stuck in the field. It was the funniest thing you'd ever see. We stuck them anyplace we could. When we got to the end and everyone was laughing, George said, 'I should have known I couldn't count on you guys.'"

Allen brought in Ed Boyton, an old hand from Los Angeles, who was better known to the players as Double O, to guard the gates of Redskin Park.

Defensive end Diron Talbert   "Double O was George's driver. George couldn't drive. He didn't have a driver's license. George would call me from his car on a Monday or a Tuesday morning. Sometimes the phone in my house would ring at five-thirty in the morning, and it would be George. He would say something like, 'Talbe, today is Billy Kilmer's birthday. Why don't you stop by and pick him up a bottle of wine and present it to him at the meeting today.' That is the kind of guy George was. But it was Double O who drove him, and who was George's security guy. George didn't allow anybody to watch practice, and Double O would walk around the field and chase people away. He also would check everyone in for breakfast every morning in training camp. You used to get fined two dollars if you didn't show up for breakfast. I'd say, 'Double O, did you check me off? You better have. I was there, you know I was there.' If you missed it again, the fine would be doubled."

Len Hauss   "Double O would make sure there were no scouts or spies from other teams watching us. George was very distrustful of people, and he thought the press might say or do things that were not in line with what his plans were. Therefore, oftentimes the press wrote negative things about him, and some of those things, like him having a security guy, which made perfect sense, they would make a big deal out of."

Brig Owens   Double O patrolled the field. He was an old, retired, military guy. He must have been about eighty years old. George had given him this job, and he took it very seriously."

Defensive end Ron McDole   "I remember one time George brought us all bicycles during training camp. I think he was on some sporting goods company board. He wanted us to ride them to practice. Most of the guys took them and sent them home, but a bunch of them put the bikes down by Double O's room, and someone stole them. George had Double O do everything. When we went to the Super Bowl, he had him walk around the top of the stadium and write down numbers of the airplanes flying overhead so he could check on them."

Allen, however, wasn't above spying himself.

Safety Mike Bass   "George once sent Double O to check on the sunset times for the Super Bowl. He also had spies everywhere to spy on other teams, so when he came up with something, we knew that it was based on accurate information. You never put anything past George."

. . .

Allen's quirks and paranoia helped contribute to his coaching persona, which had captured the attention of Washington fans and kickstarted the momentum that Lombardi had started two years earlier. It was as if Bill Austin had never been there. And the way the Redskins opened the season certainly helped the momentum that Allen's presence brought to Washington—even though it would be four weeks before Redskins fans got to see the Over the Hill Gang live.

They opened the season in St. Louis against the Cardinals and their talented passer, Jim Hart. He would be overmatched against the Allen prototype defense that counted on making the other team turn the ball over and then capitalizing on those turnovers. The old man, Richie Petitbon, intercepted a pass in the first quarter in St. Louis territory and took it down to the 1-yard line, where Larry Brown took the ball over for a 7–0 Washington lead. In the second quarter, the Cardinals came back with two scores, an 8-yard touchdown pass from Hart and a 25-yard field goal by Jim Bakken, taking a 10–7 lead into the locker room at halftime. Again, it was a turnover in the third quarter that allowed the Redskins to come back and take the lead, when linebacker Chris Hanburger picked up a fumble by the Cardinals' Sid Edwards and ran 16 yards for a touchdown and a 14–10 lead. The defense wasn't done yet, though. Washington safety Brig Owens intercepted a pass at the Cardinals' 39-yard line, and Billy Kilmer connected on a 31-yard touchdown pass to Jerry Smith for a 21–10 lead. St. Louis, with Hart now out of the game with an injury, closed the gap to 21–17 on a pass from backup quarterback Bobby Beathard, who would someday became a very familiar figure to Redskins fans. But Curt Knight added a 25-yard field goal, and the Allen era began with a 24–17 victory.

Washington fans already had a pretty good idea of how their team would win under Allen. In the second week, they saw how their team played under Allen: hard nosed and aggressive. The Redskins headed to New York to face the Giants at Yankee Stadium. The scoreboard showed that the Redskins easily handled the Giants 30–3. But they needed ringside judges to score this brawl-filled game.

New York, remarkably, opened the game with a 3–0 lead on an 18-yard field goal by Pete Gogolak. It would not last long. Kilmer hit Charley Taylor on a 71-yard touchdown pass, and linebacker Jack

Pardee intercepted a Fran Tarkenton pass and returned it 20 yards for the second score and a 14–3 lead when the first quarter ended. The scoreboard didn't reflect all the scores, though. Larry Brown scored a twenty-stitch cut on his right hand when he tried to punch Giants defensive tackle Bob Lurtsema on the first play from scrimmage for the Redskins and was called for unsportsmanlike conduct. Then, Giants Paul Laaveg and Redskins defensive end Verlon Biggs were thrown out of the game for fighting. A 52-yard Knight field goal in the second quarter gave Washington a 17–3 lead. Tarkenton added to the bad blood after being sacked three times, the third time by backup defensive end Jimmy Jones, because Biggs got tossed. Tarkenton got up from the Jones sack and threw the ball at Jones's helmet. Tarkenton joined the crowd who had drawn unsportsmanlike conduct flags.

Jimmy Jones wasn't very well known among football fans, but Allen knew who he was, and he saw him as a pass-rushing specialist not being utilized by the team who had drafted him, the New York Jets. Jones came to Washington not just with talent for rushing the passer but also with information that would help shape the Redskins defense. He basically brought Verlon Biggs with him.

Defensive end Jimmy Jones   "I was drafted by the Jets in the fifth round in 1969. They were the world champions at the time. I was there for two years. George Allen was here—it was his first year in Washington. He had seen some of my ability to rush the quarterback and traded for me in 1971. I was pretty light. I probably weighed about 230 pounds. I started out as an outside linebacker with the Jets and ended up coming to Washington as a special teams player. George Allen made me the first designated pass rusher. He told me he didn't trade for me to come in and play every down. He wanted me in pass situations, to rush the quarterback.

"I was in New York with Verlon. The press there thought Verlon had signed his contract with the Jets there, but I knew he had not signed, and when I went to Washington, I told George Allen that Verlon wasn't signed, and that he was looking to leave the Jets. Lo and behold, the next week he was down in Washington."

The win over the Giants was particularly satisfying for Allen, because he took pleasure in beating them, especially in New York.

. . .

Brig Owens "George loved going to New York and beating the Giants, and in turn beating the New York press. It was always the Giants and the New York press. They wouldn't have much to say when they got beat, so George would say after we beat them, 'Let's see what the New York press has to say now.'"

Bigger than a New York win, though, would be a victory the following week—the third straight on the road—against the hated Cowboys in Dallas. The Redskins-Cowboys rivalry developed for a number of different reasons. You could make the case that it started right from the beginning of the Dallas franchise, and continued with the personal animosity between Washington owner George Marshall and Dallas owner Clint Murchinson, who took a personal shot at Marshall by buying the rights to the Redskins' theme song—the very song that Marshall's wife, Corrine Griffith, wrote the lyrics to.

But it also developed because of the origins of so many of the Washington players.

Diron Talbert "When George was with the Rams, we used to play Dallas every year in the *Los Angeles Times* charity game. Then we practiced against them. We were in Fullerton, California, and they were at Thousand Oaks. So we used to have a three-ring circus with them. We knew them very well by the time we got to Washington."

Redskins fans knew Dallas very well, too, and it was not a pleasant relationship. They had watched their team be beaten by the Cowboys six straight times, with three different head coaches in charge. But right from the start of this game at the Cotton Bowl before a crowd of more than 61,000, Washington fans watching back at home saw that things were about to change. On the second play the Redskins offense ran, fullback Charley Harraway took a pitch from Kilmer and ran 57 yards for a touchdown. The Redskins led 7–0 and never fell behind in the game. The Cowboys got on the board with a field goal early in the second quarter, but Washington responded with a 50-yard touchdown pass from Kilmer to Roy Jefferson. It was the only pass that Kilmer completed in the first half, but he made the most of it. The Cowboys managed 2 more field goals before the first half ended, but were behind 14–9 going into the locker room. When Allen had a lead at halftime, you could be sure what the game plan would be the rest of the day: tough defense and very conservative offense.

The Redskins defense, which had already stifled Cowboys starting quarterback Craig Morton, who had thrown the ball twenty-five times in the first half, delivered by holding the Cowboys scoreless in the third quarter, while Knight added a 25-yard field goal for a 17–9 lead going into the fourth quarter. Knight added another field goal, this one a 32-yarder, and defensive end Bill Brundige delivered the crowning blow with a 29-yard sack of a scrambling Roger Staubach, brought in to replace Morton and who had appeared to bring some life to the Dallas offense. Calvin Hill scored a touchdown on a 1-yard run, ending a Dallas drive with about three minutes left in the game, but the Redskins controlled the ball the rest of the game and came away with a 20–16 victory. Kilmer had thrown the ball just ten times, but the Redskins offense controlled the ball with the running attack—Harraway had 111 yards on 18 carries and Brown had 81 yards on 21 carries. After the game, Allen told reporters that it was a "great, great victory, a complete victory."

The Redskins returned home to a city that was coming down with a big case of Redskins fever. They were the talk of the town, and now Washington fans wanted to see firsthand their new team do what it had done on the road. The Redskins did not disappoint, delivering a 22–13 victory over the Houston Oilers before the hometown crowd at RFK Stadium. And they got a firsthand look at Allen's version of offense—not what they had been used to during the high-powered scoring days in years past, when Jurgensen was leading an offense with Taylor, Smith, and Bobby Mitchell that was putting points on the board—but losing. Washington fans were more than happy to take the tradeoff of a 22–13 win, where 15 of the points came on Knight field goals, and a 4-0 start. The only touchdown was scored when defensive end Ron McDole intercepted a Charley Johnson pass at the Houston 18-yard line and went in for the score. Six of the Oilers points came on field goals kicked by someone who would someday become a Redskins fan favorite: a young Mark Moseley.

By week five, the town was starting to work itself into a frenzy as it witnessed another defensive victory by the Redskins. Three interceptions by linebacker Jack Pardee and a total of seven turnovers by St.

Louis led to a 20–0 win over the Cardinals before more than 53,000 fans at RFK Stadium, and countless more watching on television and listening to the radio–lawyers and waitresses, cops and criminals, judges and juries, all united in their passion for Washington's football team.

So when the Redskins' winning streak finally ended in Kansas City, with a 27–20 loss to the Super Bowl–defending Chiefs–and the loss for the season of All-Pro receiver Charley Taylor with a broken ankle when he was tackled after his second touchdown catch of the day–Redskins fans were expected to come down to earth.

Instead, you would have thought they were returning as NFL champions. There were an estimated 20,000 fans waiting at Dulles Airport to greet their team and show their love for the Redskins.

Mike Bragg   "We were flying into Dulles, and you could see from the plane that traffic had come to a halt on Dulles Airport Road. There were cars lining the highway. They couldn't walk us through the terminal. We had to go through a freight terminal to get to our bus. When everyone found that out, they all rushed over there. All the television stations were there. George made a speech, and it was an amazing thing."

Receiver Roy Jefferson   "We saw all those cars along the road, and it was unbelievable. I had never seen anything like that before. We couldn't figure out what was going on. We thought there was some kind of major accident or something. It was three hours before we got in and out of Redskin Park because of those crowds. That was seriously exciting."

But this was more than typical fan passion. This was hope in a place full of hopelessness. There had not been much to be happy about in the nation's capital over the last few years, for sports fans in particular and for the population in general. The glory of 1969–when Vince Lombardi coached the Redskins and Ted Williams managed a winning Senators team–was gone, lost in the death of Lombardi, the losing 1970 season, and finally the loss of a major league baseball team, with the Senators moving to Arlington, Texas, and being renamed the Texas Rangers. But the gloom covered far more than the athletic fields. The country was still suffering from the deep divide that the war in Vietnam had created, and Washington was the center of that division, with marches and protests often resulting in scenes of chaos and violence surrounding the nation's institutions. These were the postcards from Washington.

Then there was race. Washington was one of the cities that went up in flames after Dr. Martin Luther King was assassinated in 1968, and the scars of those riots still ran deep in the city, as it dealt with the issue of the growth of the suburbs and the abandonment of the city. There was not much to feel good about in Washington in 1971. Now there was.

Mike Bragg   "When we went back to practice on Tuesday, Mayor Walter Washington showed up, unannounced. He came all the way out to Dulles to talk to us. He said to George, 'Coach, I want to talk to the team. Is that okay?' George was famous for staging things like this, but after it happened, everyone concluded that George didn't stage this one. It wasn't planned. Mayor Washington said, 'Fellows, I've got to tell you something. We're going through a tough time in our city right now. We're out of money. I can't pay people. The city is divided along economic and racial lines. We have a drug problem. We are facing a workers' strike. But you know what? You guys are making my job easier. Every Monday morning, instead of talking about all the problems in the city, people are talking about the Redskins. They are watching what you are doing on the field and how you are playing as a group, and that is carrying over to the people in the city. I want to thank you for that. Keep up the good work.' Everyone was surprised by that. It made us feel good."

Pat Fischer   "We had the support of the mayor and the schools. The players would go out and give talks in the schools in the city. There was tremendous support for us, at a time when the community was going through some pretty tough times. What we were doing gave people something in common to rally around."

The outpouring of support was widespread. One of the biggest businesses in the region, Giant Foods, took out a full-page newspaper ad to congratulate the team: "We of the Giant Food family know that we echo the sentiment of every family in Washington, in suburban Maryland and Virginia, when we say . . . Redskins, you are beautiful, and we love each and every blooming one of you."

Finally, the nation's number-one sports fan offered his own kudos following the loss to the Chiefs. President Richard Nixon sent the following note to Allen: "A truly great team just proved that it can be great in defeat as well as in victory. The Redskins proved they were a great team yesterday."

The Redskins showed their appreciation by keeping their undefeated record at home intact, beating the New Orleans Saints 24–14, despite turning the ball over six times. They controlled the ball and scored on a 1-yard run by Kilmer, a 36-yard touchdown pass from Kilmer to Brown, a 47-yard Knight field goal in the fourth quarter, and a clinching 53-yard touchdown on an interception return by Pat Fischer—a fan favorite in Washington because everyone could see that this was a 5-foot-9, 170-pound football player who played the game as if he were 6 inches taller and 50 pounds heavier. He would take on all comers and cover receivers bigger than he week after week. He played for the Redskins from 1968 to 1977, missing just three games over that span, and he had 27 career interceptions and 412 interception yards, with 53 of them coming in that win over the Saints.

Roy Jefferson "Pat Fischer and I played against each other when I was in Pittsburgh. We got into at least one fight every year, a serious fight, really going after each other. But he was a real pro. He used his intelligence, and had quick feet. In practice, you wouldn't beat him too often, because he knew everything you would be running, unless Sonny called a play off of a play, something that we didn't generally run off a particular formation or set. We would catch him every once in a while with something like that, and he would yell, 'You guys don't do that. Don't do that.'"

Besides the players who showed up in the scoring summary, there was another factor that was now contributing to wins like the one against the Saints: the 53,041 fans at RFK Stadium. Playing in Washington was a new experience for visiting teams. There was always tremendous support for the Redskins, but now it had reached rabid levels, and the stadium rocked, rolled, and roared like never before. There was truly a twelfth man now for Washington at home, and it was no accident. George Allen recruited those fans for that role like he recruited players.

· · ·

Brig Owens   George Allen was the first coach in the game who really challenged fans to back their home team, to really use the fans against the opponents. Sure you had fans in other cities who supported their teams, but George said, 'This is your team, and when we come out, we want a standing ovation when the team is introduced.' We had teams come in and players would ask, 'How come these fans give you guys standing ovations?' We became the team that players wanted to come and play for, and we also became the place where other teams didn't want to come to play. We would go on the road, and our goal was to turn the fans against their own team and cheer us for our play. That was the fun of it."

The fun hit a bump, though. The next week, in front of the home-town fans, was a 7–7 tie against the Philadelphia Eagles, in which Washington turned the ball over seven times—3 fumbles and 4 inter-ceptions. That was not George Allen football. And Redskins fever—the fans now obsessions with their team—had taken a turn that the coach wasn't happy with.

Before the Eagles game, Sonny Jurgensen was activated, coming back from the broken bone he suffered in the exhibition game against Miami. With Kilmer having such a poor game and Jurgensen being the darling of Redskins fans, the calls started for Allen to bench Kilmer and play Jurgensen. The calls gained momentum in Chicago the following week, where the Redskins lost to the Bears 16–15, and the game ended when Knight attempted his sixth field goal of the game, a 45-yarder than went wide left. Who put the Redskins in position for that last field goal attempt? Jurgensen, whom Allen inserted in the closing minutes of the game to replace an ineffective Kilmer.

It got worse—much worse—the following week back home at RFK Stadium, where the Cowboys manhandled the Redskins 13–0, holding them to just 65 yards rushing. And again, with the team down 10–0 in the fourth quarter, Allen brought Jurgensen in to try to save the game, but the rusty quarterback was intercepted on his first pass attempt.

Redskins fever had taken hold with the 5-1 start. Now, with the team 5-4, it had taken a different form. The town was in the grip of the mother of all quarterback controversies, the one that started it all—Sonny or Billy? Bumper stickers started showing up on cars declaring "I love Billy" and "I love Sonny." The *Washington Daily News* conducted a poll to determine whom fans wanted to start as quarter-back for the Redskins. Jurgensen got 1,225 votes to just 594 for Kilmer. Allen, though, brought Kilmer in because he wanted him to run his conservative offense, and he felt that he could not trust Jurgensen to do that. However, if Kilmer was making mistakes, as he had been with the turnovers, he was not fulfilling his role. So Allen gave Jurgensen the start the following week in Philadelphia against the Eagles. And again, Jurgensen suffered another shoulder injury while scrambling early in the second quarter. He would be out for much of the season, so the debate had the wind knocked out of it. Kilmer capitalized on it, leading Washington to a 20–13 win, with 2 Knight field goals, a 27-yard touchdown pass from Kilmer to Jefferson, and a 38-yard pass interception return for a score by Mike Bass.

The Sonny or Billy argument quieted down while Jurgensen was injured, but while it had become the hotly debated issue in the city, players insisted it divided neither the team nor the two quarterbacks.

Mike Bragg   "Sonny versus Billy, that's typical Washington. Democrats versus Republicans. Liberals versus conservatives. The city thrives on that kind of controversy. It's the way it is in this town . . . but Sonny and Billy were close, and they helped each other a lot with what they were doing on the field."

Linebacker Rusty Tillman   "Billy and Sonny became friends. We were lucky to have Billy when Sonny went down. They were different type players. Billy was the more vocal leader and rah-rah type of guy, while Sonny was the best quarterback I ever saw. When Sonny was in the ballgame, you knew the offense would move. I have never seen anyone throw as pretty a pass as Sonny did. Those two stayed friends throughout the whole thing."

Linebacker Chris Hanburger   "Sonny versus Billy, we never got involved in that. We knew we were in good hands, whoever it was. We had some first-class people on the team, and the maturity of the team was so strong that those kind of issues had no bearing on the way we played."

. . .

Jimmy Jones "We knew Sonny had more talent than Billy. But we stood behind Billy. He was a leader. He didn't have as much physical ability as Sonny, but he was such a leader. . . . George's theory was that too many bad things could happen when you threw the ball 50 yards down the field. He preferred the control-passing game. Sonny and George didn't see eye to eye on that."

Len Hauss "Around 1971, Walter Rock and I were spending a lot of time together, and during some of this controversy, one time after practice we got Sonny and Billy together and said, 'Hey, let's go sit down and talk.' We had some pretty good heart-to-heart talks, and I think by the time we were through, we had gotten us all thinking together that the team was the most important thing and that these guys were good enough football players and strong enough individuals that regardless of who played, it would be to the advantage of the team that we could win with either one of them."

Jurgensen and Allen was a marriage that was just not meant to be. Allen made his quarterbacks, even the ones who were not going to play, watch game films to make sure they were ready in case they were needed. So while Jurgensen was playing behind Kilmer, he had to prepare the same way. One time the preparation didn't go very well.

Diron Talbert "Jurgensen took some films home, and George told him, 'You better get those reels back on time, and make sure they don't get lost.' George didn't like anyone fooling with his films. This one time, Jurgensen brought the films out to his car to bring back. He was going to put them in the trunk. Well, he puts them on the edge of the car, closes the trunk, and forgets to put them in. Those films wound up being spread all over the road. George was mad. He had three or four games' worth of films all over the highway."

Jurgensen, though, didn't let his problems with Allen get in the way of his relationship with Kilmer, despite all the quarterback controversies.

Sonny Jurgensen "We were friends. We respected each other because we were competitors and we appreciated each other."

. . .

Two points to be made, though: Jurgensen and Kilmer would become even closer in a few years, with the arrival of a new Redskin; and though the Sonny versus Billy debate didn't divide the team, it did leave lingering questions in some players' minds years later, when they thought back as to what could have been—in one game in particular.

The team's winning ways continued the next week back at RFK Stadium, where the defense tortured the Giants in a 23–7 victory with five interceptions. Following that game would be a week full of drama for the Redskins. It began after the Redskins-Giants game, when Kilmer, after a night of celebrating, stopped at the Toddle House in Arlington, Virginia, early Monday morning for breakfast. The toast of the town went to pay for his $4 breakfast bill with the smallest denomination of money he had: a $100 bill. The Toddle House waitress wasn't crazy about trying to make $96 change, so she and Kilmer got into an argument, and then an off-duty officer joined in to get Kilmer to calm down. The end result was that Kilmer—who denied he was drunk—was arrested and charged with being drunk in public, and spent several hours in jail. It was front-page news. "Pete Rozelle will probably put that whole chain of coffee houses off limits," Kilmer joked with reporters.

Then came George Allen's homecoming to Los Angeles to face his old team, the Rams, a game that was full of drama before the opening kickoff. The game began in the papers, when Deacon Jones declared that "the Rams will blow the Redskins out of the Coliseum," and Allen delivered his own broadside against his replacement, Tommy Prothro, when he called the Rams "a great gadget team."

What added to the drama was that it was *Monday Night Football* and that the outcome would decide whether or not the Redskins would be playing in the NFL postseason contest for the first time since 1945.

It was a wild game, starting with Kermit Alexander picking off a Kilmer pass and running 82 yards for the touchdown and giving Los Angeles a 7–0 lead early in the game. But the Redskins came right back when Kilmer hit Jefferson on a 70-yard touchdown pass to tie the game at 7–7. At the end of the quarter, the Rams added a 32-yard field goal by David Ray for a 10–7 lead. Washington tied the game early in the second quarter when Knight managed to leg out a 52-yard field goal, tying the club record held by John Aveni. The Redskins defense then stopped the Rams twice down near their end zone. On fourth down and 1 at the Washington 18-yard line, the Rams went for the first down, and McDole and Pardee ran down Gabriel short of the first down. Washington took over, but the Rams got the ball back on the Redskins' 45-yard line on a fumble by Charley Harraway. But again the Redskins defense came through when Ted Vactor blocked a 29-yard field goal attempt by Ray. You only get so many chances against this opportunistic Redskins team. Kilmer led a drive with a 27-yard pass to Jefferson and followed with a 32-yard touchdown to a diving Clifton McNeil in the end zone, putting Washington on top 17–10 just before the end of the first half. On the kickoff to the Rams, return man Roger Williams bobbled the ball, and Vactor—one of Allen's special teams stars—recovered the ball on the Los Angeles 4-yard line. Larry Brown took it over from the 1-yard line, and the Redskins went into the locker room with a 24–10 lead.

The Redskins defense kept the pressure on in the third quarter. Bass intercepted a Gabriel pass and took it back to the Rams' 45-yard line. Kilmer connected with McNeil on a 36-yard pass and then with another scoring pass on a 5-yarder to Jefferson, giving the Redskins a 31–10 lead. But Los Angeles came back when Bob Klein recovered a fumbled punt by Washington at midfield. Gabriel hit Matt Maslowski and Lance Rentzel with completions to move the ball to the 3-yard line and then tossed it to Klein in the end zone to cut the Washington lead to 31–17. The Rams defense held and the offense brought the Redskins' lead to 31–24 when Willie Ellison, who the week before had set an NFL record by rushing for 247 yards against the New Orleans Saints, crossed the goal line early in the fourth quarter. It stayed that way as both teams battled throughout the fourth quarter until Gabriel, leading a drive with less than a minute left to play, threw to fullback Larry Smith. But Washington defensive back Speedy Duncan stepped in, pulled down the pass, and took off 46 yards for the score with just seconds left in the game, sealing a 38–24 victory and the Redskins' first playoff berth since the end of World War II.

The Redskins locker room was a raucous scene, with Allen leading the postgame cheers and telling reporters about the guts and the glory of the Over the Hill Gang. "It was a complete game victory," Allen told reporters. "This Redskins team has tremendous character. We've overcome adversity all year. When it looked like we might fold, we pulled together and won." Kilmer had a remarkable game, completing 14 of 19 passes with 246 yards and 3 touchdowns, and was awarded a game ball, as was Jefferson for his 8 catches for 137 yards and 2 touchdowns. Duncan got a game ball for his last-minute interception. Chaplain Tom Skinner got one for his inspirational talk, and finally, George Allen was awarded a game ball by his team.

Washington, with a record of 9-3-1, had clinched a playoff spot but still had one more game left to play at home in the season finale against the Cleveland Browns. After the emotional win in Los Angeles, they went into the game flat and committed four turnovers in a 20–13 loss to the Browns. It was an afterthought, because the Redskins were going to the playoffs; they were traveling to San Francisco to play the 49ers, and the whole town was buzzing–even the White House. President Nixon reportedly called Allen on Christmas Day, the day before the playoff game against the 49ers, to suggest an end-around play for Roy Jefferson. The play did not work, as Jefferson lost 13 yards, and not enough worked in general that day at Candlestick Park, as Washington lost 24–20. They had taken the lead in the first quarter when they blocked the punt of Steve Spurrier, a former Heisman Trophy winner and future Redskins coach, and Kilmer threw a 5-yard touchdown pass to Jerry Smith for a 7–0 lead. The teams traded field goals in the second quarter, and Washington came off the field at the end of the first half with a 10–3 lead, but the game was lost in the third quarter. In a change of personality, Allen, on a fourth down and inches play at the San Francisco 11-yard line, went for the first down instead of the field goal, and Larry Brown was tackled for a 2-yard loss. San Francisco quarterback John Brodie capitalized on that play by hooking up with Gene Washington for a 78-yard touchdown pass to tie the game at 10–10. Rosey Taylor intercepted a Kilmer pass, and Brodie found tight end Bob Windsor in the end zone on a 2-yard touchdown pass and a 17–10 lead. Knight closed the gap to 17–13 with a 36-yard field goal late in the third quarter, and the teams traded touchdowns in the final quarter, with the game ending on a sack of Kilmer by 49ers defensive end Cedrick Hardman.

The season was over, but hopes and expectations were running high and carried over to the start of training camp in 1972, as the city buzzed with the idea that their team no longer simply expected to be good–they expected to be champions. In the fifth preseason game, when the Redskins defeated by 27–24 the team that had gone to the Super Bowl the year before and lost to Dallas, the American Football Conference (AFC) champion Miami Dolphins, Brig Owens and Jim Kiick said to each other as they left the field, "See you at the Super Bowl."

The Redskins were among the stars of the NFL, a winning team with a high-profile coach and an identity—the Over the Hill Gang—that made them a prime franchise to showcase on television. So in its third year of existence, ABC's *Monday Night Football* opened with the Redskins facing the powerful Minnesota Vikings, when the Vikings still played outdoors in Bloomington, Minnesota.

It turned out to be a vintage George Allen win, with a special teams player, Bill Malinchak, leading the way by blocking a punt on the first series by Vikings punter Mike Eischeid, then picking the ball up at the Minnesota 16-yard line and taking it in for a touchdown two minutes into the game. Malinchak had another key play later in the game when Vikings Clint Jones fumbled a kickoff, and Malinchak recovered the fumble. Two plays later, fullback Charley Harraway carried the ball in to give Washington a 24–14 lead, which they held onto for a 24–21 victory.

Allen was the first NFL coach to put a premium on special teams. He was the first to hire a special teams coach—a familiar name to football fans: Marv Levy. Levy was a young coach who would go on to lead the Buffalo Bills to four AFC championships. Allen would also be the first coach to have his special teams introduced in pregame introductions on national television.

Brig Owens "George Allen made special teams special. This was the only city where you would have guys on special teams with their own radio and television shows. When he wanted his special teams introduced before the game on *Monday Night Football*, the league went bananas. But George insisted. He said, 'Our special teams are doing great things for us, and they deserve to be introduced.' That was a combination of going against the establishment, and also the fact that we were very proud of our special teams.

"I can remember when George brought Malinchak out of retirement [in 1976]. We were getting ready to go into the playoffs. George had brought Malinchak [who retired after the 1974 season] for a visit to Redskin Park. George joked around that he was going to bring him back because he can block at least two field goals or punts that will help get you to the playoffs. The next day Bill Malinchak was in a practice uniform."

Two weeks later, in a 37–14 win against the Cowboys in Dallas, Malinchak blocked a Danny White punt that led to a Washington touchdown.

The special teams embraced their identity. They began their own pregame meeting rituals in the showers at RFK Stadium. These meetings were emotional sessions that would carry on into the Joe Gibbs era and reach new heights under special teams coach Wayne Sevier. Rusty Tillman was one of Allen's special teams' standouts.

Rusty Tillman "The shower thing started when George came. All of us on special teams—myself, Bill Malinchak, Bob Brunet, Ted Vactor—realized how much importance George put on the kicking game. Before our first game [in 1971], Malinchak got up and made a speech to the special teams. 'Hey, this guy really believes in us. He thinks we are as important as the offense and the defense. We need to go out there and do the best we can.' That was the start of the shower huddle. We used to get really fired up. George would come back and talk to me before a game and tell me how important I was to the winning effort and how I had to make a big play, and I thought I was the most important guy on the team. But every other guy felt the same way. George made every guy feel like he was the most important guy out there. He had a tremendous talent."

Special teams players were special in other ways; they were characters with their own set of eccentricities. Vactor, who was so good at blocking punts that buttons were being sold around Washington saying "Vactor's a factor," was known for running a clothing store out of the trunk of his car at Redskin Park.

Rusty Tillman "Ted Vactor had all the latest fashions. I bought a couple of pairs of slacks from Teddy. I don't know where he was getting them from. Who knows what the deal was. They were double knits to play golf in. I think I still got them."

. . .

Mike Bragg   "Ted Vactor used to sell clothes out of his car. We used to call it 'Boutique 29.' His number was 29. I don't know where the stuff came from. He would dress the whole team. It was funny. Then he ran his little business out of the empty locker between him and Speedy Duncan. Teddy had a real knack for blocking field goals. He was always taking a chance, and he had a unique way to come around the corner and then block the kick."

The special teams were another important factor in the second week of the season—a 24–10 win over the St. Louis Cardinals before a hometown crowd of 53,000 at RFK Stadium. Verlon Biggs blocked a Jim Bakken field goal attempt in the second quarter, and Mike Bass scooped it up at the St. Louis 32-yard line and took it in for a touchdown. During the game, Larry Brown became the franchise's all-time leading rusher, with 148 yards for the day, passing Don Bosseler's career mark of 3,112. In week three, it appeared the special teams would keep the Redskins' winning record intact. But they didn't get the benefit of a call by the referee. Down 24–21 to the Patriots in New England late in the game, Malinchak blocked a Pat Studstill punt deep in New England's territory. The ball rolled into the end zone, and Malinchak pounced on it as it was going out the back of the zone. But officials ruled he did not have control, calling it a safety instead of a touchdown, which would have given Washington the lead. The Redskins got the ball back on the kick and tried a 50-yard field goal, but it missed, and the Redskins fell for the first time that season, on October 1. They wouldn't lose again until December 9.

The win resulted in a shake-up by Allen, who fueled the debate of Sonny versus Billy by replacing Kilmer with Jurgensen for the game against the Eagles. And after a rusty first half of throwing 3 interceptions and going 7 for 17, he went 7 for 7 in the second half and took the Redskins to a 14–0 victory, the second score coming on a 35-yard touchdown pass to Roy Jefferson. Jurgensen was much sharper in week four, completing 13 out of 18 passes for 203 yards and leading Washington to a 33–3 win over the Cardinals in St. Louis.

With a 3-1 record, an early season showdown back in Washington against the hated Cowboys, the defending Super Bowl champions, was set up. Allen set the stage in the press for the game during what would eventually be always known as "Dallas week"—anytime the Redskins faced the Cowboys—when Allen told reporters, "We'll have a championship-type game against the Cowboys Sunday. The winner will be in the driver's seat. I only wish we had a 100,000-seat stadium this week." RFK Stadium and 53,000 people would have to do. And before the game, the fans did very well by leading loud cheers and working themselves into a frenzy during the pregame introductions.

Dallas had the first possession and marched down the field with runs by Calvin Hill and Walt Garrison, eventually putting the Cowboys in position for a 13-yard field goal by Toni Fritsch and a 3–0 lead. It grew to 10–0 in the first quarter when Charley Taylor fumbled and Cowboys linebacker Dave Edwards recovered the ball on the Washington 25-yard line. Three plays later, despite being sacked twice by the Redskins defense, Dallas quarterback Craig Morton hit a 39-yard touchdown pass to Ron Sellers. The Cowboys extended their lead to 13–0 early in the second quarter, and the crowd that had been so pumped up before the game was now nearly silent. But Jurgensen gave them something to cheer about when, after a Redskins drive, he connected on a 19-yard pass to Larry Brown to cut the Cowboys' lead to 13–7 before halftime. It was a historic completion, because it put Jurgensen over 30,000 yards passing for his career.

The second half opened pretty much like the first. The Cowboys moved the ball down the field and scored early to take a 20–7 lead. Then Jurgensen had the sort of finish that made Redskins fans believe they finally had all the ingredients they had hoped for: a great defense with the familiar explosive offense, led by a gunslinger like Jurgensen, who could still wing it even at the age of thirty-eight. He took the offense down the field, with a key 28-yard completion to Jerry Smith that ended in a 34-yard touchdown run by Larry Brown, cutting the Dallas lead to 20–14. The Redskins added a 42-yard field goal by Curt Knight late in the third quarter, and then, after the Cowboys' Toni Fritsch missed a 50-yard field goal attempt early in the fourth quarter, Jurgensen and the offense took over at the 20-yard line and began their game-winning drive. Jurgensen hit Jefferson with a 26-yard pass, then completed throws of 18 and 16 yards to Brown. The final blow came on a pitch to Charley Harraway, who took off and ran 13 yards into the Cowboys' end zone, giving the Redskins a 24–20 lead, which the defense managed to hold on to, as Mike Bass and Pat Fischer drove Bob Hayes, who pulled down a pass from Craig Morton, out of bounds at the Redskins' 38-yard line with time running out. Dallas didn't have enough time to run off another play. The fans celebrated with the players as the time expired and the Redskins beat Dallas. "We could feel the ground trembling down on the sidelines," George Allen told reporters after the game. "The fans were worth at least three points." Jurgensen proclaimed after the game what everyone in Washington felt: "We're going to be champions."

Ron McDole   "They didn't give us a chance in hell of winning that ball game. I remember Charley Harraway breaking around the outside. That really fueled the rivalry even more and upset the Cowboys, because they thought we were the same old Redskins. After that, we were at each other's throats."

One week later, at Yankee Stadium against the Giants, Jurgensen tore his Achilles tendon after completing a 13-yard pass to Jefferson, and the dream perhaps was torn then as well, though they would ultimately get close to realizing it.

The success of the team fell on Kilmer again, and the quarterback controversy was temporarily over with Jurgensen's injury. Kilmer led Washington to a 23–16 win over the Giants that Sunday and five more wins after that, giving the Redskins an impressive 11-1 record and generating national attention. After clinching the division crown 23–7 over Philadelphia, the Redskins were one step closer to the Super Bowl. Since they had secured this victory and had home-field advantage, Allen rested a number of his veteran starters, such as running back Larry Brown, and Washington lost its final two games, 24–23 to the Cowboys in Dallas and 24–17 to the Bills at home. They were well rested for a historic playoff run, and the city was on edge in anticipation.

First, there came a 16–3 win over Green Bay at RFK Stadium before 53,140 crazed fans. A 32-yard pass from Kilmer to Jefferson in the second quarter turned out to be all the scoring the Redskins needed, though they added 9 more points on 3 Knight field goals. This was a vintage Allen win, with controlled offense–Kilmer went just 7 for 14 for 100 yards, while Brown carried the ball 25 times for 100 yards–and a suffocating defense, led by the line of Verlon Biggs, Ron McDole, Diron Talbert, Bill Brundige, and Manny Sistrunk, in a five-man defensive line that put the brakes on Green Bay's powerful runner, John Brockington. The crowd went home happy and hungry–happy with the victory and hungry for the next game, one they had been waiting a long time for: a championship game at home against the Dallas Cowboys.

It was Dallas week and NFC title week all rolled into one, taking place on New Year's Eve, no less, and in the capital of the United States. From the halls of Congress to the downtown coffee shops, all anyone wanted to talk about was the Redskins and the big game against the Cowboys. The game couldn't come quick enough for Redskins fans. It was time for the rivals to beat at each other's throats, as Ron McDole had described the Cowboys-Redskins feud. It turned out that only one side got the other by the throat and didn't let go until the final gun sounded.

The dream game had finally arrived for 53,129 Redskins fans at RFK Stadium, and they roared from the time they arrived until they left and continued roaring in the streets of Washington, celebrating one of the greatest wins in the history of the franchise: a humiliating defeat of the Cowboys by the score of 26–3.

After a scoreless first quarter, the Redskins got on the board with an 18-yard Knight field goal. On the next drive, Kilmer took a chance on a third and 10 and hit Taylor with a 51-yard completion down to the Dallas 21-yard line. Three plays later, Kilmer connected with Taylor on a 15-yard touchdown pass. Toni Fritsch kicked a 35-yard field goal, as the first half ended with Washington leading 10–3. It stayed that way until the fourth quarter when, on the second play of the final quarter, Kilmer found Taylor on a 45-yard touchdown pass to put Washington further ahead 17–3. The noise now at RFK was nearly deafening, and it stayed that way throughout the rest of the game and Knight's three field goals. When the game ended, Allen was carried off the field by his players, and Redskins fans rejoiced in the first championship the franchise had won since 1942. There was no talk of quarterback controversies on this day, as Kilmer was magnificent, completing 14 of 18 for 194 yards, 2 touchdowns and no interceptions. It was a beautiful day and night, cold drizzle and all, in Washington, D.C.

Len Hauss "It seemed like everything worked for us that day. We had worked on a play, a little thing where one of the Dallas safeties would blitz and all our blocking had to be slide blocking. So often you practice things like that but never use it. But we were in the 30-yard area and a play is called, and Kilmer thinks the safeties are going to blitz. So he calls an audible for the play. I call the line blocking, and I notice the same thing he did, and we call the slide play. All of our blockers slide to the right, and they blitz their safety to the right. Billy dumps the ball over, and we get a touchdown. It was one of the easiest things you ever saw."

Charley Taylor   "That was one of my finest games as a football player. Everything was so easy for me that day, it all came so smooth."

Rusty Tillman   "After the game, Bob Brunet and I went down to Duke Ziebert's, and the whole place gave us a standing ovation."

There was just one more step to complete George Allen's goal this season: winning the Super Bowl. This was when the Super Bowl was still in its infancy, and great coaches won the game—Vince Lombardi, Weeb Ewbank, Hank Stram, and Tom Landry. Allen felt he belonged with those coaches, and he was determined—obsessed, really—not to bring a team into the biggest game of his coaching career and lose. What made it even better for Allen, but ultimately worse for his team, was that he had two full weeks to prepare for the game in Los Angeles.

Allen felt he needed to have the perfect game plan, because they were going to face the perfect team. The Miami Dolphins, led by another great coach, Don Shula, had gone 16-0 during the season, with a great running attack led by fullback Larry Csonka and running backs Mercury Morris and Jim Kiick. They were strong enough to survive the loss of starting quarterback Bob Griese, who was out with a broken right leg and a dislocated right ankle, in the fifth week of the season. Veteran quarterback Earl Morrall, at the age of thirty-eight, stepped in and kept the Dolphins winning throughout the rest of the season. Griese recovered in time to face the Pittsburgh Steelers in the AFC title game and won it 21–17, bringing the undefeated Dolphins to the Super Bowl against the Redskins.

The Dolphins had been here before, having lost to the Cowboys the prior year 24–3, so they were ready for the Super Bowl hoopla and pressure. Allen and the Redskins were not, and it showed during the game before a record crowd of more than 90,000 at the Coliseum, who saw a disappointing game between two teams that played as conservative a game as you could imagine, with each team waiting for the other one to make a mistake. The Dolphins, with Griese at quarterback and a deeper running game, were better equipped than the Redskins. Griese connected with Howard Twilley on a 28-yard touchdown pass near the end of the first quarter to take a 7–0 lead. Kilmer threw an interception to Miami linebacker Nick Buoniconti in the second quarter, and Miami took over possession on the Washington 27-yard line. Griese drove the team toward the goal line until Kiick took the ball over from the 1-yard line for a 14–0 Dolphins lead going into the locker room at halftime. The Dolphins defense, led by tackle Manny Fernandez, had effectively shut down Larry Brown and the Redskins running game.

Washington came out and played tougher defense in the second half but failed to capitalize on several scoring opportunities. Curt Knight missed a 32-yard field goal. Then, in another series of plays that will live with Redskins fans for a long time, Kilmer moved the team down to the Miami 10-yard line. When he threw a pass to wide-open Jerry Smith in the end zone, the ball hit the crossbar of the goalpost and fell incomplete. On the next play, Miami safety Jake Scott, who would be named the game's Most Valuable Player, intercepted a Kilmer pass in the end zone and brought it out to the Redskins' 48-yard line. Scott would later become a Redskin in 1976; he was George Allen's kind of player.

Several plays later, the signature play for this Super Bowl took place when Dolphins kicker Garo Yepremian—all 5-foot-7, 160 pounds of him—wound up picking up his blocked field goal attempt at the Washington 42-yard line and made the worst pass attempt in Super Bowl history. The wounded duck was pulled down by Redskins cornerback Mike Bass, who ran with it 49 yards for a touchdown and cut the Miami lead to 14–7.

Mike Bass   "Garo and I had been teammates on the taxi squad in Detroit. On this play, I was the 'spy man,' the one who had to go after the ball if a missed snap happened or something like that. I had scored a couple of touchdowns on blocked field goals during my career in Washington. Bill Brundige blocked it. I saw Garo grab the ball, and when he tried to pass it, it slipped out of his hands. He batted it, and I couldn't believe this guy was batting this ball all around the place. I just kept my eye on the ball, so it wasn't that hard to catch, because all of my concentration was on that ball. I thought I would get tackled immediately, but I didn't. The last thing I wanted was for Garo or Earl Morrall, the holder, to tackle me. I grabbed the ball and before I knew it, I was in the end zone."

The closeness of the score was not indicative of how one-sided the game was, and years later, the postmortem of the game raises several questions: Did Allen overwork his team in preparation of the game? Did some Redskins players compromise the team by too much pregame partying? What if it had been Sonny Jurgensen behind the ball instead of Kilmer?

Roy Jefferson "If Sonny had been healthy, he would have eaten them alive. Billy just had a bad game. Billy was an adequate quarterback throwing the football, but what they did was they dared him to throw. They set up their defense to stop Larry Brown. The defensive linemen, all they did was make sure they didn't get blown out, and the linebackers just ate up Larry coming through there. Billy didn't have a great passing day, and that is going to happen. But the next year we played them in the regular season, Jurgensen comes in during the third quarter, and boom, boom, boom, we go three times and score and win the game. He just ate that double zone alive. Sonny had that Achilles tendon that hadn't been healed yet.

"We got outcoached and outplayed in the Super Bowl. They scored on two big plays, one with Csonka breaking a tackle for a long run, and I forget how they got in position for the other score. But they only scored 14 points. Offensively, we just did not play well. Maybe Charley, Jerry, and I weren't as effective as we could have been, or maybe Billy wasn't as effective as he could have been. It doesn't matter. That was the difference in the game. They gave up the passing game. Charley and I were wide open down the sidelines. Jerry, of course, was open in the end zone, and as we know, Billy hit the goalpost. That was a fluke. If we had a score there, and that other score, it could have been 14–14 going down to the wire."

Brig Owens "We were thrown out of rhythm for that game. George was so worried about us staying in California, especially with the kind of guys we had who liked to roam a little bit. So he kept us in a lot of long meetings and in practice too long. We were flat. And I think we missed Sonny, too."

Ron McDole   "There's no doubt in my mind that if Sonny had been available, we would have had a chance to win that game. We didn't generate much offense."

Sonny Jurgensen   "He [Allen] didn't want me to be part of that team's success. We go to the Super Bowl, and he wouldn't even let me stand on the sideline and talk to anybody. I had to go to a booth by myself. He didn't want me to be part of any success. I played in some games that year before I got hurt, and it was always, Billy is going to start, and if we get 14 points down or so, it is Sonny's turn. If I had been healthy for that Super Bowl, I think we would have won. That was unfortunate."

Len Hauss   "We didn't play very good football that day. This was Miami's second trip to the Super Bowl. They had been there the year before and treated it a little differently than we did. We had some people who did not keep training, and one of our key people decided it was more important to go out after curfew than it was to get ready for the Super Bowl. He jumped out of his motel window and injured his knee. There were a number of things involved in that football game that took away a little bit from what it should have been."

Charley Taylor   "I think we lost that game on Thursday in practice. We practiced so strong and so hard and had the plan down so pat . . . we went out Thursday and executed it perfectly, and I think we left it there."

6

When You Lose, You Die a Little

The past for the Washington Redskins now consisted of a Super Bowl loss in January, but as far as George Allen was concerned, the future was still now, and now was 1973. The coach was determined to do whatever he had to in order to finish the job and win the NFL championship.

He was willing to bring in whomever he had to in order to accomplish that goal, and in 1973 he brought in one of the most controversial figures of the NFL in that time to Washington—a Dallas Cowboy of all people, but one of the most un-Cowboy-like players ever to play for the Cowboys: Duane Thomas.

Thomas was the talented 1970 first-round draft choice by the Cowboys out of West Texas State—probably the best running back they had at the time in the short history of the franchise. He led the Cowboys in rushing his first two seasons, carrying the ball 151 times as a rookie for 803 yards, averaging 5.3 yards per carry, and 175 carries for 793 yards in 1971, averaging 4.5 yards per carry. Thomas would help the Cowboys franchise with its first Super Bowl championship by carrying the ball 19 times for 95 yards in a 24–3 win over the Miami Dolphins in Super Bowl VI.

But Thomas was one of the most troublesome and bizarre players the league had ever seen. He refused to talk to most people, and he once called Cowboys coach Tom Landry "Plastic Man." He also came up with one of the greatest quotes in Super Bowl history. When asked about the Super Bowl being the ultimate game, Thomas replied, "If it's the ultimate game, how come they're playing it again next year?"

He struggled with a drug abuse problem and personality issues. He didn't play in 1972, and was traded to the San Diego Chargers. He refused to play for San Diego, and Allen was convinced, as he often was, that he could get the rebel player under control. So the Redskins coach took a chance and traded away what he had little use for—draft picks—to get Thomas in Washington.

It seemed to start off well. Thomas had a strong preseason in 1973 for the Redskins by gaining 70 yards on 17 carries and 1 touchdown in a memorable 37–21 preseason win over the Buffalo Bills at Rich Stadium. But he never matched his past glory. Thomas carried the ball just 32 times for 95 yards, a 3-yard-per-carry average in 1973, and had 95 carries for 347 yards and a 3.7-yard average in 1974. Too much of a different drummer for a bandleader like George Allen to even get under control, Thomas was out of the league shortly after that.

Receiver Roy Jefferson   "Duane Thomas sat between Charley Taylor and I in meetings. He would come in and never speak to anybody. I spoke to him his first day there, and he looked at me like I was some sort of fool. The next day I did the same thing, and he gave me that look again. So the third day, I came in and cursed him out. I said, 'F—k you, Duane.' Later on that morning he comes up to me and says, 'Hey, Roy, you're a crazy mother f—r' I'm thinking, 'You're the one who is crazy. I'm normal.' After that, we were decent with each other. But he gave most people that blank look all the time. He was a Muslim and a vegetarian. My wife and daughter were vegetarians at the time as well, and my wife would fix him some vegetarian meals. He loved it. Then he thought I was great.

"Duane would run two or three miles before practice every morning. He would be sitting in the whirlpool before everyone got there. He didn't lift a lot of weights, but he ran a lot. [Cowboys tackle] Rayfield Wright once told me that the best running back he ever blocked for was Duane Thomas. He said if you go to your guy and just would be on him, you didn't have to knock him all over the place. Just be on him, and Duane was gone. But he had lost a lot of weight when he came to us. He had weighed 220 pounds with the Cowboys."

. . .

The Redskins didn't seem to need Duane Thomas for their 1973 season opener or for much of anything else. The veteran defense showed no signs of slowing down when they forced three fumbles by San Diego running back Mike Garrett in the first quarter and turned all of them into touchdowns in a 38–0 blowout over the Chargers before a raucous crowd of more than 53,000 at RFK Stadium, who saw visions of a return to the Super Bowl.

But that was an illusion, because the offense, despite having 38 points on the board, struggled, particularly the passing game behind Billy Kilmer. He wasn't the only veteran quarterback struggling on the field, though. In a sad scene, former Baltimore Colts great Johnny Unitas—traded in the off season to the San Diego Chargers at the end of his career—was sacked 5 times and intercepted 3 times.

One of the touchdowns scored by the Washington defense was a 2-yard fumble recovery and scoring run by one of the most colorful characters ever to put on a Redskins uniform: defensive end Verlon Biggs.

Biggs was one of the greatest defensive ends to ever come out of the old AFL. He was a three-time Pro Bowl player there and was part of the legendary 1969 New York Jets Super Bowl squad led by Joe Namath that upset the powerful Baltimore Colts in Super Bowl III.

But he got into a contract dispute with the Jets after the 1970 season, and one of his former teammates in New York—fellow defensive end Jimmy Jones, who was now a Redskin—told Allen that Biggs had not signed a contract yet with the Jets and would love to come play for him in Washington. So Allen brought Biggs in to be part of his Over the Hill Gang.

Biggs continued to be a force at defensive end for the Redskins, but his teammates remember him for his unique and often bizarre behavior.

Defensive end Ron McDole   "Verlon was a quiet person, but he did some of the funniest things. He called me Dole, and during our first year together, playing against Houston, who had Charlie Johnson at quarterback then, Johnson tried to throw a screen on my side over me, and I picked it off. Verlon was rushing the passer on the other side. We hardly knew each other. We had just one training camp together. So normally, you would expect him to run up and block for me. Verlon comes running up alongside me, and I am heading for the end zone. This is going to be the other touchdown I score in my career. He's yelling at me, 'Dole, lateral. Dole, lateral. You're not going to make it.' I yelled back, 'If you block someone, I'll make it.' We ended up in the end zone, and he's the first one to pile on top of me. He said, 'I didn't think you would make it.'

"One time we went to play in New York, and the Giants had this offensive tackle named Joe Young. We used to call him Mighty Joe Young. Verlon was going up against him. He got a copy of the game program and was cutting out Young's picture. He had two of them, and he was taping them on the top of his shoes. I said, 'What are you doing?' The one thing you don't want to do is get the other guy you are playing against mad. So the first half is over, and it was a tough half. We come into the locker room, and normally, when you're rushing the passer, both ends usually run into each other at some point in the backfield. Verlon was sitting in front of his locker with his head in his hands. I said, 'Verlon, I haven't seen you the whole first half.' Verlon said, 'He's pissed. I can't get off the line of scrimmage against him.' I said, 'I wonder why. You went out there with his picture pasted on your shoes.'"

Biggs carried his eccentricities off the field as well.

Defensive tackle Diron Talbert   "One day Verlon invited me to his house. He was showing me how he had some nuts on the shelf by his kitchen window. He would open the window during the daytime, and he said squirrels were coming into his house and stealing his nuts. He said, 'Talbe, that son of a gun takes these nuts right here and puts them in that tree over yonder.' I asked him, 'What did you do?' He said, 'I got the ladder from the maintenance man and crawled up in that tree and stuck my hand in the hole and got my nuts back."

Punter Mike Bragg   "Verlon had a pet Doberman pinscher, and when we would go on trips, we would usually leave on Saturday night for wherever we were going, spend the night, play the game Sunday, and be back, usually within twenty-four hours. Verlon couldn't find someone to watch his dog, so he would give the dog sleeping pills to stay quiet, so he wouldn't tear up the place. He did stuff like that, drugging his dog."

Biggs made it a practice of taking teammates' lunches from their lockers. Everyone knew it, and one of his close friends on the team, Roy Jefferson, tried to make him pay several times for his food theft.

Roy Jefferson   "Verlon and I were good friends. My wife used to fix my lunch in camp. A lot of guys brought their lunches with them. She would fix pork chops, good sandwiches, elaborate lunches, and a lot of times I would share them with Jerry Smith. Biggs had a tendency to steal people's lunches, and this day my wife had fixed six pork chops and other stuff, and he got into my lunch and ate every bit of it. I was furious. We were all getting ready to go out to practice after lunch, and I was going to get him some kind of way. So I stayed back in the locker room. He stayed back because he was worried about what I was going to do. But they blew the whistle for practice, and he didn't want to be late. I didn't care at that point, because I was so mad. He left. I took every trash can in the place and dumped it in his locker, and then filled one of the trash cans with water and dumped that all over his stuff, all his clothes. He had to wear football shorts home. Then I went out to practice. He was hot, but he knew he deserved it.

"Once I had my wife fix four tuna fish sandwiches. Then I told her to fix me four other sandwiches. I left one set in the trunk of my car for three days. Then I brought them in and put them in a bag in my travel bag on the top of my locker. Sure enough, he ate them, and he was sick for two days. He was so funny, and sometimes he wasn't trying to be. But he was a good guy."

Safety Ken Houston   "There is hardly a day that goes by where I don't think about Verlon Biggs. He was the light of that team. He would steal our lunches, and one time somebody put a bunch of Ex-Lax in their lunch, and they got Vernon."

Some teammates, like Rusty Tillman, simply gave up.

Linebacker Rusty Tillman   "My wife would make me sandwiches, and Verlon Biggs would come down every day and steal my sandwiches. Finally, I had my wife make a sandwich for Verlon, too."

. . .

Biggs played for the Redskins until 1975. He died at the age of fifty-one from leukemia in 1994.

The euphoria of Washington's 38–0 win to start the 1973 season didn't last long. In St. Louis, the Cardinals beat the Redskins 34–27, in a game where, down 24–10, Allen pulled Kilmer and put in Jurgensen, who helped lead the team back in the game, along with a 97-yard kick-off return by Herb Mul-Key. Jurgensen's play earned him a start the next week in Philadelphia against the Eagles, and he responded with 2 touchdown passes in a 28–7 win. The following week they were in Dallas, and they witnessed one of the most memorable defensive plays in the history of pro football.

The two teams figured to battle, as they did the season before, for the division title and ultimately the conference championship, with Dallas coming into the game undefeated. So even though it was just the fourth game of the year, there was a playoff atmosphere at RFK Stadium, with the intensity of the Cowboys-Redskins rivalry and a pumped-up crowd of more than 54,000 Redskins fans. Plus, it was a nationally televised *Monday Night Football* event.

The game remained scoreless until near the end of the first half, when Roger Staubach connected with Otto Stowe on a 45-yard touch-down pass. Dallas kept its 7–0 lead and shut down the Redskins offense until the fourth quarter, when Jurgensen led the team on a 57-yard scoring drive that ended with a 1-yard touchdown pass to Charley Taylor to tie the game at 7–7. With about three minutes left, Brig Owens intercepted a Morton pass and ran 26 yards for the score, putting the Redskins ahead 14–7.

It appeared the Cowboys were through when the Washington defense held and Dallas had to punt with about two minutes left in the game. But the Redskins fumbled the kick and the Cowboys recovered at the Washington 31-yard line. Dallas moved the ball as time was running out. They were at the Washington 4-yard line when, on a third-down pass, Pat Fischer stopped a touchdown pass to Stowe. This set up fourth down, with twenty-four seconds left, and gave one of the game's premier defensive players his career signature play.

Ken Houston is a Hall of Fame safety and was quite possibly the best of his time at that position. He was drafted in the ninth round in

1967 by the Houston Oilers and was starting by the third game of the season. Two weeks later, in a game against the New York Jets, Houston scored 2 touchdowns, one on a 71-yard blocked field goal attempt, and the other on a 43-yard interception return. Despite being picked as All-AFL in 1969 and 1971, the Oilers shocked Houston, a native of Texas, by trading him to the Redskins in 1973.

Ken Houston   "I had been in Texas all my life. I grew up there and had great years in Houston. I remember when I signed my last contract there, they told me they were not going to trade me. They were going to rebuild the secondary around me. Sid Gilman was the general manager, and Bill Peterson was the coach. We were in minicamp, and I got a call at about 7:30 in the morning saying that Sid wanted to see me in his office at 9 A.M. I wondered why he wanted to see me in the office at 9 A.M., because we were supposed to be on the field for practice by then. I called back and asked the secretary if I had been traded. She said, 'Not to my knowledge.' I lived about ten minutes from the offices. I got there and met with Sid, and he said, 'Sit down. I got maybe some bad news for you, and maybe some good news. We traded you.' I asked, 'To who?' He said, 'The Redskins.' I said, 'I really don't want to sit down. No thanks.' I went home to tell my wife I had been traded. I didn't want to be traded, but at the time, it seemed like everyone wanted to be a Washington Redskin. They were a high-profile team and on TV all the time. Plus, it was a great place to play if you were a veteran. But at first I couldn't relate to D.C., because I had never been there. Then I learned they had traded five players for me. I thought, 'This isn't good. What if I get there and I'm not as good as they think? That won't be good.'

"When I got there and looked around at some of the players, I wondered what they had done to me. Houston had been a very athletic team and very young. I was a very aggressive player, and by the time I was twenty-seven in Houston, I was thinking about retiring. I had been pretty beaten up. But when I got to Washington, I was one of the youngest guys on the team. It turned out to be one of the best things that ever happened to me, in terms of coaching."

Houston got the most out of this one play on October 8, 1973—fourth down and goal for the Cowboys at the 4-yard line, with twenty-four seconds on the clock. Morton took the snap, went back quickly, and threw a short pass to fullback Walt Garrison—a bronco rider in the off season and one of the toughest runners in the league—right at the goal line. Houston grabbed Garrison, pulled him back from the goal line before he could get across, and dragged him down. Garrison tried to lateral as he was being tackled, but it wound up being a fumble and was recovered by the Redskins, and Washington won 14–7.

Ken Houston   "Brig Owens and I had what we called a 'combo C,' which was a combination of the free safety and the strong safety. Chris Hanburger was involved, because he was the linebacker. If the tight end would release inside and the back outside, Brig Owens and I would switch, and that is what they did. Garrison released outside, so we switched. I thought I could intercept the ball, because the quarterback had to throw it quick, and we had a blitz on. When they put it in the air, I really thought I could get between the ball and the running back. It didn't happen, but I was in perfect position to make the tackle, and I did—on *Monday Night Football*, with Howard Cosell and all that, the Cowboys and the Redskins, with the whole country watching. It was a big deal. A lot of good players made great plays that night, but that play took on a life of its own."

It was also particularly pleasing for Houston because it came against the Cowboys. Even though Houston was from Texas, he had no love for that team.

Ken Houston   "I grew up an Oilers fan. I never rooted for the Cowboys. I think in Houston we disliked the Cowboys more than they did in Washington."

It would be pretty difficult, though, to outdo the show Allen once put on for his players in the locker room to illustrate how much he hated the Cowboys.

Rusty Tillman   "The team would meet on Tuesday's at 11 A.M., after a Sunday game. It was known that George and the newspaper columnist, Jack Anderson, were taking martial arts lessons from the guy who was always on TV doing commercials for his classes, Jun Rhee. He would fight off a bunch of attackers in a parking lot and say,

'Nobody bothers me.' So one time in a meeting during Dallas week, all of a sudden we heard a gong, and Jun Rhee walked into the locker room, with about a half-dozen guys with him in full karate garb, and here came George, who was wearing his karate garb as well. The whole locker room went crazy. We were shouting, 'George, George, George.' It was electric. He talked about Dallas week and how he wanted to fly to Dallas and meet Tom Landry at midfield and fight him, and if he could beat Landry, we would win. We all kind of snickered, because we figured Landry could beat the shit out of George.

"Now he had these boards with him, and these other guys were holding the boards. He was going to break two boards with his hands, and two others with his feet, and if he could break those boards, we were going to beat Dallas. The place was going nuts, chanting, 'George, George, George.' Now he started to warm up and was making all kinds of noises and taking deep breaths. It was unbelievable. All of a sudden he screamed, came down, and broke the two boards with his hands and the other two with his feet, and the place went nuts. Then I see George's hand start to shake. He broke his hand. The trainers had to take him out of the room. And do you know what the coup de grâce was? Dallas beat the shit out of us."

Houston embraced being a Redskin. He would continue to have an outstanding career with Washington and would be selected either All-Pro or All-NFC every year from 1973 until 1979. Over his career, Houston intercepted 49 passes, recovered 21 fumbles, and scored 12 touchdowns, 9 on interceptions and 1 each on a punt return, a fumble return, and a blocked field goal return.

Safety Mike Bass   "Kenny Houston was one of the toughest defensive backs I had ever seen. I saw him bring Lawrence McClutcheon to his knees and put tears in the man's eyes. He was atypical, and that is why he is in the Hall of Fame. He was a devout team player and a tremendous athlete. I felt fortunate to be in the same backfield with him. He teased everyone a lot, but he was a positive person. I was glad our offense didn't have to play against him."

Ken Houston   "I loved playing for George. I thought he could get the most out of a player. He really cared for his players, and the game."

. . .

The Redskins went on to win the next two games that 1973 season, only to lose in an upset to New Orleans 19–3, followed by a 21–16 defeat at the hands of the up-and-coming Pittsburgh Steelers. Jurgensen was suffering from knee problems, so the ball was back in Kilmer's hands, and the offense struggled. It broke free against the San Francisco 49ers at RFK Stadium in the ninth game of the season, a 33–9 win that gave the Redskins a 6-3 record. They won their next two, 22–14 over the Baltimore Colts and 20–0 over the Lions in Detroit. But they barely defeated the Giants at home, 27–24, in a game where Washington was down 21–3 in the second quarter. The Redskins closed the lead to 21–10 going into the locker room at halftime. The score remained the same until early in the fourth quarter, when the Giants added 3 points on a 22-yard Pete Gogolak field goal. Then Kilmer hurt his ankle when he was tackled on a broken play, and the thirty-nine-year-old Jurgensen, bad knees and all, came into the game.

His first two passes fell incomplete. Then Jurgensen hit Jerry Smith with a 5-yard pass. He missed his next pass and was looking every bit the old, washed-up, and banged-up quarterback. Then he became Sonny Jurgensen again, completing 11 straight passes and leading the Redskins back to a 27–24 win, the winning touchdown coming on a 16-yard pass from Jurgensen to Larry Brown.

Jurgensen finished the game having completed 12 of 15 passes for 135 yards and 1 touchdown, and, at the seasoned age of thirty-nine, the question of why Allen refused to play Jurgensen more was asked even by a newcomer like Houston.

Ken Houston   "Sonny was the purest passer I had ever seen. The only person I ever saw who threw a purer pass was Warren Moon. I never understood why George would not play Sonny more. Billy could win, but Sonny could win big. When Sonny got in the game, the offense just seemed to click. There was always talk about that. But Billy was a winner, too. He could barely walk, and didn't throw the ball very pretty, but he was a winner. Players responded to him."

Nobody responded the next week in Dallas for the second game of that season against the Cowboys. Roger Staubach's scrambling gave the old defense fits, and the Cowboys won 27–7. Staubach had

George Preston Marshall purchased the bankrupt Duluth Eskimos franchise and moved it to Boston in 1932, but after five years of poor crowds and losing money, he moved the Redskins to Washington, D.C.

Edward Bennett Williams was a famous trial lawyer. He became an owner and team president of the Washington Redskins in 1965.

Jack Kent Cooke left, shown here with his son John watching a Redskins minicamp practice, was the driving force behind the emergence of the Redskins as one of the premier winning franchises in the league in the 1980s.

Joe Gibbs, shown here during a 2005 preseason game against the Baltimore Ravens, led the Redskins to four Super Bowls from 1981 to 1992 and then returned to the team thirteen years later.

George Allen, center, shown here on the sidelines at RFK Stadium in a Redskins 20–17 win over the Miami Dolphins, would put together a 67–30 record from 1971 to 1977, making him the second winningest coach in franchise history.

When the hard-nosed Vince Lombardi arrived in Washington in 1969, some thought he would clash with free-spirited quarterback Sonny Jurgensen. But Jurgensen embraced Lombardi's leadership, and the two developed a close relationship.

The Redskins defeated the New York Giants 33–7 in this 1956 game at Griffith Stadium.

After nearly a decade of success, 1946 would be a lean year for the Redskins, including a 20–7 loss to the Green Bay Packers in the game shown here at Griffith Stadium.

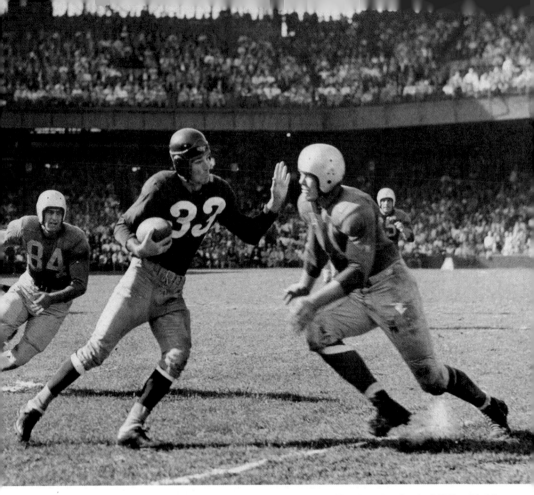

"Slinging Sammy" Baugh (holding the ball) revolutionized offensive play in the NFL with his passing skills and became one of the greatest punters in league history. He even intercepted 31 passes as a defensive back.

Billy Kilmer was brought to Washington by George Allen because the coach wanted someone more suited to his conservative style to lead his offense, which set up one of the all-time quarterback controversies between Kilmer and future Hall of Famer Sonny Jurgensen.

Joe Theismann, shown here scrambling in a 20–17 win over the Miami Dolphins at RFK Stadium in 1974, had a difficult time adjusting to the Redskins veteran squad because of his brash style.

Doug Williams, showing off his Super Bowl XXII ring, made NFL history on January 31, 1988, in addition to being the game's first black starting quarterback. In just the final six minutes of the first half, he threw for 228 yards and 4 touchdown passes. He would be named MVP.

Joe Jacoby, shown here leading the way for John Riggins in Washington's 31–7 playoff win over the Detroit Lions at RFK Stadium, would also lead the "Hogs" from 1981 to 1993.

Hall of Famer John Riggins came to Washington with a reputation as a rebel. He would become a legend in 1982, when he rushed for 444 yards in three straight home playoff victories, then earned the MVP award during the Redskins' win in Super Bowl XVII.

Larry Brown was the backbone of the Washington Redskins offense from 1969 to 1976, rushing for 5,875 yards and scoring 55 touchdowns.

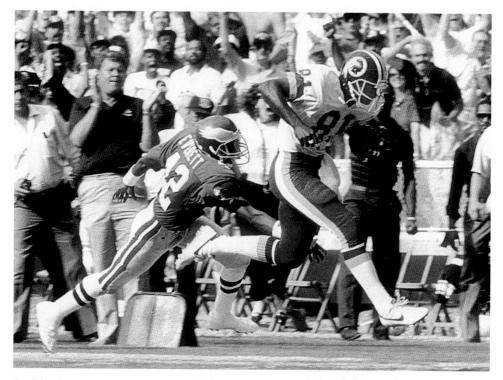

Art Monk, shown here scoring a touchdown against the Philadelphia Eagles at RFK Stadium in 1989, was a model of consistency during the Redskins' Super Bowl years.

Although he began his Redskins career as a running back, Charley Taylor would ultimately make his mark as a wide receiver, as he did here by catching a pass in the Redskins' 26–3 win over the Cowboys in the 1972 NFC championship game at RFK Stadium.

Mark Moseley was the greatest kicker in franchise history, holding the club record for points, field goals, and extra points. He was the NFL MVP in 1982.

Sam Huff earned renown on the football field as a linebacker for the New York Giants. After he was traded to the Redskins in 1964, he became a fan favorite. For the past twenty-five years he has been the heart of the Redskins' radio announcing team.

emerged as a nemesis for the Redskins and would cause them fits for the rest of the decade. He didn't join the Cowboys until he was twenty-seven years old, in the 1969 season. He was a quarterback from the U.S. Naval Academy, where he won the Heisman Trophy as a junior in 1963. Following his graduation, he spent a mandatory four years on active duty, including service in Vietnam, before he was able to turn his attention to pro football. He became a starter halfway through the 1971 season, but missed most of 1972 because of a separated shoulder. When he came back, though, he was there to stay, and he became both a hated and admired adversary for the Redskins. By the time his Hall of Fame career was done after the 1979 season, he had been involved in a number of memorable games between the two rivals, and had come to represent the Cowboys to Redskins fans more than any other player.

After the loss to the Cowboys, Washington bounced back to beat Philadelphia 38–20 in the regular season finale, with Kilmer on the field this time, tossing 4 touchdown passes, and Larry Brown running for 150 yards. It was a positive finish to a 10-4 season, with hope still alive to get back to the Super Bowl. But those hopes were left in Bloomington, Minnesota, at Metropolitan Stadium in a 27–20 division playoff loss to the Vikings and another scrambling quarterback who gave this aging team fits, Fran Tarkenton.

Four Redskins wound up making the All-NFC team that year: the newcomer Ken Houston, kick returner Herb Mul-Key, receiver Charley Taylor, and linebacker Chris Hanburger.

This was the first season that Hanburger had called the plays for the defense.

Linebacker Chris Hanburger   "We had an array of defenses, and we would call them right on the field, based on what you saw or what was going on. I think we had close to 150 audibles, with multiple defensive sets that we could go to anytime. We had total freedom out there. Everyone had to prepare if you played for George. I brought films home with me during the week and had a projector, and would go into the basement and watch films at night. George was superstitious and obsessive. Once it was around Christmas, and we were in the playoffs, and he was trying to get more film from another team, but no one would answer the phone in their offices. He was mad, and told us about it, and said, 'That's why they are losers.' Well, their season is over. They aren't in the playoffs. But he expected their coaches to be in the office so he could talk to them. That was just the way the guy thought. Sometimes the night before a game, we would go down to the coffee shop in the hotel and get a snack, and he would see you in there and come over and start drawing plays on a placemat. He always thought about football."

Allen was so intense about football that he ordered that no team photo be taken because his team did not make the NFC title game in 1973. "If the team doesn't make it to the NFC championship game, it doesn't deserve its picture taken," Allen wrote in a memo. So there is no team photo of the 1973 Redskins. Allen didn't pursue this policy, because there are team photos of the subsequent years he coached the Redskins, though none of those teams made it to the championship game.

The 1974 season would unfold pretty much the same way as the 1973 season did: a 10-4 regular season record and a first-round 19–10 loss in the playoffs against the Rams in Los Angeles. But there were a number of noteworthy moments that took place that season that are memorable in the history of this franchise. Two of them took place on the field in games that have become part of Redskins lore. Several others were business and personnel moves that would affect the future of the franchise.

Jack Kent Cooke joined the Redskins as an investor in 1961, when stockholder Milton King, a Canadian businessman, sold some of his shares. Cooke began acquiring more shares over the years until, in 1974, he obtained enough stock in the team to become the majority owner.

George Allen traded his 1974 first-round draft choice to Miami for the rights to quarterback Joe Theismann, the former Notre Dame star quarterback who had been playing in Canada for three seasons.

Theismann arrived with a swagger and attitude that rubbed the Over the Hill Gang veterans the wrong way. He wanted to play, and he let everyone know he wanted to play, even offering to field punts to get playing time.

He accomplished at least one thing in his first year in Washington: he brought Jurgensen and Kilmer even closer together.

. . .

Quarterback Sonny Jurgensen "Theismann came in and said that if he couldn't play in front of these two old guys that something was wrong. That bonded us together more than anything else. We said, 'We may be two old guys, but we'll keep him on the bench. One of us will be out there playing. He brought that on himself. Instead of coming in and listening and learning. But that wasn't his personality. He put himself in that position."

Mike Bass "Sonny rooted for Billy, and Billy rooted for Sonny, and nobody rooted for Theismann. You don't come to a veteran team acting like Theismann did. Those two guys [Sonny and Billy] had been in the league for a long time."

Quarterback Joe Theismann "Billy and Sonny are friends because of me. They have been friends for over thirty years, and it was their mutual hate for me that made them friends. I know that. It is funny. One night at the Dancing Crab [a Washington restaurant], the two of them made a pact . . . it had reached a point. . . . In the beginning, George favored Billy over Sonny. And everyone knew that Sonny was a better thrower of the football and was just more productive with the ball. I don't think they were the best of friends at that time, but they went out to dinner that night and made this pact that no matter who played, I would not play. I was referred to as 'Him.' As long as 'Him' wasn't playing, they were fine. I'm glad I was able to put two friends together. It was very rewarding to create a bond between two guys that has lasted as long as theirs has. I was an arrogant little prick, to be honest with you."

Another new arrival turned out to be an important part of the future of the team: place-kicker Mark Moseley.

Kicker Mark Moseley "I was with the Houston Oilers back in 1972. In 1971, we played the Redskins in Washington, and I kicked four field goals against the Redskins in a driving rainstorm. George Allen remembered that, and one of my buddies was Kenny Houston, who had played for Houston with me and then was traded to Washington. He was putting my name in George Allen's ear all season, and after the season was over, he was looking for a kicker, and he remembered me kicking all those field goals at RFK. He called Kenny up, found out where I was, and gave me a call. I came in here and competed against twelve other kickers to win the job. He had the film guy, Nate Fine, pull some film on me to watch the game again, and then he gave me a contract.

"What turned my career around for me when I got to Washington was the confidence that Allen instilled in me when I was there. He called me over the first day of practice, and said, 'Son, I think you have a lot of ability to be a great kicker here. I need a great kicker who I can depend on in rain, sleet, or snow. You can be that guy. You have to go out and prove yourself to the guys that you can be that kicker this year.' That was George's confidence builder for me. When we started practicing, the Over the Hill Gang lined up while I was kicking field goals for the first time. I kicked the ball, and all of a sudden I see helmets flying through the air. They were trying to knock the football out of the air. After that Diron Talbert would get a bunch of footballs when I was kicking during practice and throw them to try to knock my ball down. It taught me to concentrate and helped to make me fit in. George knew that the kickers were always the odd man out, and I had some pretty thick skin, so they would take shots at me and I learned to deal with it. It made me a better kicker. And they knew they could depend on me."

Though Theismann may have brought Jurgensen and Kilmer closer, the Sonny verses Billy debate continued for a fourth year. After starting out the 1974 season with a record of 2-2, the Redskins got a shot at a small measure of revenge for their Super Bowl loss by facing the Dolphins at RFK Stadium in the fifth game of the season. And while Jurgensen didn't get a chance to play against the Dolphins in Super Bowl VII, he got his shot against Miami this time. For the first three quarters, it looked like the best thing about that Super Bowl loss two years before was that Jurgensen didn't get a chance to embarrass himself as it appeared he was doing in this October 13, 1974, contest.

The Dolphins scored on the opening drive to take a 7–0 lead, which they carried into the locker room at halftime. Jurgensen had thrown 3 interceptions in the first half, and the crowd at RFK Stadium was both stunned and saddened by what they had witnessed. Miami added a third-quarter 32-yard field goal by Garo Yepremian for a 10–0 lead, and Washington finally got on the board with a Moseley

40-yard field goal. Then, in the fourth quarter, the forty-year-old Jurgensen showed the Dolphins and everyone else what could have been in that Super Bowl game.

The Dolphins fumbled early in the quarter on their own 33-yard line, and on the first play they had the ball, Jurgensen hit Roy Jefferson on a 33-yard scoring pass to tie the game at 10–10. They took a 13–10 lead on a 41-yard field goal. But with about two minutes left in the game, Miami quarterback Bob Griese hit Howard Twilley with a 13-yard touchdown pass to give the Dolphins a 17–13 lead. Herb Mul-Key returned the kickoff 32 yards to their 40-yard line. With 1:54 left in the game, Jurgensen hit Moses Denson with a 6-yard pass. Then he completed a 10-yarder to Jerry Smith, followed by 2 completions of 4 and 18 yards to Charley Taylor. Jurgensen's next pass was a 16-yard completion to Roy Jefferson. With time about to expire and the ball on the 6-yard line, Jurgensen's pass attempt to fullback Larry Smith was incomplete. But, with sixteen seconds on the clock, Jurgensen came right back to Smith, and this time it resulted in a touchdown and Washington winning the game 20–17. The fans went wild as the final gun sounded for what turned out to be Jurgensen's last great performance. Even though in part-time play that season Jurgensen still put up very good numbers—11 touchdowns and a 64 percent completion rate, connecting on 107 of 187 passes for 1,185 yards—he called it quits at the end of the season. In a career spanning 18 years, he threw 255 touchdowns and completed 2,433 of 4,262 passes for 32,224 yards. His career accomplishments were fully recognized when he was voted into the Hall of Fame in 1983.

Sonny Jurgensen "You couldn't ask for a better place to play than Washington. Fans were always fair. They were disappointed when we didn't win. We weren't talented enough to win all the time. But they liked the way we performed and the way we played offensively, and that made it a special relationship for me and a special place to play."

The other game that 1974 season that forever made its way into Redskins history was a Dallas game. It is one that Washington fans and players would just as soon forget.

Washington won the first game at RFK Stadium that year by 28–21, and less than two weeks later they faced the Cowboys again in Dallas on Thanksgiving Day. Any time a Cowboys-Redskins game was about to take place, it usually meant that instigator Diron Talbert took center stage.

Talbert was a big Texan who did all he could to fuel the rivalry between the two teams. In the days leading up to the nationally televised game, Talbert said they would try to knock Roger Staubach out of the game. "If Staubach runs, you like to get a good shot at him and knock him out of the game. You try to get a scrambling quarterback to scramble into the arms of somebody who's going to hurt him. If you knock him out, you got that rookie facing you. That's one of our goals. If we do that, it's great. He's all they have. They have no experienced quarterback."

"That rookie"—Clint Longley—would prove to be Talbert's worst nightmare.

The Redskins accomplished Talbert's goal of knocking Staubach out of the game when linebacker Dave Robinson gave the Dallas quarterback a nasty shot that sidelined him. At the time, Washington led 16–3, and if a game ever looked like a lock for a Redskins win, it was this one. Talbert and company were licking their chops when Longley came in for his first NFL game. But the rookie quarterback nailed them, throwing for more than 200 yards and 2 touchdowns, including a 50-yard game-winner to Drew Pearson with just 28 seconds left to play. Dallas won 24–23 and Longley immortalized as the "Mad Bomber."

Ron McDole "My locker was right next to Talbert's, and after the game, when reporters came in, they couldn't wait to get to Talbert. They asked him, 'What do you think of Clint Longley?' And Talbert asked, 'Who the hell is that?'

"I think that was the worst loss George Allen ever suffered. I don't think he ever recovered from that loss. It was hard on him, because we had the game pretty well wrapped up, and it got away from us."

Diron Talbert "I'll never forget that as long as I live. I had made those comments about knocking Staubach out of the game, and sure enough, Dave Robinson knocked Staubach out, and they put in Clint Longley, and he came in and beat us. We had some good shootouts with the Cowboys."

. . .

The team did recover, though, and won the final two games of the season, a 23–17 victory over the Rams in Los Angeles and a season finale 42–0 win at home over the Chicago Bears—a game that had a humorous mini-drama taking place on the field that featured the great defensive end Deacon Jones, who was ending his career playing for the Redskins.

Mike Bragg   "Deacon was dying to kick, and he was badgering George to kick in the last game of the season. It was against the Bears. We beat them 42–0. On the next to last time we scored, Deacon came into the huddle and declared he was going to kick the extra point. I was the kicker because Moseley was hurt and Sonny was the holder, and Sonny told him, 'Get the hell out of here and get on the sidelines.' So Deacon goes back to the sidelines, and we kick the extra point, and everything is okay. There are about two minutes left now in the game, and Deacon runs to George and says, 'If we score again, let me kick it.' George says okay. He figures we're not going to score. We're kicking off to the Bears. They will sit on it and run the clock out. But they don't. They fumble it, and Mike Bass picks it up and runs it in for a touchdown. We score, and George, true to his word, told Deacon he could go in and kick it. I knew what was going on because I had been on the sidelines watching all this. So Deacon goes in the huddle, and I see Sonny's head pop up out of the huddle. He calls time out and walks over to the sidelines and says to George, 'Do you really want to do this? Don't you think it will be rubbing salt in the Bears' wounds?' George said, 'Yeah I know, but I told him he could do it.' Sonny says, 'Well, I'm not holding it.' This was Joe Theismann's first year, so George calls out, 'Joe, go in and hold it." Deacon made the kick, and it was on the front page of the paper."

It was good for some laughs, but it was short lived. Despite beating the Rams two weeks earlier in Los Angeles, they went out there this time for the first round of the playoffs and lost to the Rams 19–10. Washington committed 6 turnovers, 3 fumbles, and 3 interceptions. The Redskins were now two years removed from the Super Bowl, and the Over the Hill Gang was getting further and further over the hill.

They failed to make the playoffs in 1975, with an 8-6 record, and finished it with disappointing losses to Dallas (31–10) and Philadelphia (26–3). Larry Brown had been surpassed by rookie Mike Thomas, who rushed for 919 yards, while Brown, at the end of his career, ran for 352 yards, banged up most of the season. Kilmer played well, throwing 23 touchdowns, while Theismann saw a little more time as quarterback, but not much—completing 10 of 22 passes for 96 yards and 1 touchdown. Charley Taylor caught 53 passes for 744 yards, including a special one in the 26–3 loss to the Eagles in the final game of the season at RFK Stadium. He broke Don Maynard's career reception record with his 634th catch and became the NFL's all-time leading receiver.

Receiver Charley Taylor   "After I caught the pass to set the all-time record, everybody left the stands. We still had about ten minutes to play. It was a rainy day and we were getting beat by the Eagles, but people hung around for that catch, and I appreciated that."

There were new faces starting to show up, even though Allen traded away as many draft choices as he could. When the Redskins did get a young player, it was through luck and opportunity. Mammoth defensive tackle Dave Butz became a Redskin in 1975 through his bad luck, and the team took advantage of the opportunity this presented.

Defensive tackle Dave Butz   "I was drafted by the St. Louis Cardinals in the first round in 1973 and played one season there. My second year I suffered a severe knee injury that was supposed to end my career. When I came back, I was a free agent and had two teams looking at me. I flew out to California and had a physical for the Raiders and passed it. I still have the doctor's report that said, 'We need to sign this boy. He is ready to play football.' The doctor and I talked for a while, and apparently I fired the doctor up some. There were two offers, though, and the other was from George Allen and the Washington Redskins. Both offers were alike, but the Redskins made the first move to sign me, and I wound up in Washington.

"I liked playing for George. He was a great motivator. When other teams had given up on players, he would take them in and get some good use out of them. My wife and I were sitting at the Dulles Marriott having lunch, and George was there eating lunch, too, during the pre-season that year. He turned my paper menu over, wrote seven things that I needed to do to play in the league for a long time, and signed it 'Coach George Allen.' I still have that menu.

"George sent my wife a rolling pin once, and it said, 'To use on Dave for motivation when needed—George Allen.' He didn't just send a regular rolling pin. He sent one with ball bearings. It wasn't a cheap one."

As big as Dave Butz was—6-foot-7 and more than 300 pounds—it was ironic that he would buddy up to one of the smallest guys on the team, cornerback Pat Fischer, who stood at 5-foot-9 and weighed 170 pounds, but had a 300-pound heart.

Dave Butz   "When I first came to the Redskins, I didn't hang out in bars. I would go home with Pat Fischer. His wife would always have a can of tuna fish for me, and I would sleep in Pat's office on a day bed that I didn't fit on, and then go to practice the next day. Pat Fischer, with all his clothes on, probably weighed about 165 pounds, with boots on and everything. He's about 5-foot-8 and is legally blind in one eye. He is one of the most impressive human beings to ever put a uniform on. They can talk about [tough guys] like [Larry] Csonka and whatever, but Pat Fischer was the toughest. [Philadelphia Eagles receiver] Harold Carmichael was about 7 or 8 inches taller than Pat, but Pat would eat him alive.

"I was sitting on the left side of the bench, which was the offensive side, which shows you what I knew. I was watching the St. Louis Cardinals sweep to their right, which would have put them right in our bench, at about the 35-yard line. Dan Dierdorf is leading the sweep, which is unusual for Dan, because he was never too fast. Pat Fischer comes up and hits Dierdorf, stopping Dan, but bounces off him vertically and gets into the backfield and tackles Terry Metcalf. Pound for pound, he was unbelievable."

When the 1975 season ended, Allen promised fans that the Redskins would return to the playoffs in 1976, and they did, going 10–4. They stepped up their running game with the unusual addition of a free agent—a rarity at the time—John Riggins, an enigmatic running back from the New York Jets.

Riggins was a farm boy from Kansas who didn't act like one. At the University of Kansas, he led the Big Eight in rushing and scoring as a senior, and during his three years there we rushed for 2,706 yards. He was the New York Jets number-one draft pick in 1971 and was in the same backfield as another small-town lad with a big-city style: Joe Namath. Riggins led the Jets in rushing and receiving his rookie season. Even though he continued to play well the next three years, at times he struggled with injuries. Regardless, he had a career year in 1975, rushing for 1,005 yards and catching 30 passes for 363 yards. He was named to the Pro Bowl for the first and last time.

The fullback was known for his antics off the field as well as his skill on the field. One year he reported to camp with an Afro hairstyle. The next time he reported with a Mohawk that had an arrow down the middle of his scalp.

Running back John Riggins   "I actually grew the Mohawk for the fun of it. I wanted to show everybody I was my own boss. I always wanted one as a kid, but my folks wouldn't let me have it."

But the Jets were never the same Joe Willie–led team that shocked the football world when they upset the Baltimore Colts in Super Bowl III. Namath couldn't stay healthy, and the Jets became a losing franchise. So Riggins played without a contract for that 1975 season, which left him a free agent to sign with another team. He signed with the Redskins, but rushed for just 572 yards in 1976 and missed nine games in 1977 because of a knee injury. Mike Thomas led the Redskins in rushing the second straight season, gaining 1,101 yards, a 4.3-yard-per-carry average.

Washington had finished the season strong, winning its last four games, including a season finale 27–14 win over the Cowboys in Dallas. But that momentum did not carry over to the playoffs, as the Vikings beat the Redskins 35–20 in the first round of the playoffs.

The 1977 season wound up being the last stand for many of the Over the Hill Gang, as well as their leader, George Allen. Running back Larry Brown called it quits during training camp, his broken body beaten down by the pounding he took and his tough running style.

. . .

Mike Bragg   "Larry Brown was one of the toughest guys that I ever knew. George loved Larry because he was tough. He wasn't coming out of the game because he got hurt. He wasn't running out of bounds to avoid taking a hit. And he was a hell of a blocker. He sacrificed his body, and maybe if he had run out of bounds more, he might have prolonged his career."

Running back Larry Brown   "What if you were George Allen, and you had the same personnel that he had, what would you have done? Hand it off to Larry Brown. When you didn't have the ball in your hands, you didn't have a chance to demonstrate your capabilities. It worked to my benefit, because if you don't carry the ball, it's likely you won't be around long, but the more you carry it, the more punishment you take.

"One day in training camp I was running, and I felt a sharp pain in my right foot. After all the bumps and bruises I had at that point, this was the one that put me over the top. I had just had it. I walked over to Coach Allen and said, 'That's enough. I've had it.' At the time I was in a backup role, and I was not carrying the ball as much. The feeling was no longer there."

When Brown retired, he was regarded as one of the greatest running backs of that era. From 1969 to 1976, Brown rushed for 5,875 yards, caught 238 passes for 2,485 yards, and scored 58 career touchdowns. His greatest season was 1972, when he gained 1,216 yards in 12 games and won NFL Player of the Year honors.

The Redskins opened the 1977 season with a tough 20–17 loss to the Giants, then won their next three over Atlanta, St. Louis, and Tampa Bay. But then they lost 34–16 to the Cowboys in Dallas and 17–6 to the Giants at RFK Stadium, which seemed to signal that the end was near for the Allen era. Allen had beaten the Giants eleven straight times, but had now lost three in a row to New York, and, next to the Cowboys, Allen considered the Giants to be right behind his hatred of Dallas. After the game, the coach told reporters that he "couldn't ever remember a loss this devastating." Future Redskins general manager Charley Casserly remembers the speech Allen gave when the team met the Monday after that loss.

. . .

Charley Casserly   "He called the whole organization together—coaches, scouts, secretaries, and staff. He walked into the room, looking like he hadn't slept all night. He said, 'We win together, we lose together. This is the lowest we have ever been, and we're going to find a way to come out of this thing.' He made everyone feel like it was everyone's fault that we lost that game. And when we won, he had a way of making everyone feel like they were part of the win."

   The fact that Casserly was there and part of it at Redskin Park that day is the stuff of legend. He was a high school football coach who wrote to all twenty-eight NFL teams looking for a job. He landed one with the Redskins—a job where he did everything they asked of him and got paid zero for it. But he was there watching George Allen coach football behind the scenes, and that was a priceless education.

Charley Casserly   "In April 1977, I wrote a letter to all twenty-eight teams looking for a job and got twenty-two responses. Out of those, I got twenty rejections and two interviews, one with the Patriots with Chuck Fairbanks and one with George Allen. I was thrilled that I got answers. I was thrilled to have the autographs of these great people: Don Shula, Bart Starr, and Chuck Noll. I got an interview with George in May. He was my hero, and here I was getting a chance to meet the guy. The first thing he said was, 'Write up three ways you can help the Redskins.' I'm thinking, 'Wait a minute, Coach. You've got this backward. You're going to help me. How am I going to help you? I'm a high school coach from Massachusetts.' I wrote up my three ways, and we spent quite a bit of time together that day. At the end of the day he told me he wanted me to go home and rewrite the three ways I could help the Redskins, in more detail—what I haven't done in football and what I'd like to do, and what changes I would make in the National Football League. This was his standard three questions for everyone he interviewed, but I didn't know that at the time. I went home and wrote it up and mailed it to him. I met with the Patriots the next week, and they offered me a position with no salary. Then the Redskins offered me a position as well—to work for nothing.

   "I came here at the end of June 1977. I lived in the YMCA in Alexandria for $8 a night until training camp started. At training camp I was the 'gofer' among other things. I answered the phones for George. I was the 'Turk' [the person who tells a player to bring his playbook when he is being cut by the coach] in training camp. I ran errands. I worked in the public relations department. And I worked in scouting. I did preseason scouting. I did film breakdowns. I did a little bit of everything.

"In the fall, as the tradition had been, since I was not the first one to do this job, they put you on the road in college scouting. We didn't have any draft choices, though, and the next year our first draft choice wasn't until the sixth round. But they paid your expenses on the road, which allowed you to survive financially. That took me through the fall."

Casserly's roommate, safety Mark Murphy, also arrived in Washington that year through his one unique path, thanks to Allen.

Safety Mark Murphy "I was a senior at Colgate in the spring. I didn't know if I would be drafted or not, but I got a call from George Allen. Back then, it was twelve rounds held over two days. He called me and said, 'We really like you, Mark. We want to have you here. We want to draft you. We're going to get you an airplane ticket and fly you down here and have a press conference and announce you.' So they flew me down the first day of the draft, and I thought this was great. They put me up at a hotel near Dulles Airport. I didn't really know what was going on. I watched television and saw that the Redskins had two picks in the draft on the first day, and I wasn't one of them. I figured I would be drafted on the second day. Then early that day they got me up and about a half-dozen other players they had there. They drove us around in a van and gave us a tour of the city. None of us really knew what was going on. We had lunch downtown and saw Washington, and later in the afternoon they took us out to Redskin Park.

"They put us all in one room, and then called us in for a meeting, one at a time. They told us that the draft had just ended. You haven't been drafted, but we want to sign you as a free agent. George was hiding us, hoping that no other teams would get in touch with us. I called back home and spoke to my girlfriend, who is now my wife, and she said, 'Where have you been? I've been calling the hotel trying to get you, and they keep saying there is no Mark Murphy registered there.' I had given her the phone number for the hotel, but the Redskins had given the hotel instructions to say there was no Mark Murphy staying there. She said there were six other teams that had called me at home wanting to sign me as a free agent. Fortunately, I got in touch with some of them before I did finally sign with the Redskins. One of the guys who was with me there was Nat Turan, from Rutgers. There were about five or six of us. George called me his thirteenth-round draft pick.

"Despite that, I really came to like George Allen. I played for him just one season, but it was one of the best things that happened to my career, being a defensive player. His knowledge of defense and his preparation, I learned so much that first year not just from him but from the veterans I played with, on how to play defense. He had a passion that was unbelievable, and he was such a character. Everyone got a kick out of him. He was so exuberant. It was like a college atmosphere. He was very competitive and would do anything to win."

In his rookie year, Murphy had another job besides playing football.

Mark Murphy "I was the designated driver for Talbert and Kilmer. It was worth it just to be around them, they were so funny."

The laughs and good times would soon end, though. The team continued to struggle after that Giants loss, and, despite winning the final three games of the year—10–0 over Buffalo, 26–20 over St. Louis, and fittingly, 17–14 over Los Angeles—the team finished with a 9-5 record and was out of the playoffs. This was the seventh and final season of George Allen's contract, and it was time to move on.

The Redskins didn't really move on, however. They just tried to create another version of Allen and the Over the Hill Gang by hiring one of the old Ramskins as head coach: former Redskins linebacker Jack Pardee. He had been one of Allen's favorites, both in Los Angeles and in Washington, and was like a coach on the field. He had been an assistant coach for several years under Allen in Washington, and then he was hired as head coach of the Orlando Blazers in the short-lived World Football League. His success there resulted in a head coaching job with the Chicago Bears in 1975, and he turned that team around from 4-12 into a winning, playoff squad with a 9-5 record in 1977 (he was named NFC Coach of the Year), just beating out the Redskins. He pressured the Bears to let him out of his contract when the Redskins job opened up, because it seemed so natural for him to follow Allen and keep the tradition alive.

But franchise owners Jack Kent Cooke and Edward Bennett Williams also made another hire that would eventually take the organization, which had been decimated by all the draft choices that Allen had traded away, out of the Allen influence and into the new era of football. They hired the organization's first true general manager: former NFL quarterback Bobby Beathard. He had much more success in the front office than on the football field, however, working as a scout for the Kansas City Chiefs and the Atlanta Falcons before being named director of player personnel for the Miami Dolphins in 1972.

The two hires represented a franchise trying to hold onto its past but needing to move forward, and the two would clash.

Though there were still several veterans on the club, a number of them had called it quits. Charley Taylor retired after the 1977 season, leaving behind a Hall of Fame legacy—649 receptions for 9,140 yards and 79 touchdowns between 1964 and 1977. Fischer left as well, as did Jerry Smith, a tragic figure who lived with the pain of keeping a secret for his entire life, knowing that if the truth had ever been revealed publicly—though it was known or suspected throughout the game—his career would have likely been over much earlier. He was one of the best tight ends of his time, catching 421 passes for 5,496 yards and 60 touchdowns. He was also gay, and ten years after he stopped playing, he died from AIDS-related complications.

While declaring his homosexuality would have been perhaps the most difficult act a player of that time could have done, a number of Smith's former teammates said they would have supported him if he had.

Chris Hanburger   "I knew Jerry very well. It was a sad story, and for a lot of us, we kind of wondered about him. But had we known, it would not have made any difference. If we had known, we would have been highly protective of him, at least I would have. There may have been some players who knew for sure, but I didn't know at the time. I had suspicions, but we didn't talk about it. When the AIDS thing became known, because it was so new and there was so much about the disease we didn't know, there was some fear. We didn't know if we could shake hands with him or what. As things went on, we understood better. But as a team, I don't think it would have made a lick of difference. I know from my point of view it would not have made any difference."

. . .

Roy Jefferson   "Jerry Smith, we would have speaking engagements, and sometimes I couldn't make one, or he couldn't make one, and he would call me and ask if I could fill in for him, and we would do that for each other. I also bought a couple of townhouses that he and his brother had built. They were building homes then. He was a beautiful guy. I was at his bedside three or four days before he died, and he told me, 'You know what? We're taught all our lives that if you work hard enough, you can overcome anything. But there is nothing I can do now. If there was something I could do, I'd do it. But there is nothing I can do.' I was standing there crying. If there was something he could have done, whatever it was, he would have done it if he could."

Mike Bass   "I measured Jerry by what he did on the football field. What he did outside was his own business. It had nothing to do with me. He didn't drop a ball because of his sexual orientation, and that never bothered me anyway. I didn't care. The man could do whatever he wanted to do, as long as he came to play on Sunday. He was a football player, and I was very proud to be on the same field with him. I had heard some things. Dave Kopay was on our team, but these guys came to play, and I didn't care what they did off the field."

As the roster changed that 1978 season, others were either cut or demoted, which presented an awkward situation for Pardee that he never fully came to grips with, since some of these players were his former teammates.

Linebacker Rusty Tillman   "Jack Pardee was a very tough guy as a player. He was the guy who cut me, and I still have a bad taste in my mouth over that. He didn't communicate it very well. I found out through another player that I had been cut."

Pardee also made the move of naming Theismann as the starting quarterback over Kilmer, and the brash quarterback seemed to be making the most of it. The Redskins started the 1978 season 6-0. But this would be a team that played two different seasons. They finished 2-6 for an overall mark of 8-8.

. . .

Joe Theismann   "We were the toast of the town. We were 6-0, and I was on the cover of magazines. Then we went 2-6 and wound up 8-8. It was a strange season."

More changes came in 1979. Kilmer was gone, as were Chris Hanburger and Ron McDole. Regardless, Beathard, despite not drafting until the fourth round, found a number of players who would be instrumental in the future success of the franchise: linebackers Monte Coleman, Rich Milot, and Neal Olkewicz, safety Tony Peters, and tight end Don Warren.

Washington opened the 1979 at home against the Houston Oilers and Earl Campbell, who scored the winning touchdown for the Oilers on a 3-yard run with about two minutes left in the game for a 29–27 Houston victory. It was a game the Redskins led at halftime by 17–6. They led 27–13 early in the fourth quarter when the game fell apart. Dan Pastorini connected with Billy "White Shoes" Johnson on a 14-yard pass, and the Oilers stopped the Washington offense, got the ball back quickly, and moved it into position for a 26-yard Tony Fritsch field goal: Fritsch had just missed the extra point after the Johnson touchdown. With the score 27–22, Washington had the ball and appeared to have the game in hand when Riggins fumbled on the Redskins' 29-yard line. Campbell pounded the ball toward the goal line until he scored the go-ahead touchdown.

The following week they nearly did it again, squandering a 24–3 lead and allowing 21 points against the Detroit Lions in the Pontiac Silverdome. Riggins had another key fourth-quarter fumble that led to a Lions touchdown, and the Lions tied the game at 24–24 with about two minutes left. This time, though, Theismann moved the team into position for a 41-yard Mark Moseley field goal to win the game.

The margin of victory was a little wider the next week, a 27–0 win over the Giants at RFK Stadium, followed by victories over St. Louis and Atlanta. With a 4–1 record, the Redskins went to Philadelphia to play the improved Eagles, under coach Dick Vermeil. Wilbert Montgomery ran roughshod over the Redskins defense, scoring 4 touchdowns in a 28–17 Philadelphia win. Washington bounced back with wins over Cleveland and Philadelphia. In their rematch with the Eagles in Washington, they stopped Montgomery by holding him to

33 yards rushing and taking a 17–7 victory over the Eagles, behind the running of Riggins, who had 120 yards on 19 carries.

With a 6–2 mark, the Redskins were pummeled by the Saints the next week 14–10, as the New Orleans defense sacked Theismann seven times, and there was a feeling that this might be 1978 all over again, because the Redskins looked bad against the Saints and even worse in a 38–7 beating at the hands of the Steelers. They were now 6-4 and heading toward mediocrity again—especially since they nearly blew another big lead the following week against St. Louis. The Redskins led 27–7 in the fourth quarter when Cardinals quarterback Jim Hart drove his team to 3 touchdowns and a 28–27 lead with less than two minutes remaining. Theismann, though, had been through this before; he moved the team into position for another game-winning field goal by Moseley, this one a 39-yard kick with thirty-six seconds left and a 30–28 win.

It turned out to be the victory that saved the season for Washington. A loss would have left them 6–5 and demoralized. As it was, Washington started off the game against the Cowboys, at RFK Stadium with a 4-yard touchdown pass to end a drive by Theismann, one of 3 touchdown passes he threw, and Moseley had 2 field goals in a 34–20 win before the boisterous hometown crowd of more than 55,000 fans.

The Redskins kept the momentum going with three straight wins and a 10–5 record as they prepared for the last game of the season, which was in Dallas, against the Cowboys, with the playoffs being on the line for Washington. A win would give them the division title, and even with a loss, the Chicago Bears would have to beat the Cardinals by more than 33 points to edge the Redskins out of a wild-card position. The day would end in disappointment for Redskins fans, but they were taken for a wild ride along the way.

The Redskins recovered three Dallas fumbles to take a 17–0 lead in the second quarter, and then Theismann hit Benny Malone with a 55-yard touchdown pass. But the Cowboys scored 2 touchdowns in the second quarter to close the gap to 17–14 at halftime. The Cowboys took a 21–17 lead at halftime, and the teams traded scores in the fourth quarter. Clarence Harmon fumbled at the Cowboys' 42-yard line, handing the ball over to Dallas, which led to a 26-yard touchdown pass from Roger Staubach to Ron Springs. Washington failed to move the ball on its next possession and was forced to punt. With Staubach leading the charge, the Cowboys drove down the field and connected on the winning score with a 7-yard pass from Staubach to Tony Hill for a 35–34 lead, the victory, and the end of Washington's playoff hopes. Of all things, the Bears defeated the Cardinals by 36 points.

Despite the loss and the third straight season the Redskins had missed the playoffs, there was much to be optimistic about. Theismann came into his own, throwing for 20 touchdowns. Riggins came back to have his best season, rushing for 1,153 yards and averaging 4.4 yards per carry. Moseley hit 25 of 33 field goals for 114 points. Pardee won his second NFC Coach of the Year honors. There were plenty of reasons to feel good about the Redskins going into the 1980 season.

Those reasons were forgotten in training camp, when Riggins heard a tune in his head that said he wasn't getting paid what he was worth, and if he wasn't getting paid, he wasn't playing. So he left Carlisle, went home to Kansas, and didn't return that year.

It was Diron Talbert's last Carlisle training camp, and Riggins made it a memorable one.

Diron Talbert   "It was four in the morning, and Riggins was banging on my door. He wanted to get in. He was yelling, 'Talbe, let me in. These guys ain't giving me no money.' He beat on the door and huffed and puffed, so I let him in and we talked for a while. He comes to the conclusion, 'Talbe, they're not going to give me the money I want. I'm going home.' I said, 'Well, get on out of here and go home.' So he left. The next morning I went to practice, and someone asked me, 'Did you hear about Riggo? He's in Washington at the Dulles Marriott and is fixing to get on a plane to go home.' He had driven back to Washington after he left my room. The next time I talked to him was two days later, and he was in Kansas. 'I told you I was going home,' he said. 'They ain't paying me.' And he stayed out the whole year."

The team never recovered from Riggins's departure, losing five of its first six games and ending the season with a 6–10 record. Plus, there was a growing animosity between Pardee and his players and Pardee and Beathard, his general manager. There had been at least one positive development: a rookie receiver from Syracuse named Art Monk, who caught 58 passes for 797 yards receiving. He was the future of the franchise, and Jack Kent Cooke, who was now taking over full control of the Redskins, as Edward Bennett Williams bowed out to devote all his time to the Baltimore Orioles, wanted to cut ties with the past and move into the future. So Pardee was fired.

Kicker Mark Moseley   "Pardee's downfall was that he was such a nice guy and loved the players, many of whom were his old team-mates, and he couldn't cut them. We had a lot of the Over the Hill Gang who were getting up there in age and were going to have to be let go. Guys like Ron McDole, who rode to work with Pardee every day. He had to cut Ron, and that was hard for him. That was his downfall in Washington, that he was such a nice guy that some of the guys who weren't real dedicated to the game took advantage of him and got away with a lot of stuff, and it really began to disrupt the team."

Dave Butz   "I didn't like playing for Jack Pardee. We weren't as confident or unified. I told Bobby Beathard that I could no longer play and lose like we were. [Pardee] did a lot of stuff that he didn't even do as a player. One of his biggest thrills was to set up two cones and have an offensive and defensive guy go at it and a running back to tackle. It was an unnecessary drill. It was so old school it was pathetic. If guys can't hit by the time they get to the pros, they shouldn't even be on the team. It was a waste. We were doing cone drills right up to the end, and Pardee wanted to do it one more time. Ted Fritsch was our long snapper, and Neal Olkewicz was the linebacker against each other in this drill. Ted came off the line, and Neal hit him with a forearm that knocked him out. Ted Fritsch was never the same after that. He was never a consistent long-ball snapper again, and that ended his career.

"One day [Pardee] asked for everyone to see him before going home, so I went to his office. He was sitting there with a big-ass cigar and started saying somebody said you said . . . and when I heard that bullshit, I said, 'Stop right there. You get the person in here right now, across the table from me, and we will continue this discussion. But if you're not going to get the person who said I said something, in here with me and you, we have nothing more to talk about.' He wouldn't do it, so I left. Pardee used spies on the team, and I didn't appreciate that at all. Somebody saying something that I said was bullshit. That is not the way to start a conversation with me."

Pardee had his supporters as well.

. . .

Mark Murphy "I really liked playing for Jack. Like George, he was primarily a defensive coach. He was George's signal caller. I owed a lot to Jack. He gave me my first chance to play regularly, and he had confidence in me, particularly in calling signals. I was able to flourish with him as a coach."

There were not enough Mark Murphys, though—that is, players who were flourishing. It was time for the franchise to adopt a new identity. For this, they turned to an anonymous offensive assistant coach from San Diego, a name that players, let alone fans, barely recognized: Joe Gibbs.

7

Champions

Joe Gibbs had a long but obscure coaching career when Washington Redskins general manager Bobby Beathard brought him to Washington. It was not the typical Redskins hire, not the high-profile name like a Vince Lombardi or a George Allen, or even a Jack Pardee. The players had little or no knowledge about their new head coach, other than his association with Don Coryell and his high-profile offense in San Diego.

Linebacker Monte Coleman   "I didn't know anything about Joe Gibbs when he came. We had played San Diego and beat them at RFK Stadium, but you know more about the head coaches than the assistant coaches, so I knew more about Don Coryell. I didn't know anything about Joe Gibbs."

Tight end Rick Walker   "I didn't know anything about Joe, but he had been endorsed by people who knew the game. He had a great pedigree and was around a genius in Don Coryell. Sid Gilman was the godfather. I grew up in southern California, so I knew what the Chargers meant."

Kicker Mark Moseley   "Gibbs was really an unknown when he came here. No one had really paid attention to him before. We had heard he was this great offensive mind who had coached with Don Coryell in San Diego."

Safety Mark Murphy "I didn't really know a lot about Joe Gibbs when he came here. I knew he was a very respected offensive coordinator. But nobody really knew much about him."

Defensive tackle Dave Butz "Joe Gibbs was with Don Coryell when I started with the St. Louis Cardinals. I can remember one time coming off the field at about the 45-yard line, going toward the dugout where we went in at St. Louis, and Don Coryell asking Joe Gibbs to go get him a Coke. I thought that was kind of ironic that Coryell couldn't get his own Coke."

Gibbs probably didn't mind getting Coryell a Coke. He had known the Chargers head coach for so long, and his career was so closely connected to Coryell, that it probably seemed perfectly normal. Gibbs played tight end and linebacker at San Diego State from 1961 to 1963 for Coryell, then began his coaching career there in 1964, working as a graduate assistant on Coryell's staff. He coached the offensive line, and during his time with the Aztecs, they won 27 of 31 games, including an 11-0 season in 1966. He left to coach the offensive line for Bill Peterson at Florida State in 1967, and during Gibbs's two years there the Seminoles went 15-4-1. He went back to the West Coast in 1969 to coach at the University of Southern California with John McKay. The winning continued, as the Trojans also had a 15-4-1 record while Gibbs was there. He kept moving, though, going to Arkansas to join Frank Broyles's coaching staff in 1971, where the Razorbacks went 14-8-1 in the two seasons Gibbs coached there.

It was an impressive college resume, coaching with some of the great names in the sport—Coryell, McKay, and Broyles—and Gibbs made enough of an impression on two of those coaches that when they were putting together staffs to coach in the NFL, they wanted Gibbs to be part of it. Coryell made Gibbs the offensive backfield coach for the St. Louis Cardinals in 1973. They won two NFC East titles and had a 42-27-1 record in the five years Gibbs coached for the Cardinals—a remarkable record for a franchise with a track record of futility. Gibbs moved on to another great coach from his past, joining McKay's staff in Tampa Bay as the Bucs offensive coordinator, but was back with Coryell a year later as part of the coach's staff in San Diego in 1979, where he helped direct the explosive "Air Coryell" offense, with quarterback Dan Fouts and a receiving corps of John Jefferson, Charlie Joyner, and Kellen Winslow, winning two AFC West titles.

These were the football influences that shaped Gibbs's life. There was another strong influence that would shape his life as well, one that would become such a strong guiding force that it would sometimes become a source of controversy in the locker room: his faith in God.

Gibbs grew up in a small town in the mountains of North Carolina and was drawn to his religion at an early age. With his grandmother's influence, he became a devout Christian at the age of nine. He grew up reading the Bible, but after leaving home to go to college and then to start his coaching career, he had let his commitment to religion fade. Then, in 1972, while coaching at Arkansas, he met a Sunday school teacher from Fayetteville named George Tharel who helped Gibbs rededicate his commitment to his faith, and since then it has played a role in everything Gibbs has done.

Gibbs was hired to coach the Washington Redskins on January 13, 1981. Beathard said, "I closely followed his career and I feel that he has prepared himself for this position as well or better than any coach in the NFL. He has a track record that speaks for itself. Besides being bright and a terrific *x*'s and *o*'s man, Joe has demonstrated leadership. You can find a lot of fine assistant coaches, but there are few assistants who can lead. Joe has an unusual talent to get along with players."

Because Gibbs was such an unknown, in a town that placed such value on star power, owner Jack Kent Cooke tried to reassure Redskins fans that they had the right man for the job. "I was satisfied that he had an inner intensity that matched any man I'd run into in the coaching ranks," Cooke said.

He would need that intensity. First, to have the pounding running game that he desired, Gibbs would have to convince John Riggins to return to the Redskins after he had unceremoniously left the team as a holdout the year before. So he made the trip to Lawrence, Kansas, and met with Riggins, and the two men hit it off. Before long, Riggins showed up ready for training camp, proclaiming, "I'm broke, I'm bored, and I'm back."

Riggins was a welcomed familiar face in Carlisle in the summer of 1981, as there were several new faces—twenty-two in all when the season started—under the Gibbs regime. Beathard had what turned out to be one of the most productive drafts in franchise history. They moved up in the first round of the draft from twentieth place to ninth in a deal with the Los Angeles Rams for a group of later-round selections and used that ninth pick to tab offensive tackle Mark May from Pittsburgh. Beathard came away from that draft with three other future Redskin starters: receiver Charlie Brown, lineman Darryl Grant, and defensive end Dexter Manley, one of the most controversial and talented players ever to play in Washington.

Manley was a man-child, a 6-foot-4, 270-pound pass rusher with tremendous strength and remarkable speed for such a big man. He went to college at Oklahoma State, but he received no education there, at least not in the classroom. As has been well documented over Manley's tumultuous life, he was dyslexic, unable to read or write, and emotionally immature—put simply, he was not equipped to deal with everyday life, let alone the life of a superstar athlete. But he could play, and he had caught the eye of Beathard.

Defensive end Dexter Manley   "I saw Bobby Beathard at the combine in Tampa in 1981. He pulled me into a room and told me he was going to draft me. He didn't tell me which round, but he said he was going to draft me. I did great at the combine, and I thought I would be drafted in the top three rounds. But there were people questioning my character. I got in trouble at Oklahoma State, and I was on probation. The word was I was taking stuff or giving stuff or something.

"I was in Stillwater, Oklahoma, the first day of the draft, waiting to hear. They stopped after the fourth round on the first day and I hadn't been picked yet. My agent told me they were questioning my character. I got on my knees and said a prayer. As soon as I got off my knees, the phone rang and it was Bobby Beathard. He had drafted me.

"I didn't know what to expect. People told me that the Redskins were an easy team to make. But Joe Gibbs was new and wanted a whole new football team, so the theory of it being easy to make the Redskins was not true anymore. I didn't necessarily buy that anyway, so I worked my tail off. I was real hungry. I had a passion for football. I knew I could play in the NFL. I could not believe it when I got off the plane at Dulles Airport. I could feel the energy and excitement from the fans at minicamp. I knew I couldn't ask for a better place to be."

. . .

Another deal Beathard made on draft day also helped shape the new Gibbs Redskins: Washington traded its second-round draft choice for Baltimore Colts running back Joe Washington.

Running back Joe Washington   "I got into a contract dispute with the Baltimore Colts and Bob Irsay. I thought I had a deal with the Colts, but they called up at the last minute to make some changes. I thought it was probably time for me to move on. Plus, they drafted Curtis Dickey, who they were paying more than me. I told them I wanted to be traded, and on draft day the Colts called me and told me I had been traded to the Redskins, and then later that day I got a call from Joe Gibbs.

"Washington was one of the places I wanted to go because Joe Gibbs had gone there and I knew about him from his days in San Diego. I called San Diego to pass the word to Gibbs that I wanted to go to Washington. The year I made the Pro Bowl in Baltimore, the coaching staff for the game was the San Diego coaching staff, which included Gibbs, and I thought the offense and what they did worked real well. I couldn't talk to the Redskins, it wasn't allowed, so I called the Chargers and talked to Don Coryell. I'm sure he made it known to Joe that I was trying to get out of Baltimore.

"Gibbs told me they traded for me and that they were excited about it, and I was excited about it, too. I had been depressed about my situation, but after I talked to Joe Gibbs, I went outside in the hot Texas sun and started working out. It felt great."

When an unknown free agent arrived in Carlisle for Gibbs's first training camp, he nearly blocked the sun. He was another new face who would become one of the building blocks of the success of the franchise for the next ten years. Joe Jacoby—6-foot-7 and more than 300 pounds, a very large man by 1981 football standards—had been a relatively unheralded lineman at the University of Louisville but had managed to catch the attention of Washington Redskins scout Charley Casserly.

Scout Charley Casserly   "Louisville had just played Pittsburgh and Florida in the previous two games. It was their last game of the season.

I had seen [Jacoby] as a junior and rated him as a free agent like a lot of other scouts did. I saw him late in the year against highly rated guys, and he played them pretty good. These guys were not making plays, not getting to the quarterback, and he was blocking them. He was a big guy who could stand on his feet, and I thought, 'This guy must be a lot better than all of us think he is, because he is blocking these guys who are going to be high-rated draft choices.' I met Joe and told him that he needed to get on the weights and work hard in the off season and that we would be coming back in April to see him.

"Joe Bugel and I went back in April. It was a Saturday morning. Jacoby walked in, and he completely blocked the light coming through the door. He had completely transformed his body. He didn't weigh any more, but now he had a massive chest that he didn't have when I saw him in the fall. He was a guy who we had to take a shot at, a big guy with balance and strength and who was competitive.

"When people asked him if he was disappointed that he didn't get into any of the college All-Star games, he said that while those other guys were at the All-Star games, he was back lifting weights and getting ready for the draft. He took a negative and made it into a positive."

To mold this team with all the new players, Gibbs picked a coaching staff that would be teachers and that he could trust to delegate authority to while still carrying out the head coach's goals and philosophies. He didn't pick a group of Joe Gibbs clones, though. It was a very different mix that would form Gibbs's staff.

One of his most important decisions was to heed Beathard's recommendation and keep defensive coordinator Richie Petitbon on the staff. Petitbon, who went back to the start of the George Allen era, was brought to Washington as part of the group of Ramskins—former Rams who helped shape the Over the Hill Gang. The other staff members were offensive line coach Joe Bugel, who had spent four years coaching the offensive line for the Houston Oilers when the team set records for rushing and passing; running backs coach Don Breaux, who coached in Arkansas for Lou Holtz, worked on coaching staffs at Florida State, Texas, and Florida, and spent a season with the Houston Oilers; linebacker coach Larry Peccatiello, who coached linebackers for the Seattle Seahawks and Houston Oilers; special teams coach Wayne Sevier, a teammate of Gibbs from his days at San Diego State and colleague from the Coryell coaching staffs in St. Louis and

San Diego; Lavern "Torgy" Torgeson, a former Redskins linebacker who left the Rams coaching staff to join Gibbs and return to Washington for a third coaching stint, having started coaching with the Redskins in 1959 and then joined George Allen in 1971; and legendary receiver Charley Taylor, a familiar face to Washington fans, to coach the receivers.

Of all the pressured debuts Gibbs would have to make as the new coach, none could be more difficult for him to face than the Cowboys at RFK Stadium to open the season. It was Gibbs's first week, and it was Dallas week. It wouldn't go well. His team turned the ball over six times in a 26–10 loss to the Cowboys before more than 55,000 fans, who had more questions than answers about the new head coach by the time the game ended.

The answers they got the following week were even more disturbing—a 17–7 loss to the New York Giants before the home crowd. Washington fumbled the ball twice, leading to 2 Giants touchdowns, and went an embarrassing 0 for 16 on third-down conversions. At least the damage in week three took place away from home. It was a 40–30 loss to the Cardinals in St. Louis, a game that saw the Redskins take a 10–3 lead in the first quarter, then the Cardinals went on a 37–7 run.

Zero and 3 became 0 and 4 in Philadelphia, a 36–13 loss to the Eagles, who scored 22 points in the fourth quarter to put away a confused Redskins team. Things didn't appear to get any better in week five. Coming back home to present Redskins fans with a 30–17 loss to San Francisco, the questions now were not what kind of coach would Gibbs be, but how much longer could he survive in the job?

Those were the questions being asked from the outside. Inside the organization, however, from the owner down to the players, they believed they still had the right man, and the players could sense a turnaround coming.

Joe Gibbs "That first year had so many emotions to it. We start off bad, the worst period I ever experienced in my career. But in life, when you go through those times—thinking they are the worst things that ever happened to you—a lot of times, you'll find out later that if you go through them the right way, they wind up being a blessing down the road, and it's something you wouldn't trade. That's really what that time was, because 0-5 was one of the worst experiences I ever had, just a completely demoralizing experience. Now, looking back on it, I think it motivitated our team. It gave me a chance to analyze the people around me and see what our owner was like under severe difficulty. All those things are wrapped up in that 0-5 start. It was just one of the most emotional times in my life, with tremendous lows.

"Mr. Cooke was at his best when things were at their worst. He had been through tough times himself. Many times, when I was at my lowest, he would come in my office, and I would think he was going to jump me, that is, when he would surprise me and come in and say, 'Look, things are going to be okay. We're going to get through this.' That's exactly what happened during that 0-5 start. Every time I thought he was going to fire me, he would try to find a way to talk to me and pick me up. Now, other times he would surprise me and nail me on something. But normally, during those tough times, he was at his best."

There was no panic in the locker room, either.

Kick returner Mike Nelms "I am an optimistic person. It is hard to beat me down. I would have felt differently when we got off to that 0–5 start if I didn't think we had the players to compete, but I knew that we did. It was just a question of when, not if. You hear a lot of coaches say, 'We win together, we lose together.' He was emphatic about that. He said, 'I do not want any finger pointing. When we lose, it is not one play that determines the game. I don't care who you are, you start that finger-pointing stuff, you are going to hit the road.' A couple of guys caught a bullet because of that. They were pointing fingers after a game, and their lockers were soon empty.

"It was just a question of could we do what he was asking us to do, and I felt we had the personnel. I never questioned him or his ability. It was more on us. I had confidence that we were capable of competing and not end up on the losing end so often."

Dave Butz "When Gibbs came to the Redskins, he took an offense that was extremely simple and made it as complex as the defense was, got the proper personnel, and really turned things around. There was the time when we had lost our first five games in the first year with him, and he stopped me after practice, between the grass field and the artificial field, next to Nate Fine's tower, and he said, 'You won't believe this, but we are so close to being a good team. I want you to hang with me. Keep working as hard as you are, and we will turn this around. Trust me. We are so close.'"

Tight end Rick Walker   "Joe brought about four or five of us in for a meeting. He drew up something . . . to me, I've never seen anyone do what Joe does on the board, how his mind functions in developing formations and sets based on what the opponent does. I could see in the beginning he had a very good sense of how to utilize people and how to attack certain areas. That was on a day off. We came in, and he drew up what he had in mind, certain things we would have to do, certain requirements . . . and that was it. There was a warm-up game, and then we were very close. You could tell there was a change coming about."

Quarterback Joe Theismann   "I was really excited when he got here. He had come out of San Diego, where Dan Fouts had been throwing all over the place, and there was a new concept of offense, with two tights ends. Through 1981 I led the league in everything: pass attempts, pass completions, and interceptions. I led them in all positive and negative categories. So we lose to San Francisco the fifth game of the season.

"It's funny that you can be in a room with someone, and you either know whether you are connecting or not connecting, and I would sit in those meeting rooms and would talk to Coach Gibbs. Now keep in mind, at that time I was doing television shows, I opened a restaurant, I was the Washington Redskins, the public face of the team. I found this out about Joe Gibbs: Joe is extremely loyal to 'his people.' I wasn't one of his. What he means by his people are the people he chooses to be on the team or the people he drafts. You really have to play above just good for Joe to keep you. He wouldn't think twice about unloading you and finding somebody else who would have been one of his guys. That's fine with me. I never minded competition. They brought guys in. They drafted Tom Flick in the second round to try to take my job. They kept trying to give my job away in 1981. After the fifth game of the season we were 0–5, and I got a sense that Joe and I were just not on the same page. After the San Francisco game, I went home and was very restless. I hopped in my car and drove to his house. I guarantee you he was shocked to see me standing at his door at about 7 P.M. We sat down and I explained to him that I would give up everything . . . I wanted him to understand how committed I was to being his quarterback, but I wanted that commitment from him as well. We sat down and talked for a number of hours. After that conversation, everything changed."

It changed in Chicago at Soldier Field, on October 5, when the Redskins played a Bears team that was a very willing participant in the turnaround. The Bears turned the ball over three times. Joe Lavander intercepted a pass by Vince Evans in the first quarter that led to a Mark Moseley field goal and a 3–0 lead. A minute later, linebacker Neil Olkewicz intercepted another Evans pass and ran it in from the Bears' 10-yard line for a 10–0 Redskins lead. And to illustrate how truly a bad day Evans was having, tackle Dave Butz intercepted a pass before the end of the first half, missing a chance to score when he was tackled at the 1-yard line. John Riggins took it in for the touchdown, and the Redskins went into the locker room with a 17–0 lead. They made it 24–0 with about five minutes left in the game on a 2-yard run by Riggins, and the Bears finally got on the board when replacement quarterback Mike Phipps connected with Marcus Anderson on a 43-yard touchdown pass with less than two minutes left in the game. It was a 24–7 victory and Joe Gibbs's first regular season victory as an NFL head coach.

What pleased Gibbs most was the running game—watching Riggins rush for 126 yards. This would be the blueprint for success in Gibbs's offense. "We proved that we can run the ball, that we can move it out from the goal line in tough situations and that we can control it for a long time," he told reporters after the game.

They lost the following week in Miami to the Dolphins and a young quarterback named David Woodley—a preview of a historic matchup that would come the following season—by 13–10 on a fourth-quarter 25-yard field goal by Uve von Schamann. The defeat did not stop the momentum that had finally started the week before, nor did it shake the confidence of this team in their rookie head coach.

Washington went on a four-game winning streak, with victories over New England (24–22), St. Louis (42–21), Detroit (33–31), and the division rival New York Giants in overtime (30–27). Three of those four wins came by a margin of 3 points or less, which is important to note, because it serves notice that the most significant offensive weapon the Redskins had in the early days of the Joe Gibbs's regime was kicker Mark Moseley. That was clear in the overtime victory over the Giants. With the rain coming down hard at Giants Stadium, Moseley kicked a 49-yard field goal to tie the game at 27–27 and send it into overtime, and then nailed a 48-yard kick for the victory. But they lost the following week—another Dallas week—to the Cowboys at Texas Stadium, taking a 24–10 beating. Another loss the next week in Buffalo (21–14) to the Bills was reminiscent of the early season defeats with several turnovers, but they were also done in by a number of questionable calls by officials. With a record of 5-8, the verdict was still out on Gibbs.

He provided enough evidence to make his case in the final three games of the 1981 season, two of which took place before the home-town fans at RFK Stadium: a 15–13 win over the Eagles, a 38–14 victory over the Baltimore Colts, and, in the season finale in Los Angeles, a 30–7 win over the Rams, which saw 502 yards of total Redskins offense. They finished the season with an 8-8 record, having won eight of their last eleven games after the frightening 0-5 start.

Theismann recovered from an erratic first half to finish with 19 touchdown passes, though he had thrown 20 interceptions. But he found a reliable target in Art Monk, a quiet second-year receiver from Syracuse who caught 56 passes, averaging 16 yards a catch, for 6 touchdowns. The rust from sitting out the season before eventually shook off Riggins, who carried the ball 195 times for 714 yards, and was a red-zone machine, scoring 13 touchdowns. Joe Washington ran for 916 yards, averaging 4.4 yards per carry, and the two of them made a good rushing combination, both on and off the field.

Joe Washington   "John was tough, endearing, unique, and very passionate about things. He had firm beliefs that he didn't waver from. He was very principled. We had a good relationship. I told him the first time I met him that I thought he was black all these years. I really did. For a long time, I thought he was black.

"When I first got to the Redskins, our lockers were next to each other. The equipment managers and trainers in Washington always had everything ready and out in front of our lockers before the game. They had your pads, the extra tape, anything you had asked for. They were great. When I would come into the locker room, I would see all of John's stuff laid out and I would notice something in a green tube called "Fleet." It was always in a tube, and it was always gone. The same thing, game after game. Finally, I asked him, 'Riggo, what is this "Fleet" stuff I always see?' He grinned and said, 'Hey Little Joe, I'm not the same type of runner as you. I don't have that shiftiness. If I happen to get a real good hit, I don't want to lose control.' I asked, 'What?' Then I found out it was an enema. Before every game, John Riggins used an enema so he wouldn't lose any body control when he got hit or when he hit somebody else."

After the 1981 season, Joe Gibbs and Bobby Beathard had a better idea of what they wanted and whom they wanted to succeed. One of their priorities was conditioning—particularly strength training—and they targeted a hard-working strength coach at Penn State by the name of Dan Riley.

Strength coach Dan Riley   "I came to the organization in January 1982. I was the strength coach at Penn State before that, and Bobby Beathard and the scouts, when they came through there, I think they saw what was happening as the program developed there. They wanted some of the same things with the Redskins.

"Bobby Beathard and [trainer] Bubba Tyer had come down to Penn State the year before and spent some time talking to some players, and I think I got favorable responses, and that led to having any interest in hiring me. So at the end of the season at Penn State they called, and Joe said he was interested and wanted me to come up for an interview. I met with him and all the coaches. He offered me the job right away. I came back to Penn State for a couple more weekends before I decided to go. It was because of Joe that I went there. At the time, strength coaches were kind of a novel item—I think there was only one part-time guy in the league—and I was told by people that I would just be a token, because NFL players wouldn't work hard. I told Joe that I didn't want to be a token, and I wasn't. He was as supportive as he could be from the very beginning, and that allowed me to do my thing.

"Initially, when they offered me the job, I turned it down. I wasn't sure I was going to leave Penn State and have the same degree of respect and authority in Washington that I had there. Joe was the one who convinced me to come back to look at Washington one more time, which I did with my family, and he sold me on the kind of support I would have.

"Joe tells this story, but he tells it differently than it really happened. He tells the story that when I visited there, the facility was bad, and he kept preparing me for it, because all the coaches were with us at Redskin Park. We get to the weight room, and before he opens the door, he says, 'Remember: we are going to build a new room, so keep that in mind.' We walked in and I did a 360 in slow motion and said, 'This sucks. This is terrible.' He agreed, and I said to him, 'I can train an athlete with just cement cans, but you need equipment to get the job done thoroughly.' I submitted a budget the first year for $50,000 and every year after that I kept badgering him for more equipment, and I got it.

"He tells the story that I said I could train the Redskins with cement cans, and once I got there, I came to him and asked for $50,000 worth of equipment. He laughs when he tells the story and says that I was the crazy one. Well, I would say to him, you stay here every night, you don't see your family, your kids grow up without you, you say that you have to work on a game plan for Sunday's game, and then, in a game, we run three plays, 40-gut, 50-gut, and Charlie hitch. Whenever I say that, and I was up there just a couple of months ago and spoke to the whole staff, half the coaches there are scared to death of Joe, and when they heard me talking to him like that, they thought that was kind of funny. Who is the crazy one? I would go home and be with my family, and you would stay here and work on a game plan that you don't even use."

Riley said his program would make great demands on the players, and at the time, weight training the way he wanted to do it—a full-time program—was still a novelty in the NFL. He needed the help of certain players to sell it to the team, and he got it from John Riggins.

Dan Riley "In the early days, leaders on the team who really helped me sell what we were doing were players like John Riggins. He had never really trained with weights, and I was still kind of learning the system that we had, and he took to the system because John was, and is, a really hard worker. For him to accept it and for guys to see him train hard, it helped me gain credibility quick.

"Riggins was one of the team leaders, and he and I were close friends and still are. He was respected because of his performances on the field, even before he got to the Redskins. You can't be well respected unless you perform at a high level. He never ran out of bounds, and when he did score, he would just hand the ball to the official. With John, it was always about the team. He was one of the most intelligent players I have ever seen. He is extremely smart, and when he does say something, it is worth listening to. He is an unbelievably tough person who doesn't walk around showing it. He is a cult hero in Washington, but he would act just the opposite among a group of people or friends, and instead of talking about himself, he would engage everybody else into the conversation and make them feel really comfortable. He respects the game of football, but he didn't make it something more than it was, and he didn't make himself something more than he was.

"I was lucky. It was a really good group of guys, and you know the guys Joe wanted and brought in, they had a great work ethic and were good guys to be around. There wasn't a lot of organized strength training going on, and it needed Joe's support. We had a lot of young players, and I grew up and matured with them, like Joe Jacoby, Charles Mann, and guys like that.

"The weight room was an area for spontaneous interaction. It was not the classroom, and there were opportunities for a player to interact with another player who he might not spend a lot of time with, like an offensive lineman and a defensive back. Once the season starts, they are pretty much locked up in meetings in separate rooms and work out in groups, and there is not a lot of time for conversation. The weight room became a place where guys would hang out. Russ Grimm was always holding court—him, Riggins, and Ron Saul back in the early days. For sure, when Russ Grimm was in there, you knew it. He was always trying to irritate somebody."

Riley wound up building a strong influence on the players.

Rick Walker "Everyone was trying to get the Ironman T-shirt from Dan Riley, who, in my personal opinion, was the single most important factor to our run. He had more interaction and a better relationship with most of the players because of the position he was in. It was so incredible, how much personal time he gave. I would meet him on Sunday afternoon, Sunday night, to work out. He was compassionate to what you wanted to do. He was a cyborg. Now they can't even get people to show up for camp."

When players did come to camp in 1982, they needed a scorecard to recognize even more new names. Joe Gibbs wanted his guys, and Bobby Beathard got more of them in his second season. The Redskins had put together a championship team, even though it didn't appear so after losing all four of their preseason games.

Gibbs made it clear that he was going to use youngsters over veterans who didn't produce. He cut running back Terry Metcalf, whom he had been close to from their days in St. Louis. He made backup linebacker Rich Milot a starter, as well as rookie cornerback Vernon Dean. He cut receiver Carl Powell, a top draft choice, in favor of unheralded Alvin Garrett. He brought in veteran defensive end Tony McGee to replace Mat Mendenhal and shore up the pass rush. And, most important, Gibbs opted to keep place-kicker Mark Moseley for the 1982 season and cut highly touted rookie kicker Dan Miller, who had missed two field goals in the final preseason game.

Cornerback Vernon Dean "When I was drafted, I knew I was going to a team that had struggled early but finished strong the year before, and because of that, we knew in training camp that this was going to be a pretty good team. There was great anticipation within the team going into the season. When I came out of school, I was really a safety playing the corner. But I was able to make plays. I had good speed, but not great speed. I had speed suited for a safety, but a corner's body. I played corner, but I also played safety in certain situations. I would have liked to move over there at the end of my career, but we had players there like Todd Bowles and Alvin Walton, pretty good players.

"As a youngster, you always expect training camp to be hard. It's two-a-days, and nobody likes two-a-days. You really had to work to earn a spot on the team, no matter where you were drafted. It was more mentally tough than physically tough. The amount of information that had to be processed, in addition to having to excel physically, that was tough.

"Coach Gibbs ran a pretty tight ship, but he put us in position to play well, to excel. The game was much faster than college, but Coach

Gibbs and his staff, Richie Petitbon and the others, did a great job preparing me and the whole team. Because they made it simple to process the information you needed, it helped prepare you and slow the game down a little bit. And I had those veterans who wouldn't allow me to be overwhelmed."

Defensive end Tony McGee   "I was drafted out of Bishop College, a small school out of Dallas, by the Chicago Bears in the third round in 1971. I was traded to New England in 1974 and played there until 1981. Then I was traded to Washington in 1982 and played here until 1984. I had over 106 sacks. In the three years I was here, we went to two Super Bowls and one division playoff.

"When I first got to Washington, I saw that this team was focused on doing something. We weren't the biggest or the most talented team, but we were a team, and you could tell the way they put the team together that it was important to them. They brought me in when they had a young defensive end like Dexter Manley, and then the next year they brought Charles Mann in. I had the opportunity to watch those young men grow and work with them. I saw Perry Brooks play a whole game against Dallas with a broken leg. I saw Darryl Grant develop from an offensive tackle to one of the best defensive tackles around. The Hogs were impressive, the Riggo drill, the wide receivers, the way Charlie Brown emerged—this team was built for success. It is hard to do again because of the salary cap.

"Chicago, everything was tough, tough guys, the Monsters of the Midway, good defense, no offense, and we never won that much. In New England, we were very talented, but we never won anything. In Chicago during training camp, we hit just to hit. In New England, we would hit like game conditions. But when I got here, the training camps here were a combination of both—we hit and it was very much like game situations. It was a tough, competitive camp."

Mark Moseley   "I wasn't even supposed to be on that team. I was supposed to be cut that year. They drafted a kicker and told him the job was his. But I wasn't going to give up. I kept fighting and making the most of my chances, and it came down to the last game of the pre-season that year, before they made their decision. They were going to let Dan Miller do all the kicking, but he had a rough game, and that opened the door for me. Then the rest of the season was mine."

. . .

Dave Butz   " Mark Moseley was an excellent head-on kicker. If I wanted someone to kick for me in a game, I would pick Mark. He was good on kickoffs, had good hang time, and could put the ball in the end zone every time. He was a roommate of mine for seven or eight years. One time, in the middle of the night, I heard this fluttering noise, and I thought we had a moth stuck in the window shade or something. I got up and found Mark brushing his hair in front of the mirror with the lights out. He was asleep. It was pitch black in the room, about 2 A.M. I said, 'Mark, you better get to bed.' He didn't realize he was doing it.

One time the sheets blew up straight from the bed, and Mark started coming toward me. He was having a bad dream. I said, 'Mark you take one more step toward me and I'm going to drop you.'"

The training camp at Carlisle in 1982 was also particularly noteworthy because it was the birth of the Hogs, the legendary moniker for the Redskins offensive line, christened so by line coach Joe Bugel.

Center Jeff Bostic   "Joe Bugel was looking at Russ Grimm's body, and he called us all hogs. He said, 'Hey, you bunch of hogs, let's go,' to what he called his bullpen, which was the most remote place on the practice field at Carlisle. That was where we worked. It kind of started as a joke, and on his own Bugs had T-shirts made, with this nasty looking hog wearing Redskins colors in between the goalposts. He passed them out in a meeting at training camp. It gave us a sense of identity. We were all young—Grimm, Joe Jacoby, Mark May was in his second year, and I was in my third. It gave a bunch of young guys a lot to rally around. We had no idea what it would turn into. It really exploded, with T-shirts, towels, and hog noses. It took the town by storm, and it kept going for years."

Tackle Joe Jacoby   "We were all young and only had one senior member, George Starke, though Ron Saul was there. George was the one we looked to to kind of keep everybody in line. Joe Bugel did the job as far as preparing us and getting all the guys in the right positions, and the right group of guys starting. It was a strange group to get together, with draft choices like Russ Grimm and Mark May and free agents like Jeff Bostic and myself thrown into that mix. It turned out to be the right timing, with everything coming into place."

· · ·

Despite all the warm feelings about identity, there were a lot of questions going into the 1982 season, particularly after the 0–4 preseason record. And another question came up when their leading rusher from the year before went down for the season with a knee injury.

Joe Washington   "I got hurt in a preseason game. I made a cut, and it was just time for it to go. When you look at the years that I played and my running style and all the cuts that I made, it was just time. But I wasn't ready for it, not at that point."

It looked as if they could have used Joe Washington and some other talented players as well when the season opened in Philadelphia against the Eagles. The Eagles scored 10 points in the first quarter and shut down the Redskins offense, and, after Tony Franklin kicked a 44-yard field goal, Washington kick returner Mike Nelms fumbled the kickoff, giving the Eagles the ball back again on the Redskins' 18-yard line. But running back Wilbert Montgomery coughed the ball up on the 15-yard line and the Redskins recovered. Theismann drove the Redskins to two scores, a 5-yard touchdown pass to Art Monk and a 6-yard touchdown reception by Charlie Brown. The Redskins had a 14–10 lead with less than a minute left in the first half, but Philadelphia added another 44-yard field goal by Franklin when Eagles quarterback Ron Jaworski hit Harold Carmichael on a 46-yard pass.

The third quarter was nearly a replay of the first–Philadelphia dominance, with 14 points on a 2-yard run by Montgomery and a 42-yard touchdown pass from Jaworski to Montgomery for a 27–14 Philadelphia lead after three quarters. Theismann came up with a big play, finding Brown for a 78-yard touchdown pass. After the Washington defense held, the Eagles punted, and Nelms returned it 28 yards to the Philadelphia 48-yard line. Four plays later, Riggins took the ball in from the 2-yard line, and Moseley's extra point gave Washington a 28–27 lead. A fake punt attempt by the Eagles backfired, and the Redskins got the ball down by the Philadelphia 30-yard line, which led to a Moseley field goal and a 31–27 lead with less than three minutes left in the game. But the Eagles quickly moved down the field on a 14-play, 90-yard scoring drive, culminating in a 4-yard touchdown pass to Carmichael for a 34–31 Eagles lead with 58 seconds remaining.

Nelms returned the Eagles kickoff to the Washington 37-yard line. The-ismann found Monk on a 10-yard pass, and then the Redskins quarter-back scrambled down to the Eagles' 31-yard line. Moseley nailed a 48-yard field goal to tie the game at 34–34 with the clock running out.

Washington got the ball in overtime, and, after several Theismann to Monk connections, Moseley was put in position to win the game, which he would do time and time again in the 1982 season, and he did on this September Sunday afternoon with a 26-yard field goal and a 37–34 victory to open the season.

Joe Gibbs "Philly had a heck of a football team. They had been to the playoffs the year before and went to the Super Bowl two years earlier. When we went up there to play them, I felt that that was one of the key turning points in all of our games that we ever played with the Redskins. It was a tremendous victory that got us rolling."

The Redskins were indeed rolling, coming away with a 21–13 win over Tampa Bay in a drenching rainstorm that served notice to the league about the strength of the Redskins' special teams, Moseley's foot, and the Diesel (John Riggins). Curtis Jordan blocked a Bucs punt on the messy field before the end of the first half for a score, Moseley kicked 3 field goals, and Riggins carried the ball 34 times for 136 yards.

Cornerback Curtis Jordan "We had thought of blocking one all week, after looking at the films. We worked on it a lot. Now the team is 2-0, and we've got the momentum."

Next on the schedule was finally a home game to show off this momentum against the St. Louis Cardinals. But, unfortunately, Wash-ington was all dressed up, with no place to go. The next day, everyone got the word: the NFL players were going on strike, because a dispute between the league and the union that had been going on since Febru-ary was not even close to being resolved.

Joe Gibbs was obviously distraught about what would happen to his team while they were on strike. "Nothing could have been worse than going 0-5," he told reporters. "But at least that was something I had control over. With the strike, I'm just a concerned bystander."

Gibbs had to put his team in the hands of his players. It was in good hands.

The Redskins may have won the 1982 NFL championship during the seven weeks they didn't play. While many players on other teams went back home or were spread around the country, the Redskins made a concerted effort to stay close together and not let the strike be divisive or a detour to practicing.

Monte Coleman   "What propelled us that year was our ability to stay together during the strike. We would have team meetings and practices, some seven on seven as a team, and we stayed in contact as a team. When we came back to play, it was like we hadn't missed a beat."

Rick Walker   "Joe [Gibbs] told us during the strike that no matter what, just stay together. We worked together in Herndon. Theismann's leadership skills were superb in that. [Theismann had crossed the picket line in his rookie season in 1974.] We had almost all the guys, except for a couple who lived far away. We were running what we ran in practice, and pretty much practicing as a complete team. When we came back, we had never really departed."

Mark Murphy   "What made the 1982 season unique for me was the strike, because I was so involved in the Players Association. We worked to stay together as a team during the strike and it benefited us."

Joe Jacoby   "At first, the strike didn't look like it would be settled, and guys were starting to get ready to go home. I was going to head back to Kentucky, and Russ Grimm was heading back to Pittsburgh. It was getting to the point where in another week or two, the season would have been over. But they settled it, and we had managed to stay together. We had dinners together, played cards together . . . we were young and just out of college, and to us it was still a college atmosphere. We kind of bonded together then."

When the season started up, the Redskins were on the road again. It was November 21, and Washington fans still had not seen their team up close yet during the regular season. Moseley kicked 2 field goals, and the Redskins beat the Giants 27–17. Finally, on November 28, Redskins fans could watch their team that year at RFK Stadium. Rainy weather and a tough Eagles defense kept the Redskins offense bogged down, but the Redskins defense was better, with 4 interceptions. The offense again was Moseley, with 45- and 43-yard field goals, and the special teams, with returner Mike Nelms running back a 58-yard kickoff to put Moseley in position for one of those field goals, which led the Redskins to a 13–9 win over Philadelphia. With a 4–0 record, the Redskins prepared for Dallas week and a home game. They emerged from Dallas week bruised, battered, and no longer undefeated.

The Cowboys opened up a 17–0 lead after three quarters on an 8-yard touchdown pass from Danny White to Ron Springs, a Rafael Septien 31-yard field goal, and a 14-yard scoring run by Timmy Newsome. But the Redskins staged what appeared to be a memorable fourth-quarter comeback. Moseley connected on a 38-yard field goal, and Theismann found Charlie Brown with a 17-yard touchdown pass. With the Cowboys' lead cut to 17–10, the 55,000 fans at RFK Stadium were in a frenzy, and it appeared that Dallas was ready to hand the game over, fumbling the ball twice in the fourth quarter, but Washington failed to recover either of those fumbles. Then, in a crowning insult, White, going back to punt with a fourth and 21, instead took off and ran for a first down. Springs put Washington away with a 46-yard run for a 24–10 Cowboys win.

A loss to Dallas at home will always bring out the grumbling, but what truly raised concern was that, even though they had a 4–1 record, Washington had scored just 23 points in the two games coming back from the strike, and those concerns remained the following week, even though the Redskins beat the Cardinals in St. Louis, because the score was just 12–7. What kept the hope alive, though, was Moseley. He was carrying the offense, with 4 field goals, giving him 18 straight, including the final 3 he kicked in 1981.

The Redskins came home for an important divisional game against the Giants. A win would guarantee them a playoff spot. As the snow fell in Washington, creating terrible field conditions, the Redskins played as if the last thing they wanted was a spot in the playoffs, doing everything they could to help the Giants win. They turned the ball over five times, including 4 Theismann interceptions, giving New York a 14–3 lead in the first half. Of course, Washington's only score came on a 20-yard Moseley field goal. But Gibbs found a way to get his team to recover coming out for the second half. Over the course of his career, Gibbs would become known for making locker room adjustments at halftime to put his players in position to win. Washington began moving the ball on the ground more, and engineered a 10-play, 80-yard scoring drive in the third quarter that ended when Joe Washington, back in active duty, attempted a halfback option pass to Art Monk. When Monk was covered, Washington instead took off down the field 22 yards for the touchdown. Remarkably, Moseley missed the extra point, and the score was now Giants 14, Redskins 9.

Gibbs kept the ball on the ground, running Riggins 8 times on a 10-play drive that led to Moseley's fourth field goal, a 31-yard kick, closing the gap to 14–12. It was Moseley's twentieth straight field goal, tying Garo Yepremian's record. While the Redskins were mounting their comeback and overcoming their own turnovers, the defense was keeping the Giants in check by sacking New York quarterback Scott Brunner five times for the day. Another last-minute drive gave Moseley the chance to break the record and win the game with his fifth field goal; with nine seconds left, he kicked a 42-yarder for the 15–14 win and a spot in the playoffs.

Mark Moseley   "In 1982, when I had all those winning field goals, if I had missed any of those field goals, we would not have made the playoffs that year, because I was scoring all the points. We were scoring them all with field goals.

"The biggest thing about the Giants game was the snow that day. The snow was really coming down hard. It was a nasty day, and one of those typical Redskins-Giants games. The scoring was low, and our offense had been struggling all year. It looked like it was going to do that same thing. I had to kick 3 field goals that day to set the new record, and the third one looked like it was going to be a game winner. There was a lot riding on that kick.

"Because of the weather I really had to concentrate. I remember how quiet it was. It was amazing. You could hear a pin drop for a couple of seconds. I walked out and made sure I had my footing right and had a good place for the ball and where my plant foot would be good and solid. I had seen myself kicking that field goal during the week. I did a lot of this mental preparation in practice, going out on the field and envisioning myself kicking the game-winning field goal. I had a dream that week that I did kick the game-winning field goal. I had already seen it happen once, so it was like a repeat of what I had already seen.

"We liked RFK because it was our field. It was our turf, our mud, our slush. It was the wind blowing when they opened the tunnel down at the far end. We knew that when teams came to RFK, they had better be ready to play football because they were going to get the best from us. We took a lot of pride in that. RFK was a very special place for us. We loved playing there. That was our field, and we would do everything we could to win there. And the fans backed it up. They would make those stands rock, and they were loud. Quarterbacks hated coming to RFK because of the fan noise.

"We were not going to be denied that year. That was such an emotional year. There were so many games that maybe we should have lost, but we won. We would score just enough points to win."

Washington momentum kept growing with a 27–10 win over the Saints in New Orleans. Moseley connected on 2 more field goals, of 36 and 45 yards, to run his streak to 23, and, thanks to an Eagles 24–20 upset of the Cowboys, the Redskins 7-1 record put them in a position to get home-field advantage for the playoffs. They closed the deal emphatically with a 28–0 win over the St. Louis Cardinals at RFK Stadium. It was a defensive masterpiece, as they recorded 5 sacks for the second straight week and finished the season allowing just 128 points over 9 games, the lowest total in the league.

It was not all good news. Moseley's field goal streak ended at 23 when he missed one in the final seconds of the first half. The miss did nothing to diminish Moseley's remarkable season, as he was named the NFL's Most Valuable Player for the 1982 season—a remarkable achievement for a kicker.

There would be more accolades. Gibbs was named NFL Coach of the Year. Five players were named to the Pro Bowl: Theismann, Moseley, Charlie Brown, Mike Nelms, and safety Tony Peters.

But the atmosphere was hardly festive around Redskin Park, because the team suffered a huge loss in the win over the Cardinals. Art Monk went down with a stress fracture in his right foot. It had been discovered two days before the Cardinals game, but doctors determined that he could play and not risk more severe injury. Then, in the first quarter of the game, the stress fracture became a total fracture, and there would be no Art Monk for Joe Theismann to count on in the playoffs. He was leading the team in receptions with 35 for 447 yards, a 12.8-yard-per-catch average. He was, as he would be throughout his career, the team's most reliable receiver, the one they looked to when it was third down.

They would have to look elsewhere for help for this upcoming playoff run, with the Detroit Lions first on the agenda. They found someone to step in, 5-foot-7 Alvin Garrett, one of the so-called Smurfs of the Redskins small backup receiving unit. Garrett was a Gibbs favorite, plucked off waivers when the Giants cut him ten weeks into the 1981 season. But there was more than one Smurf to carry the load.

John Riggins did not play in that final game against St. Louis because he was resting a bruised thigh. But at the age of thirty-three, he felt the sand slipping through the hourglass, and he didn't know how much time he would have left or how many chances he would get to experience a championship season. He wanted to control his destiny as much as he could—and to carry the ball as much as Gibbs would give it to him.

He didn't talk to Gibbs much, so he went to Joe Bugel and asked, "Will you tell Gibbs I want the ball more?"

To which Bugel replied, "Tell him yourself."

So Riggins met with Gibbs. "I'm really getting down the road," he told Gibbs. "I don't have many of these left. I've been out for two weeks, and I'm ready. Give me the ball."

He did, and Riggins took the city of Washington on the greatest three-week ride it has ever seen.

Detroit, with a 4-5 record in this bizarre 1982 strike season, was coming to RFK Stadium for the first round of the playoffs, and they simply couldn't play with a Redskins team that was starting a legendary roll. Cornerback Jeris White intercepted an Eric Hipple pass and ran 77 yards for a touchdown. Alvin Garrett, playing for the injured Art Monk, caught 6 passes for 110 yards and 2 touchdowns. And Riggins delivered, carrying the ball 25 times for 119 yards.

Joe Theismann   "In the Detroit [playoff] game, they actually moved the ball down the field. When Jeris White picked off a pass and ran it back for a touchdown, that set the whole scoring binge in motion. We didn't know how good a football team we were in 1982. Joe had just instituted the offense. Our defense was fabulous through those years. In 1982 and 1983, the Redskins defense was no different from the New England Patriots. In the Detroit game, the interception turned things around early, and then we started doing our thing."

. . .

Next up, the Minnesota Vikings and their star quarterback, Tommy Kramer. The Redskins felt so good about themselves during this stretch that it even motivated Dave Butz, who was normally quiet and reserved, to speak up in the team meeting the night before the game and make a guarantee.

Dave Butz   "The night before the Minnesota game I stood up and told the team, without the coaches in there, that if we beat Minnesota, we would win the Super Bowl. I just knew it."

Tony McGee   "My biggest sack of my career was in the playoff game against Minnesota. They were driving down the field, and Kramer had the ball. It was fourth down and they were in our territory. If they had scored, we would have lost. I was able to sack Kramer. Out of all of my 106 sacks, that was my only sack in the playoffs."

It would help the Redskins to a 21–7 win over Minnesota and another playoff victory before the hometown fans, who after Theismann hit Don Warren in the first quarter for a 3-yard touchdown score and a 7–0 lead, began chanting, "We want Dallas! We want Dallas!" It was a performance more than a game, the prequel to what would be perhaps the greatest single day in Washington sports history. They would get Dallas, and Riggins would deliver the win to Redskins fans on a silver platter, carrying the ball 37 times for 185 yards against the Vikings defense. When the Diesel was taken out with the score 21–7 in the fourth quarter, the crowd was nearly deafening in its approval of what their hero had accomplished that day. He reciprocated in Riggins-like fashion: he stopped on the field and bowed to all four sections of the stadium. "It seemed like the appropriate thing to do," Riggins told reporters after the game.

The performance was the perfect setup for the NFC title game: Redskins versus Cowboys at RFK Stadium. The city could barely contain its anticipation, with the press going back and forth between both teams in the week leading up to the game. The Cowboys had been to the NFC title game the two previous years and lost each time. "When you've gotten the booby prize two years in a row, you're starving for it," said Dallas receiver Preston Pearson.

"They've been a thorn in our sides since I've been here," said Russ

Grimm. "I'd like to do something about it. We don't like them and they don't like us."

The situation was ripe for Dexter Manley to spout off. He was the king trash talker of the team, so much so that he was often dressed down by teammates and coaches for mouthing off too much. And he did his share of talking before the Cowboys game, despite being warned to keep his mouth in check. "I hope they run at me every play," he declared. He showed up for the Dallas game wearing his "I Hate Dallas" hat and declaring, "This is our Super Bowl. This is the game we have all waited a long time for. How can it get any bigger than this?"

Dexter Manley "The Cowboys were such prima donnas. They thought they were the greatest thing since sliced bread. I really resented that. They didn't have respect for the Redskins and our players.

"Before the game Joe Gibbs had called me into his office and told me that this is a team sport and chewed me out about giving them bulletin board clippings to fire them up. But I always thought it was what you do on the field that was important. I wasn't looking at it from Gibbs's perspective. I really disliked the Cowboys. I had grown up loving the Cowboys. I loved people like Walt Garrison, Duane Thomas, Bob Hayes, and all those guys. I always had great respect for Tom Landry. But then Tex Schramm had started this whole 'America's Team' stuff, and I didn't like it."

Redskin fans, though, loved it. They were all for raising the hype for the Dallas game. The week before the NFC title contest, people were hanging signs from office windows and holding rallies downtown during the lunch hour.

Charley Casserly "I go to the Senior Bowl that week to scout. I'm gone the whole week. I get back, and as I am pulling into Redskin Park, the buildings along the way were covered with signs for the Redskins. It was like a high school pep rally. It was unbelievable. I got goose bumps driving to work. Employees from various businesses would come over in the afternoon and sing 'Hail to the Redskins' in our parking lot. Somebody had a sign on Constitution Avenue that said, 'Honk if you hate Dallas.' It paralyzed Constitution Avenue."

. . .

The game would take place on Saturday, January 22, 1983–the best day in the history of Washington sports. And it began with Redskins fans chanting, "We want Dallas! We want Dallas!" more than an hour before the game, working themselves into a frenzy at the sight of the Cowboys the during pregame warm-up. When the game started, the Cowboys won the toss. Getting the ball first, they drove down the field and got on the board first with a 27-yard field goal by Rafael Septien for a 3–0 Dallas lead. But it did little to discourage Redskins fans, particularly when their team got the ball and the first offensive play was a handoff to Riggins, who ran for 7 yards.

Joe Jacoby "The first play of the Dallas game was a straight handoff up the middle, and it looked like a nothing play, maybe a yard or two. The next thing you know the whole pile is moving forward. That's how pumped up we were. It was like a scrum in a rugby game. They couldn't get John down, and we all kept moving. It was that kind of game, with plays like that."

There would be wars between the Hogs and the Dallas defensive line. Joe Washington said the battles between Mark May and Randy White were memorable.

Joe Washington "Those Hogs were a unique group of guys. Mark May and Randy White were always into it. They were talking about each other's mothers, and any heritage. They would spit on each other, push on each other. You needed a raincoat if you were playing near them. It was funny. It was unreal. To watch Mark continuously go up against Randy White was amazing. You grow to admire a guy who goes up against one of the best tackles ever, an All-Pro every year who plays hard from the time he steps on the field, and Mark May being a young kid, that is special. I was impressed by him."

The Hogs marched down the field 86 yards and answered back with a 19-yard touchdown pass from Theismann to Charlie Brown, giving the Redskins the 7–3 lead. In the second quarter, Dallas's Rod Hill mishandled a punt at their 11-yard line. Several plays later, Riggins carried it in for a 1-yard touchdown, and the Redskins led 14–3. The play Redskins fans remember, though, was a defensive play before the end of the first half. Before the game, Dexter Manley said that he was going to get Cowboys quarterback Danny White, and he did, sacking him hard with about twenty-three seconds left and knocking him out of the game.

Going into the locker at halftime, Washington led 14–3 and had forced the Cowboys to go to backup quarterback Gary Hogeboom. It seemed everything was lining up for Washington, but then Mike Nelms fumbled the kickoff, and though the Redskins recovered, it put them deep in their own territory. When the Cowboys got the ball back, it was on the Redskins' 38-yard line. Six plays later, Dallas scored on a 6-yard touchdown pass from Hogeboom to Drew Pearson to close the gap at 14–10 early in the third quarter. Nelms made the most of his chance at redemption by taking the kickoff and running the ball back 76 yards to the Cowboys' 21-yard line. A few plays later, Riggins took it over from the 4-yard line for a 21–10 Redskins lead. Hogeboom proved up to the task, though, keeping his team in the game by leading a 14-play, 84-yard drive that resulted in a 23-yard touchdown connection to Butch Johnson, and Washington led by the slim margin of 21–17 with about three minutes left in the third quarter. It would be the defense that would widen the margin and deliver the victory of a lifetime for a generation of Washington fans. Linebacker Mel Kaufman intercepted a Hogeboom pass that set up a 29-yard Moseley field goal for a 24–17 lead. Then, when the Cowboys tried to run a delayed screen play, Manley put on a strong rush, tipping the ball into the air, and defensive tackle Darryl Grant intercepted it and ran it in from the 10-yard line for a 31–17 lead. The stadium felt as if it was about to collapse as the stands rocked up and down from the fans stomping and chanting, "We want Dallas! We want Dallas!" Washington got the ball back with about five minutes left and put the game away by turning the Diesel loose and running the Riggo drill.

Joe Jacoby   "We're killing them with that last drive, and all it was was a 40 or 50 gut. Really, the last eight or nine plays were 50 gut. We're running to Russ's [Grimm] and my side against Randy White and Harvey Martin. The other two guys, Jeff [Bostic] and Mark [May], were telling the defense where the play was going, and they still couldn't stop it. Ernie Stautner, the Cowboys defensive line coach, was yelling at his linemen, 'Dig in! Dig in!' But they couldn't stop us, even when we were telling them where the play was coming. That line just came together during that playoff run."

. . .

Much to the delight of Redskins fans, the Cowboys, suffered one final insult. As Theismann was tackled on fourth down with the seconds running out on the clock, fans, believing that the game was over, stormed the field and started taking down the goalposts. But there was still time remaining, and the officials had to force the Dallas offense to take one final snap, which Drew Pearson did. The game ended, and the Redskins were going back to the Super Bowl.

For some players, they had already played their Super Bowl in this NFC title game against Dallas.

Tony McGee   "The Super Bowl was big, don't get me wrong. But that Dallas championship game was so tremendous. The moment that you know you are going to the Super Bowl for the first time is a moment that you never forget."

Mike Nelms   "Beating Dallas in that playoff game was satisfying to me. Dallas scored, and that let a little air out of us. But I live for those kind of moments. I thought, 'This is sweet.' I wanted to go, and surprise, they kicked the ball to me. I took off to the side that we were supposed to be blocking on, and the guys made a nice hole, and I shot through it. I set an NFC kickoff return record in that game. A couple of plays later, we scored and never looked back. That was a thrill for me. For a defining moment for me, it was being an integral part in that game against Dallas."

Dave Butz   "We sure provided a lot for our fans over those three weeks. When we beat Dallas to go to the Super Bowl, my wife and I drove through Georgetown to get to the George Washington Parkway to get out to Reston, and people were in the streets, bouncing off the car, and yelling, 'We're going to the Super Bowl!' They had no idea that I was a player who helped them get to the Super Bowl, which my wife and I thought was an awesome thing to watch."

Joe Gibbs   "If I had to pick one game over my career where my team was the most emotional, and the fans were the most emotional, it was that Dallas game."

. . .

Mark Murphy "The Super Bowls are great, but that conference championship game against Dallas, I have never played in a more electric atmosphere. Those were three great games in three weeks."

But there was unfinished business—the Super Bowl—and appropriately, the Redskins would be facing the team that they had faced the last time they went to the Super Bowl: the Miami Dolphins. That 1972 Dolphins team that had beaten George Allen's Redskins have since gone down in history as the only team to go undefeated throughout an entire year in NFL history, going 17-0, with future Hall of Famers like Larry Csonka, Bob Griese, and Paul Warfield. The Dolphins squad these Redskins would face in Super Bowl XVII on January 30 in Pasadena were not so legendary, going 10-2 and led by a very average quarterback named David Woodley and a swarming defense known as the Killer Bees (the Dolphins defense had six starters whose last names started with the letter B). So it would be the Killer Bees against the Smurfs, the Hogs, and the receiving corps known as the Fun Bunch. It was the nickname Super Bowl.

Riggins, who had rushed for 464 yards in those three playoff games at RFK Stadium, brought his own style to the dance when he showed up in a top hat and tails at a party during Super Bowl week thrown by Redskins owner Jack Kent Cooke. This had been his stage during the playoffs, and he was about to step out for the final act.

Other Redskins players found different ways to stay loose

Dan Riley "One of my most fond memories came in the Super Bowl, the first one in Los Angeles. All the coaches got courtesy cars. My family didn't come out until Thursday, and I didn't go out at night, so Neal Olkewicz and Richie Milot—Richie played when I was at Penn State and I was close to him—called and asked if they could borrow my car. I said, 'Sure, just be careful.' I was in my room getting ready to go to bed when I got a call from Richie that my car was in the ocean. I was a little stunned. I said, 'What do you mean?' He said they went down to the beach—him and Neal and Donnie Warren was in another car with a group of them—and they got too close to the beach where the wet sand was, and the waves kept coming in. Water was coming into the car, so they left it there because they were worried about getting back for curfew. I laughed at first but I knew I had to get that car back. So they got a couple of tow trucks and pulled it out of the ocean. I got in it on Thursday when my family came to town to go out to dinner, and we couldn't drive it—the seats were soaked and there was sand all over the place."

More than 106,000 fans filled the Rose Bowl that Sunday, and they saw Miami score first midway through the opening quarter on a 76-yard touchdown from Woodley to Jimmy Cefalo—the second longest in the history of the game. Washington came back early in the second quarter when Dexter Manley sacked Woodley, causing a fumble that Dave Butz recovered down in Miami territory, and Moseley kicked a 21-yard field goal. Miami kept the pressure on with a 20-yard field goal by Uve von Schamann. Washington capped off a scoring drive with a 4-yard touchdown pass to Alvin Garrett. It appeared it would stay that way going into the locker room, but Dolphins kick returner Fulton Walker, who had already returned one kick 42 yards, took this one 98 yards for a touchdown and a 17–10 Dolphins lead.

The Redskins came out in the second half having made the typical Gibbs halftime adjustments with a series of plays that included two flea flickers, a tight end around, a fake end around, and much more movement that threw off the Killer Bees defense. A 61-yard scoring drive ended with a 20-yard Moseley field goal, cutting Miami's lead to 17–13. Then the team traded interceptions—Theismann intercepted by A. J. Duhe on the Redskins' 47-yard line, and Mark Murphy intercepted Woodley at Washington's 5-yard line. After several runs by Riggins brought the ball out to Miami's 18-yard line, the most important play for both teams took place. The play that is often immortalized from that game is the 43-yard fourth-quarter touchdown run by Riggins, but the pass attempt by Theismann in the third quarter is where the game could have turned.

With time running out in the third quarter, Theismann tried to hit Brown on a first-down pass, but right defensive end Kim Bokamper tipped the ball into the air, and it looked as if it would wind up in Bokamper's hands. But Theismann reached out and knocked the ball to the ground. If he hadn't, Bokamper likely would have scored, and Miami would have had a 24–13 lead going into the final quarter.

. . .

Joe Gibbs   "The two big things in that game for us was Riggins breaking off tackle and Theismann knocking down that pass."

Joe Theismann   "Knocking the ball away from Kim Bokamper at that time in the game gave us an opportunity to continue our game plan. I didn't realize how big a moment it was then. I turned to my right to throw a hitch. I didn't like it so I backed up a little bit, turned back to my left, and Kim knocked it up in the air, and all of a sudden my feet were in quicksand. Everything went into slow motion. I looked up and found the ball, and I saw Kim running toward it with his arms open. I knew I could get up to knock it down, so as I started to make a leap toward it, I just tried to get my hand in between his and to time it when the ball hit my hand and to strip it away, and I was able to do that."

Charley Casserly   "Riggins won the MVP, and the Hogs certainly dominated the game as the game wore on, but Theismann's play was as big a play as there was in that game. He never got the recognition for that play. It was an instinctive, athletic play that not a lot of guys could have made."

The tip pass set the stage for the Riggins run in the fourth quarter, when Washington had the ball on the Miami 43-yard line, with fourth down and 1 yard to go. Gibbs wanted to go for the first down, and Miami called time out.

Joe Gibbs   "It would have been a risky field goal. We felt we would take our best play and go at them. We felt we didn't want to lose a Super Bowl game by not being tough enough."

Their best play was a misdirection and handoff to Riggins, who shook off right cornerback Don McNeal and didn't stop running until he reached the end zone with ten minutes left in the game. Washington led 20–17 and put it away in the final minutes with a 59-yard scoring drive that culminated with a 6-yard touchdown pass from Theismann to Brown for a 27–17 victory and the first Super Bowl championship for the Redskins. Riggins, who had carried the ball 38 times for 166 yards, was named the NFL's Most Valuable Player, but it was the Redskins defense that was just as valuable, holding the Dolphins to just 176 yards in total offense. Riggins, though, was indeed the man of the hour, and in the locker room after the game, surrounded by all the celebration and after President Ronald Reagan had made his congratulatory phone call, the running back declared, "Ron may be the president, but at least for tonight I'm the king."

The Redskins were treated like royalty when they returned to Washington, where more than 500,000 fans filled the streets for a parade to honor their champions. As far as Joe Gibbs was concerned, the fans deserved to be honored as well.

Joe Gibbs   "They say fans are the same all over, but our fans were always going to be there for us. They were there, they were vocal, and they helped us emotionally. They had been through tough times, and they were battle-tested. They cheered special teams. They understood what defense was. It's a knowledgeable fan in Washington and not somebody who just buys a ticket and shows up for the game and doesn't understand the past heritage of the Redskins. That is what is special about Redskins fans."

8

Staying on Top

It was great to be a Washington Redskins fan going into the 1983 season. The Redskins were the reigning Super Bowl champions, and they showed an explosive enough offense during the preseason to make fans believe that the team would have a lot more ways of winning this upcoming season other than relying on Mark Moseley field goals.

After two full seasons under Joe Gibbs's offense, the team had come together to seemingly make the most of the game plans they were given, with Joe Theismann leading the way. The offensive line had two full seasons together, and the identity of the Hogs had turned them into a tight-knit unit.

There was a rookie in camp whose speed was making heads turn, a small cornerback named Darrell Green. And Redskins tradition would be honored when Bobby Mitchell and Sonny Jurgensen were inducted into the Pro Football Hall of Fame on June 30.

It wasn't all positive, however. Two Redskins—safety Tony Peters and running back Clarence Harmon—were arrested in separate incidents for cocaine possession, a preview of problems that the Redskins and all of sports and society would face throughout the decade. But those were just blips on the Redskins juggernaut that had now consumed the Washington region, with fans still basking in the glow of the team's Super Bowl victory.

What could heighten the hype? How about opening up on *Monday Night Football* at RFK Stadium against the Dallas Cowboys? What could be better than that? How about leading the Cowboys 23–3 at halftime on national television?

It seemed like a carryover from the celebration of the NFC title game back in January. This high-octane Redskins offense ran roughshod over the Dallas defense, amassing 261 yards while the Washington defense held the Cowboys to just 85 yards in the first half.

Moseley put Washington on the board first with a 23-yard field goal. Then a Redskins drive ended with a 1-yard run by John Riggins for a 10–0 Washington lead. Then Darrell Green stepped up to begin the first chapter of the legend that the Redskins cornerback would become.

Green, who was a star track sprinter at Texas A&M, chased down Dallas running back Tony Dorsett from behind after Dorsett broke free at the Washington 17-yard line and was heading for the end zone early in the second quarter. That left the Cowboys with a 28-yard Rafael Septien field goal, their only score of the half.

There were 2 more field goals by Moseley—a 30-yarder and a 39-yarder—and a 41-yard touchdown pass from Theismann to Charlie Brown, and as the Cowboys went into the locker room at RFK, the fans were bouncing in the seats, chanting, "We want Dallas! We want Dallas!"

In the second half, they got Dallas—a lot more Dallas than they would have liked.

Danny White hit Tony Hill on a 75-yard touchdown pass to open the third quarter and came back with about six minutes left in the quarter to score on another long bomb to Hill, this one a 51-yard touchdown pass, and now the score was just 23–17 Redskins.

Nothing was going right for Washington. Moseley missed a 31-yard field goal attempt with just under 10 minutes left in the game, and the Cowboys drove 80 yards down the field in 12 plays, and now Washington found itself down by 1 point after White ran the ball over for the go-ahead score, putting Dallas on top 24–23.

The Redskins still had time to mount their own go-ahead drive with two minutes left, but cornerback Ron Fellows intercepted a Theismann pass and returned the ball to the Washington 4-yard line. White threw his third touchdown pass of the day, a 1-yarder to tight end Doug Cosbie, and the Cowboys increased their lead 31–23.

Washington did manage to score one more time when a drive ended with a 1-yard touchdown pass to tight end Don Warren, but with ten seconds left, it just made it a 31–30 defeat instead of a 31–23 loss.

It was a disappointing way to open the season. Little did Redskins fans know that would be the last time they saw their team lose at RFK Stadium until a year later.

The loss would be overshadowed by the controversy that took place in the *Monday Night Football* announcer's booth, where Howard Cosell created a national furor and incensed Washington's black leaders when he referred to Redskins receiver Alvin Garrett as "that little monkey" when describing Garrett's pass catching and running ability.

Washington bounced back the following week with a 23–13 win over Philadelphia, followed by a 27–17 victory over Seattle. Then they engaged in one of the wildest games ever seen at RFK Stadium against the Los Angeles Raiders. The Raiders, like the Redskins, had posted an 8–1 regular season record the year before but were upset by the Jets in the second round of the AFC playoffs, and they felt they were every bit as good as the Redskins. They may have been right.

It didn't start off as a wild affair. Raiders quarterback Jim Plunkett's first two passes fell incomplete, and his third one was intercepted by Curtis Jordan, who ran it back to the Los Angeles 11-yard line. Three straight carries by Riggins, and the Redskins were on the board with a 7–0 lead. Another interception by Plunkett in the second quarter resulted in a 28-yard field goal by Moseley for a 10–0 Washington lead. An exchange of punts put the Raiders on their own 1-yard line, but Plunkett hit Cliff Branch at their 44-yard line, and Branch sprinted into the end zone for a 99-yard touchdown pass, cutting Washington's lead to 10–7. Washington marched back with a scoring drive that ended with a 5-yard touchdown pass from Theismann, who was under constant pressure by the Raiders pass rush, including 3 sacks by Howie Long, to Joe Washington. The first half ended with the Redskins leading 17–7. They added a 29-yard field goal quickly in the third quarter for a 20–7 Washington lead. And then all hell broke loose.

Plunkett, who had thrown 3 first-half interceptions, started finding his own receivers. He hit Calvin Muhammad on a 25-yard touchdown pass, followed by a 22-yard scoring connection. Another Los Angeles drive ended with a 2-yard touchdown pass from Plunkett to Todd Christensen. Then Greg Pruitt returned a 97-yard punt early in the fourth quarter for another score. Now the Raiders seemingly had the game in hand, leading 35–20 halfway through the final quarter. But this was a Redskins offense that had fully come to grasp their coach's offensive schemes and were operating now as a high-powered Joe Gibbs machine. In the final seven minutes, the Redskins scored 17 points on an 11-yard pass from Theismann to Brown, a 34-yard field goal by Moseley, and a 5-yard pass to Washington with less than a minute left in the game. Those Redskins fans who had not left early in the fourth quarter were treated to one of the greatest comebacks ever seen at RFK Stadium—a 37–35 Washington victory, with 890 yards of total offense in a hard-fought battle that saw three unsportsmanlike conduct penalties.

It was an exhilarating Redskins win. Little did anyone know it would come back to haunt them.

The offense was now fired up, and it went to St. Louis to beat the Cardinals 38–14. The following week, they upped their offensive output to 47 points, but it wouldn't be enough to beat the Packers. Green Bay cut the Redskins defense to shreds by scoring 48 points, with a total of 1,025 yards between both teams, in another shootout, this one a 48–47 defeat, reminiscent of the days when Jurgensen and company would ring up large numbers of points and yards, only to lose because of a porous defense. The Washington offense would be among the best ever seen in the NFL, and it would have to be, because the defense was not going to win many games that season—particularly the pass defense. They had lost Tony Peters in the defensive backfield to a suspension for his arrest on drug charges. They had a talented but still unproven rookie back there in Green, and the veteran presence of cornerback Joe Lavander, who had retired, was missed.

Despite the defensive woes, the unit managed to get under control as the season went on, not giving up more than 24 points in any game the rest of the season, and that came in a 27–24 victory over the San Diego Chargers. That was enough defense to sustain an offense that would score 541 points over 16 games, while holding the other teams to 332 points. They were 12-2 when they traveled to Dallas for a rematch against the Cowboys—the infamous game when Riggins and company left Redskin Park to travel to Dallas wearing army fatigues.

Center Jeff Bostic   "It was great. Joe Gibbs was a straight-laced guy, and when he saw [special teams coach] Wayne Sevier, Joe said,

'Wayne, they've got army fatigues on.' Wayne answered, 'I guess they're pretty serious about winning this game.'"

They were. Sarge Riggins helped lead the first scoring drive, ending with a 3-yard run, for a 7–0 Washington lead, and added a second touchdown before the quarter ended with a 40-yard pass from Theismann to Clint Didier. The Cowboys got on the board with a 29-yard touchdown pass from Danny White to Doug Cosbie. And they closed it to 14–10 at halftime with a 35-yard Rafael Septien field goal. In the third quarter, there was another play that would find its way into Cowboys-Redskins lore. Dallas had the ball at near midfield on a fourth down and 1, and came out as if they were going to go for the first down. However, most everyone in Texas Stadium believed it was simply an attempt to try to get the Redskins defense to jump off sides to pick up an easy first down before a time out would be called and the Cowboys would punt. But White came up to the line and called an audible, handing the ball off to Ron Springs, who was nailed for a 2-yard loss. Cowboys coach Tom Landry could be heard on the Dallas sideline screaming, "No, Danny, no!"

For the rest of the game, it was all "yes" for the Redskins. Theismann found Art Monk for a 43-yard touchdown pass for a 21–10 Washington lead. Safety Greg Williams intercepted a White pass, and soon after a pass interference call on Cowboys cornerback Rod Hill gave the Redskins first and goal on the Dallas 4-yard line. Riggins took it in for a 28–10 Washington lead, and Moseley made the final score 31–10 with a 38-yard field goal.

Washington finished the season with a 31–22 win over the Giants at RFK Stadium, sealing home-field advantage again for the second straight year on the road to the Super Bowl. On New Year's Day 1984, Washington hosted the Los Angeles Rams and played their best game of the season, hitting on all cylinders by destroying the Rams 51–7, the largest margin of victory in any game in the history of the franchise, as the Redskins tied and set thirteen playoff records in that game and stopped star running back Eric Dickerson, who had led the league with 1,808 yards. He had just 16 yards against the Washington defense.

Washington played host to the NFC title game. The game was a matchup of two offensive geniuses—Joe Gibbs and Bill Walsh—and two of the top teams of the 1980s: the Redskins and the San Francisco

49ers. It didn't start out as a display of offensive genius, however. The first quarter was scoreless, and the only team that registered in the second quarter was the Redskins, when Riggins crossed the goal line for a 1-yard touchdown run and a 7–0 halftime lead. What was disconcerting for Washington was that Moseley missed 3 field goal attempts. In the third quarter, Darrell Green knocked the ball loose from wide receiver Freddy Solomon and recovered the fumble, which led to another drive ending in a Riggins plunge over the goal line. The game appeared to be a Redskins rout when Theismann connected with Charlie Brown on a 70-yard touchdown pass for a 21–0 Washington lead. But this was Joe Montana—granted, an early version of Montana—and the 49ers quarterback led three fourth-quarter scoring drives, hitting 3 touchdown passes to tie the score at 21–21 with about seven minutes left in the game. The Redskins, though, bounced back after two pass interference calls on Eric Wright and Ronnie Lott, and then, with forty-four seconds left, Moseley made a 25-yard field goal. Washington won 24–21 and went to the Super Bowl for the second straight season.

Quarterback Joe Theismann "Ronnie Lott continued to say that his pass interference call out of bounds was a bad call, and I said, 'You held everybody all day. Maybe it wasn't, but they had to make up for the other fifteen times that you were.'"

Super Bowl XVIII would take place in Tampa, Florida, and it would be a rematch of the Redskins and the Raiders. The way the Redskins had finished the season, the anticipation was that this would be a coronation rather than a contest, having lost just two games during the season by a total of 2 points, and that Washington would come away with its second straight Super Bowl championship. No one told the Raiders, though, who felt that their loss to the Redskins earlier in the season meant little to the outcome of this game, because this time Los Angeles would have a healthy Marcus Allen.

So much would go wrong on this day, though, that it might not have mattered who was in the Raiders' backfield. Derrick Jensen blocked a Jeff Hayes punt in the first quarter and then fell on it in the end zone, giving Los Angeles a 7–0 lead. Washington mounted a scoring drive, but Moseley missed a 44-yard field goal. When Plunkett got the ball, he hit Cliff Branch on a 50-yard pass completion and then two plays later connected with Branch on a 12-yard touchdown for a 14–0 Raiders lead.

Washington finally got on the board with a 24-yard field goal. It appeared that the score would remain 14–3 Raiders going into the locker room when Washington got the ball back on its 12-yard line with twelve seconds left. But instead of just downing the ball, Gibbs felt he could catch the Raiders off guard with a rocket screen pass to Joe Washington–the same play that resulted in a 67-yard pass in their regular season contest. This time, though, the Raiders read it perfectly and put in linebacker Jack Squirek to cover that play. He cut in front of Washington, grabbed the pass, and walked into the end zone.

Raiders 21, Redskins 3, and this game was over. There would be no Joe Gibbs halftime adjustment to change this outcome. Marcus Allen carried the ball 20 times for 191 yards, including touchdown runs of 5 and 74 yards in the third quarter, the latter erasing the Super Bowl record of 58 yards set by Baltimore's Tom Matte in Super Bowl III. When the time expired, Washington had lost 38–9. The 38 points scored by the Raiders were the highest total by a Super Bowl team. The previous high was 35 points by Green Bay in Super Bowl I.

The loss by such a wide margin left the Redskins stunned, because this was a team convinced they were the best in the NFL.

Joe Theismann   "I think we were the best team in the history of professional football. We were an unstoppable force–offense, defense, and special teams. We had everything you could possibly want. We had an unbelievable run through the playoffs, but that whole week in Tampa never felt comfortable for me. I had problems with my shoes. I had forgotten my old ones in Washington. I had packed a bunch of new ones.

"In that game, Lester Hayes and Mike Haynes played really great. The wind affected me a little bit throwing the ball. We couldn't block Mike Davis. We get a punt blocked and all of a sudden we are down 7–0 before the first possession. Boom. We had been that way before, so it was no big deal. We had beaten the Raiders earlier in the year, but they had turned the ball over something like six or seven times. I didn't personally give the Raiders enough credit for being as good a football team as they were. I spent too much time doing radio shows and not preparing for that game. I don't feel like I prepared properly for that game.

"We got to the fateful halftime decision. I threw the interception. The sequence there is somewhat humorous in itself. I walk over to the sidelines. I think we are on the 9-yard line with 11 seconds to go, something like that. I said to Joe, 'What do you want to run?' Joe said, 'I want to run Rocket Screen.' I said, 'Coach, I just don't like putting the ball in the air at this juncture of the game. There's not enough time, and I just don't like putting it in the air.' He said, 'It worked against them the last time, it'll work now.' I said, 'You don't think they know it worked? Joe Washington went for 90 yards with it.' He said, 'I want you to run it.' I started walking away and got about 5 yards out on the field, turned around, and started to open my mouth. He looked at me, pointed his finger at me, and said, 'Run it!'

"I jogged out on the field, and I thought to myself, 'I just don't have a good feeling about this.' I go out, and sure enough they drop into zone, everybody except Jack Squirek. He takes Joe Washington man to man, and as you know, they score a touchdown. For about the next four years I'm taking all the blame, so finally I caught up with Joe at a charity function and said, 'Coach, I've got a bone to pick with you.' He said, 'What's that?' I said, 'All these years, I've been taking the heat for that lousy call at halftime of the Super Bowl'. He said, 'You know what? It was a lousy call. But it was also a bad pass.' I said, 'You are absolutely right.' We kid each other often about that.

"As the game went on, we got down toward the goal line, and they played a 3–4 defense. They would bring Mike Davis off the corner after the linebacker dropped, so our guards had a double response, inside backer or outside backer. Well, if the outside backer didn't come, they turned back inside to help. Then Mike Davis came. I got ear holed at least twice. Mike Davis knocked the crap out of me. I fumbled once, I got ear holed. I walked to the sidelines, looking out of the earhole of my helmet, and my shoulder pads were about torn off me. I looked at Coach Gibbs and said, 'Who's blocking him?' Coach looked down at his board and said, 'He's supposed to be blocked.' I said, 'Look at me. Does it look like he's blocked?' That was sort of the way the day went."

Running back Joe Washington   "We had a very good football team in 1983. We beat the Raiders earlier in the year 37–35, and they didn't have Marcus Allen in that game, but I don't think that would have mattered much, because the Raiders could score so many different ways, like Greg Pruitt, who could do a lot of things. I was healthy during the game, so they could gear up and concentrate on one particular thing. But I had hurt my knee in the Dallas game that year, and I was really not effective in the Super Bowl. I played, but my knee was taped and braced.

"The Raiders did such a good job on our wide receivers in that game. We had great wide receivers, and we were shocked they had shut us down like that. I knew things were going to be bad for us when the Raiders had their first punt. The center snaps the ball high over Ray Guy's head. Guy jumps up and stabs it with one hand, does not break stride, and gets off a booming punt. I knew it would be a long day then. No matter how good you are, on any given Sunday, you can get beat like that."

Linebacker Rich Milot   "I think maybe with the exception of the 1991 team that won the Super Bowl, the team that went to the Super Bowl the following year after we won the first time was the best Redskins team. That was the best all-around team that we had. That Super Bowl was surreal. Everything went wrong for us, and everything that could go right for the Raiders did. We were shocked in the locker room after the game. It spun out of control. The whole week there were stories going around that the Raiders had spies watching us, and there were a couple of things that happened in that game that made you think. Their fullback, I think, [Frank] Hawkins, had caught two balls all year maybe. We didn't cover him tight, and I think he caught a lot of balls that game. With Al Davis, you never know."

Defensive end Tony McGee   "I think what happened in the Super Bowl that year was that we had played Los Angeles earlier in the season and beat them, and I think we just felt that we could do that again, even though that game went to overtime. I don't care what happened in the Super Bowl. We were the best team in the NFL. It is unfortunate that we didn't perform well in that Super Bowl. During that year, we had met every challenge. We had won all these games, crushed people, with the number-one offense in the league, a great defense, great special teams, a great coaching staff, and maybe sometimes you forget that the other team across the line of scrimmage might have the same things as well, or else they would not be there, even if their record may not be as good as yours.

"Things just went wrong. A lot of people say the biggest play was when Squirek intercepted that pass and went in for the touchdown. For me, the biggest play of the half was when the Raiders were punting and the ball was snapped to Ray Guy. The ball was clearly over his head, and he went up with one hand, jumped very high, and got off a great punt. Had that ball sailed over his head and we took it in for the score, we would have been right back in the game. But that kept their momentum going. Within that game, everyone talks about the run by Marcus Allen . . . that was a great run, but that was just one situation. Everything just snowballed, and it put us in such a precarious situation that I think once we finally woke up, it was too late."

Defensive end Charles Mann   "When we lost the Super Bowl, I didn't leave my hotel room after the game until we had to leave to get on the plane. I was embarrassed, very embarrassed. We won so easily that year. We beat so many people so decisively, it blew me away that we could be humiliated the way we were in the Super Bowl. I think it was the best Redskins team ever, but it was very discouraging to lose that game. I was ashamed at how we let our fans down. I didn't leave the room. I ordered room service after the game and it took three hours to come. I hadn't eaten since 3 P.M. that day, my pregame meal. This was about 1 A.M., and room service took nearly all night. My wife kept saying, 'Let's just go out and get something to eat,' and I said, 'I can't go out. Someone might recognize me. We'll just get embarrassed.'

"I think it was arrogance. We had just beaten Los Angeles earlier that year, with a 15-point turnaround in a matter of four and a half minutes or so. We felt at that point we could beat anybody. When we faced them again, we played like all we had to do was show up. We were killing people that year. It was easy. We walked into a buzz saw, and before we knew it, we were down, and finally when folks woke up maybe in the second half, it was too late. Los Angeles knew how to finish somebody, show them no mercy, which they didn't."

Defensive tackle Dave Butz   "The Raiders were having fights during practice leading up to the Super Bowl, and when I heard that, I knew we were in trouble. A team that gets to the Super Bowl and has fights in practice before the game has to be reckoned with. One of the things we did not have during that Super Bowl week was a bed check, and we did not move out of the official hotel and go to a separate hotel, like we usually did. Gibbs thought he was dealing with grownups, but he wasn't. There were a hell of a lot of doors opening between 1 A.M. and 4 A.M.

"Darryl Grant went down with a concussion on the second play of the game against the Raiders. Dean Hamel came in to take his place. He did not know the defenses because he did not expect to play, because Darryl had never been hurt before, and he always took a step to his right before he went up field, which always made him late. When the Raiders found out that he wasn't up to the caliber that he should have been playing in the Super Bowl, they literally beat the hell out of me. I have never been so physically beat up in my life than I was in that game. There were more people hitting me than I could ever remember. To illustrate how tired and beat up I was, my friends got to the game late, and so they had to park real far away. On the way to the car, I had to take a knee on stone [got down on one knee to rest] just to get to the car. That was the most spent I have ever been for a game."

Coach Joe Gibbs   "That was probably the best team we ever had. That team was probably the most efficient and strongest we had, if I ever had to pick one. Yet we went and played that game in Florida and got beat by the Raiders. It was one of those things. We had a game on a particular day, and we didn't play real well. But if you look at the stats of that team, it was awesome."

In three years, Joe Gibbs had changed the entire landscape of this Redskins franchise. In three years, they had posted a 30-11 regular season record, with two trips to the Super Bowl and one Super Bowl title. And they would continue that impressive record with an 11-5 mark in 1984, with Art Monk leading the way with his record-setting 106 catches that year. But their playoff run stopped in their first game against a devastating Chicago Bears defense, losing 23–19, with the Redskins rushing game held to under 100 yards and Theismann sacked 7 times.

Still, the momentum was well under way, bringing back the excitement of the Over the Hill Gang years and George Allen, when winning was routine and the playoffs came every season. Under Allen, however, the Redskins' legacy was defense. Offense was an afterthought. Now, though, Gibbs had turned the franchise into an offensive juggernaut, without abandoning the other side of the line. The defense, under Richie Petitbon, may not have been as stifling as Allen's Over the Hill Gang, but it was still tough and effective and often overlooked because of the high-powered offense.

One legacy, though, that carried through from the Allen years to the Gibbs era was the special teams. Allen was the first coach to have a special teams coach, with future Buffalo Bills head coach Marv Levy in that role, and Wayne Sevier, under Gibbs, took it to a new level. Sevier was a legendary special teams coach and motivator, and one particular game during the 1984 season illustrates why special teams players loved playing for Sevier, who passed away in October 1999.

Tight end Rick Walker   "Wayne would take everybody back in the shower. Joe [Gibbs] would do his *x*'s and *o*'s, and Petitbon was a great strategist. But Wayne Sevier talked to you like a convict. He was the best. He could translate anger and passion and a great desire to go out there and annihilate the opposition, and take no prisoners. People got so jacked up, and with Pete Cronin and Otis Wonsley and Dexter Manley . . . there were very few people who weren't in that shower, that is why it was always so crammed up in there. We had starters who would play on special teams. We had Art Monk and Jeris White on the corners on punt returns, taking on the charge guys. They destroyed people. Art was a lunatic. The job they did on other guys was amazing. Wayne Sevier would challenge everyone in practice every day. He would walk up to Joe Jacoby and say, 'Hey, Dexter says he is going to kill you.' He would come and tell me, 'Hey, Monte Coleman says he is going to bust you up today.'

"Wayne would kick to everybody. Joe would say, 'Let's be smart about this thing. Willie Gault [Chicago Bears] is a world-class sprinter, and we're going to kick this thing away,' and that's what Joe had to do. That was his job. Joe would leave, and Wayne would say, 'We're going to kick it right to him,' and he would be cursing that we're going to kick the shit out of this guy and this guy, and we would be screaming crazy. We get on the field, kick to Willie Gault, and I think he went 100-some yards. I've never been so embarrassed in my life. Wayne would say, 'Do you want to kick away from this guy?' and we would say, 'Hell, no, let's go kill Willie.' I was humiliated. We were coming off the field and looked over at Wayne, and Joe gave him a look that only old friends could have in the heat of the battle. Thank goodness Joe controlled himself, but I will never forget that look. We felt so bad because nobody wanted to let Wayne down.

"Another time we were playing the Cardinals in the final game of the 1984 season. They had Stump Mitchell. We needed this game to win the division. We won the toss, and we kicked, just to send the dogs after people, and that was another exciting thing, because our kickoff coverage was about humiliating people. Wayne, same thing. Joe says be careful, stay in your lanes. Joe leaves, and Wayne takes us back in the shower, and the dogs go back in the dungeon, and I am telling you Wayne started talking stuff about Stump and what we were going to do to him. We were going to kick it right to him. We did, and Otis Wonsley knocked him out. He laid on the field, the first play of the game, and I saw those bleachers rocking, and those maniacs we had at RFK. Everytime I see *Braveheart*, the hair stands up on the back of my neck; we had moments like that at RFK. If they had let the people run on the field at that moment, they would have eaten the Cardinals alive. I knew there was no way anybody could beat us that day.

"We had professional special teams players who took great pride in it. The system allowed that we could keep seven or eight guys, promised to Wayne, just for special teams. One year we cut Carl Powell, a second-round wide receiver, in camp. It was a defining moment that money didn't matter. It was a message that was sent.

"The last I saw Wayne alive, we were at Camden Yards at an Orioles game. Wherever he was, when I would see him, I would say, 'Hey, Stud.' He stopped and turned around. He knew you were talking to him. He was that kind of guy. He smiled and we hugged. That was Wayne Sevier. You never went into a game better prepared emotionally, from a psychotic standpoint, than with Wayne Sevier."

The 1985 season would be one of transition. John Riggins was in the final year of his Hall of Fame career, and Bobby Beathard traded their number-one pick for New Orleans running back George Rogers, who was seen as the heir to Riggins in the Gibbs big back system. Gary Clark came over from the United States Football League (USFL). Charlie Brown was traded to the Atlanta Falcons for guard R. C. Thielemann, and safety Mark Murphy was waived.

Safety Mark Murphy "In the second game of the 1984 season, I sprained ligaments in my knee. They put me on injured reserve, but

I think the Redskins used it as a way to get rid of me. I can't prove it, but at the time I was one of the leaders of the players union. I had played eight years, and I wanted to keep playing, but I had been accepted to law school and had a job offer from the NFL Players Association, and looking back on it, it was probably the best thing that happened to me. My career was over quickly, and I got started working toward my law degree. The last time I had really played was in 1983, and I was a starter in the Pro Bowl and led the NFL in interceptions. I played two games the next year and never really played again.

"About a week after my injury, Cooke was at one of our practices, and he walks over to me and asks me, 'How's the knee?' I said it would be a few weeks, and he answered, 'Well, it doesn't really matter, Mark. You'll never play again.' And I never played again."

They also picked up a lineman in the eleventh round of the draft who would become one of the future mainstays of the offensive line and a Hog, although it would take time for Raleigh McKenzie to fit in.

Guard Raleigh McKenzie   "I was coming into an established group of guys, the Hogs, and that whole thing was kind of hard—who is this little lineman trying to break into our group? But I think once practice started, Bugs saw something in me where I could be a gamer for him. It didn't take the other guys a lot of time to take me in. They gave me the rookie hard time, especially when they felt I was going to make the team. It seems like those are the guys they give a whole lot more grief to.

I had to go through two levels of acceptance: with the team and then with the inner group, the Hogs. But once I was one of the Hogs, it had a domino effect with the respect level I received.

Joe Bugel was very intense. He was a tremendous teacher who demanded a high level of play and practice from his guys. I had played on teams where they stressed teamwork, but this was one organization where I really felt those were important—teamwork, family, loyalty to each other, picking each other up, and not letting your teammate down, on or off the field. Families hung out together. It was pretty amazing to see and be part of."

Change wouldn't come easy, and the biggest transition would be one Redskins fans would never forget. The Redskins were battered by the Cowboys in the season opener, losing 44–14, with Theismann throwing 5 interceptions. They barely beat Houston 16–13, but then lost two straight, 19–6 to the Eagles and a 45–10 thrashing by the Bears at Soldier Field. They won five of their next seven games and suffered division losses to the Giants and the Cowboys. Washington had a chance to redeem one of those losses when the Giants came to RFK Stadium for a *Monday Night Football* contest on November 18.

Theismann, who had been struggling through his worst season with the Redskins, hit tight end Don Warren on a 10-yard touchdown pass for a 7–0 Washington lead. The Giants tied the game 7–7 when Joe Morris peeled off a 56-yard run. At the start of the second quarter, Washington had the ball, first and 10 on their own 46-yard line, Joe Gibbs ordered a 50-gut throwback, which called for Riggins to take a handoff from Theismann, then turn back and pitch the ball back to Theismann for a loss. But the play broke down when Giants linebacker Harry Carson forced Theismann to scramble. Lawrence Taylor—the nemesis of the Redskins in the 1980s—had Theismann in his sights and came down on the Redskins quarterback with the tackle—a play that would be seared in the minds of anyone who was on the field or who watched it on television. Theismann's leg was bent at a horrible angle, and the snapping sound was heard across the field. Taylor jumped up and started waving in a panic mode for the trainers to get out on the field, but this was beyond the scope of any trainer. Joe Theismann—who had started 71 consecutive games and still holds the Redskins career mark for passing yards in a career, with 25,206— was done not just for the season but for his career with one of the worst broken legs ever seen in the NFL.

Joe Theismann "I have vivid memories of the entire night. We weren't really playing that well as a team. I wasn't really playing that well, either, coming off the previous years that I had. I wasn't playing at the standard that I considered that I should be playing at. I saw this game as a tremendous opportunity to get back on track and play the way I thought I could play football. Going into the game, I was very excited. It was *Monday Night Football.* It was our archrivals, the Giants, who had become as much as a rival as the Cowboys at the time. I was all excited about the football game. I felt it would be a banner night. I think I was seven for ten in the first quarter.

"Then we turned to start the second quarter, and the flea flicker, and the moment that my leg was broken, you could say that changed my life completely. I had become a very self-centered egotistical person who really didn't gave a darn about anybody but me. The only thing that mattered to me was being a football star—not playing football, not being a part of a team, but being a football star. That was the only thing that mattered to me. I was at the point in my career and my life that you could say even though I had all these material things, as a person I was probably as low as you could get, looking back on that time.

"I remember all the movements in the pocket. I remember somebody grabbing my shoulder. I remember the pain. It's funny, people come up to me and ask, 'Did it really hurt?' Yeah, it hurt a lot. I can still close my eyes today and picture [trainer] Bubba Tyer on my left side and Joe Gibbs on my right. I can feel the moisture on my back. I can see the Longines clock. I think it was 10:10. I remember when they put me on the stretcher. The doctor came out and I asked how bad it was, and he said, pretty bad, and I said, 'Can you put it back together?' He said it already is. It snapped like a toothpick, and when they moved it, I guess it sort of went back in. I had no feeling from my knee down. It was completely numb.

"The series of events that happened after that are a little humorous. They started to wheel me out of the stadium. Harry Carson was going to retire. I turned and looked at Harry and said, 'Harry, I understand you're thinking of retiring?' He said, 'Yeah, I am.' I said, 'Well, don't you go retiring because I'm coming back.' He said, 'That may be the case, but it ain't going to be tonight.' As they wheeled me out of that stadium, I got an ovation that I had never heard before in my life. All those people poured their hearts out to this selfish, self-centered guy. I was so appreciative of the outpouring of care and concern, not only after my injury . . . the subsequent weeks and months after that, the letters and cards, everyone was so nice. And then it became a question of rebuilding my life.

"I had signed a brand new contract the year before. That was going to be it. That was going to set me up for my life. All of a sudden, that was gone. My career was gone. I had broadcast the Super Bowl the year before for ABC, and I really liked television, and I was hoping that was where I could go, and as it turned out, I had.

"I wanted to come back to play. I called five or six different football teams and told them I would sign an injury waiver. I said, 'Look, I will be happy to sign a waiver. If I get hurt, you don't pay me anything. All I want is a chance to go back and play.' I had broken my leg in 1972 in Canada, and having never seen the video, I didn't know the severity of the injury. To me, it was a broken leg, two bones instead of one, big deal. But at the age of thirty-five, it is so hard to rehab. Joe Gibbs was ready to move on. He encouraged me to leave the game. I would always say to him, 'You don't understand. It isn't about money.' All of a sudden, I had a love for the game again. I had always had a love for the game but now I had an appreciation for it, I guess you could say. Into my 50s, I still throw for different teams now. For the Baltimore Ravens in the week of the Super Bowl in 2000, I threw their defensive drills during Wednesday's practice. I have thrown for New England on occasion, and the Redskins when Norv [Turner] was there. God blessed me with an arm that never really ran out of gas."

The other part of the story is that Theismann was replaced with an untested project of a quarterback, a former baseball-pitching prospect named Jay Schroeder, who was drafted in the third round out of UCLA in 1984. He was up to the task, hitting on 13 of 20 passes for 221 yards, 1 touchdown, and no interceptions, and leading the Redskins to a 23–21 win. He would show much promise the rest of the year, as the team won four of its final five games. But their 10-6 record was not good enough to make the playoffs. Like Theismann, they were done, but just for the year. Theismann was done for good. He was an enigmatic personality—outspoken, talented, annoying, and, by his own admission, self-absorbed. He wasn't very close to many of his teammates off the field. But on the field, he was respected for his toughness and leadership ability.

Dave Butz "Ron McDole said you could ask Joe Theismann a question, go downtown, get a haircut, do a little shopping, come back, and he will still be on the same question. He never saw a mike he didn't like. Joe is a self-promoter. Joe is out for Joe, which is okay, but footballwise, he was a great competitor and had a lot of moxie."

Joe Washington "I thought Theismann was one of the toughest quarterbacks I ever saw, certainly one of the best passers in bad weather. Out of all the quarterbacks I worked with, he and I were on the same page. Most of the time he knew what I was going to do. He could see the same things in the open field that I would see. I had a lot of respect for Joe. He did talk a little bit every now and then, but he was always a good guy to me, and you can only go by how a guy treats you. Anybody who was willing to stay in the pocket like he was, with the big defensive linemen bearing down on you and a 174-pound running back to protect you, hats off to him. He never wavered as far as confidence in me protecting him. I was probably one of the better pass blockers around, but still, when you are talking about a 174-pound back, and you are going to stand in the pocket and throw deep routes, you have a lot of guts to do that."

Receiver Gary Clark   "The Joe T. play was a pass to me, a trick play. Fortunately for me, I wasn't in a position to see what happened to Joe. Knowing Joe T. and his commitment for the game, we figured he would be back the next year, and he probably thought so as well. But it wasn't in the cards for him to come back. I only had him my rookie year, but he was a great team leader. He probably had something to do with me getting the start by the sixth game of my first year. I'm sure that Joe T. nudged that along."

Linebacker Rich Milot   "Joe Theismann was an underrated quarterback. He was a great athlete. I remember one time we played one-on-one basketball, and I think he beat me 11–0. I don't think he missed a shot. I don't think he was ever fully appreciated, because he would sometimes put his foot in his mouth."

Kicker Mark Moseley   "I am probably as close to Joe as anyone on the team ever was. He was my holder, and our families were close. We would go to the games together and hang out together after the games. Joe is a guy you have to be around and know him to really appreciate. Most people have the wrong impression of him. He is a great guy, but just a very high-intensity-level kind of guy. He has a huge amount of ability. He is very intelligent. People misinterpreted his confidence for cockiness. He was always talking. He always had something to say, but he could always back it up. He didn't say something if he didn't mean it.

"I had him chewing me out all the way off the field, but if you had someone else go out there and hold for me, or if you needed someone to win a game, he would be right there. He would be out there if he had a broken arm. He had the heart of a lion. He was like a brother to me on the team. He is an honest person, and if I ever needed anything, he would be there for me."

There would be another familiar face gone after 1985. John Riggins would call it quits. The running back who was seen as a troublemaker while with the Jets changed his entire image under Joe Gibbs and finished his career as a Hall of Famer. He carried 2,916 times for 11,352 yards and 104 touchdowns during his career. He also caught 250 passes for 2,090 yards and 12 touchdowns. His 13,435 combined net yards are among the best ever, as are his 116 touchdowns by rushing and receiving. He rushed over 1,000 yards 5 times in his career and over 100 yards in 35 games, including a then-record 6 in postseason. He rushed 251 times for 996 yards and 12 touchdowns in 9 postseason contests. He made his mark on the field and off, with his colorful antics, from telling Supreme Court Justice Sandra Day O'Connor to "Loosen up, Sandy baby" at a function, to showing up in top hat and tails at one of Jack Kent Cooke's Super Bowl parties. But only his teammates knew him well—particularly the Hogs, as he was a member, even though he was a running back—and he was as respected and admired as any player who ever put on a uniform for the Redskins.

Tackle Joe Jacoby "John would hang out with us at the Five O' Clock Club, the little shed off the field at Redskin Park where the linemen would meet for liquid refreshments and food and get things off our chest and just talk. It was part of keeping the team together and building something."

Jeff Bostic "John would sit in the meetings and watch films with us. He wanted to see where the blocking schemes were coming from and where he needed to be. John liked hanging out with us."

It was now Jay Schroeder as quarterback and George Rogers as running back in the 1986 season. But there would be some new faces that would change that dynamic. The collapse of the USFL brought running back Kelvin Bryant, receiver Ricky Sanders, and former Tampa Bay quarterback Doug Williams to the Redskins. Bryant would never live up to his potential, as he failed to stay healthy enough to play for any length of time. Williams, though, would play a pivotal role in the future of this franchise and make history in the process.

Schroeder and Rogers both seemed up to the task, leading the Redskins to a 12-4 season. Schroeder had 22 touchdowns, 22 interceptions, and 4,109 yards passing, while Rogers carried the ball 303 times for 1,203 yards and 18 touchdowns. But there were problems. After fourteen years in a Redskins uniform, Moseley was cut after a 30–6 loss to Dallas on October 12, and the Redskins were never able to find someone the rest of the year to effectively take his place, using Max Zendejas and then former Maryland kicker Jeff Atkinson, who was working as a mortgage banker in Annapolis when he got the call from the Redskins in December.

Atkinson came through in the playoffs, with 4 field goals in a 19–7 victory over the Rams in the first round, and then 2 fourth-quarter field goals in Chicago in a 27–13 win. But this was the New York Giants' season, and their devastating defense, led by Lawrence Taylor, crushed the Redskins 17–0 at Giants Stadium.

There was change and upheaval entering the 1987 season, and labor clouds were forming on the horizon again. Wayne Sevier left to join the San Diego Chargers coaching staff. The personal problems of Dexter Manley had reached the point where he entered a drug rehabilitation center. Dave Butz was holding out. Atkinson suffered a dislocated ankle, leaving the Redskins scrambling for another kicker. And the league was bracing for another players' strike—only this time they were preparing by lining up replacement players.

Washington opened the season against the Eagles at home, but the starting quarterback for the Redskins was not Schroeder, who had a shoulder injury. It was Williams, who threw for 272 yards and 2 touchdowns for a 34–24 win. He had 3 touchdown passes in the second game against Atlanta, but new kicker Ali Haji-Sheikh struggled, and Jeff Bostic fumbled a snap on an extra point, opening the door to a 21–20 Falcons victory.

By week three the players were on strike. There was a whole new cast of players at Redskin Park wearing Redskins uniforms. These unknowns would play a major role in the success the striking players would enjoy later that year.

First, they would face the Cardinals at home, and St. Louis still had a handful of veterans on the roster, because the players were divided about the strike. But the replacement Redskins, led by quarterback Ed

Rubbert, running back Lionel Vital—who caught 7 passes for 255 yards—and receiver Anthony Allen, came out on top 28–21. They won their next game against the Giants in New York, as Allen rushed for 128 yards in a 38–12 victory. But their toughest game was against the Cowboys in Dallas. The strike was falling apart, and players were starting to cross the line and report to their teams. Many of the Cowboys rushed back to play, but the Redskins wanted to stick together as a team, as they did during the 1982 strike. So they wanted to report as a team, and by the time they did that, it was too late for them to play in the Cowboys game.

It would be a bunch of players who weren't good enough to make an NFL roster that would go up against Danny White and the real Cowboys. Remarkably, though, the scrubs beat the stars, 13–7, as Redskins fill-in quarterback Tony Robinson completed 11 of 18 passes for 152 yards and Vital ran for 136 yards, while the scrubs defense caused 2 Dallas fumbles.

When the Redskins veterans returned, they came back to a team that had gone from 1-1 to 4-1. One could make the case that the credit for the success of the 1987 Redskins should go to the replacement players, who would later be the inspiration for the movie *The Replacements*.

Assistant general manager Charley Casserly   "The strike in 1987 was not a pleasant thing. I don't think anyone wanted to be involved with bringing in a replacement team. But you had a job to do. None of us knew how long the strike would go on, but we were right in the middle of a division schedule. One game was canceled, but we went to St. Louis, New York, and Dallas, and we were 1-1 at the time. That was going to make or break our season, those three games.

"We went to work day and night trying to find players. We were fortunate to have a great coaching staff. We beat St. Louis in that first game, and they had a lot of veterans, too. And then, to beat Dallas on a *Monday Night* game, when they had Danny White, Tony Dorsett, Randy White, and Too Tall Jones, who had all come back, was amazing. Our veterans had voted to return, but it was after the deadline and [Cowboys president] Tex Schramm said they couldn't play. Eventually, the league lost that case in court and had to pay the players who they wouldn't let play. To beat them down there, in a game that nobody thought we had a chance to win, was a big moment for us. We didn't think we had much of a chance, but Joe got those kids believing in themselves, and they played great. You could tell that Dallas didn't want to be there that night.

"We had mixed emotions that night, but we came out of the strike 4-1. The Giants were 0-3 during the strike games, and they had lost their first two that season. Remember, they were the defending Super Bowl champions, and at the end of that we were 4-1 and they were 0-5. They got it going at the end of the season, but by then they were out of it. Philadelphia went 0-3. The Cardinals weren't going to be contenders, and they went 1-2. Dallas went 2-1, losing to us. They had won the division the year before, but that was their last great shot. When we beat the Cowboys, that took the heart out of them and they fell apart the rest of the season. At that point, we coasted home with the division title."

They didn't exactly coast. Their first game was at home against the New York Jets, and the Redskins were losing 13–7 going into the fourth quarter. But they came back to score 10 points in a 17–16 win, with the key play coming when Dave Butz sacked Jets quarterback Ken O'Brien, stopping a Jets drive with less than four minutes left in the game. What made that play remarkable was that just twelve hours before, Butz was in Arlington Hospital, hooked up to an IV that was filling him with 11 quarts of fluid. He had been suffering from a stomach disorder that caused him to lose a massive amount of weight in one week.

Dave Butz "I had two different types of parasites and went from 315 pounds to 272 pounds in one week. On a Friday night, the night before we had to go to the hotel before a game, I drank a glass of water, and it just shot out of my mouth like in the *Exorcist*. I couldn't hold down water, so I told my wife to call the doctor, who met us at the hospital, and from 9 P.M. that night until 9 A.M. the next day, I received 11 quarts of fluid. They were pumping saline into my veins, but the pump couldn't get it in fast enough, so they took a 16-gauge needle, and I was getting a quart of fluid an hour. I was paid to play, and in the old school we did that. We got ready. The next day my blood levels were close to normal. I played the whole game, sacked the quarterback, kept them out of field-goal range, went back to the hospital after the game, and received another 6 quarts of fluid. But I missed no practices and no meetings. Guys that had a lot simpler things happen to them didn't make their practice.

"Once I had a thumb that I broke. I felt my thumb hit the back part of my wrist. I said, 'That's unusual, that has never happened.' It was sitting there off to the side, and I went up to the team doctor, Dr. Levine. I tapped him on the shoulder. He was kind of irritated, because he was watching the game. I said, 'I think I have a problem.' He turned around and yelled, 'Jesus, let me fix that for you.' He set it on the field, and then we went into the tunnel, where he put a cast on it. My wife came down and wondered what the problem was. I said I was getting a cast put on this thing so I could go back in and play. I missed seven defensive plays, and came back in and played. The following Monday they took $3\frac{1}{4}$-inch pins and used a hand drill and drilled two $3\frac{1}{4}$-inch pins into my thumb and wrist, to hold my thumb to my wrist. They didn't like the first two they put in, so they took a pair of pliers and pulled them out. They drilled two more holes. I asked, 'Doc, I understand why you are holding the thumb together, but why did you bend the wires over at the end.' He said, 'Dave, that is in case you hit somebody or somebody hits you, we don't have to cut your flesh apart to get the pins out.' I said, 'That makes sense.' There was no way you could have taped that up enough to keep people from holding on to it, and there are many pictures where there were offensive linemen holding on to the pad."

Rich Milot   "Dave Butz, when he wanted to play, he could take over the game pretty much like no one else in that era. He was so big. The teams that he would get fired up for, he would absolutely dominate, whether it be Dallas or St. Louis, where he had come from, he would tear them up. He didn't give a very good locker room speech. I remember a few times he tried to give some pep up speeches, and they would make you laugh more than fire you up."

Washington went 2-2 over the next four games. Gibbs made a fateful decision by benching Schroeder, and declaring that Williams would be his starting quarterback. The Redskins won five of their final seven games, including the season finale, a 27–24 overtime victory against the Vikings in Minnesota, with Barry Wilburn intercepting a pass in the end zone and taking it all the way down the field for a touchdown, and Haji-Sheikh coming through with 2 field goals, including the game winner. Three weeks later, they faced the Vikings again in the NFC title game, and another cornerback, Darrell Green, was the deciding factor in the Redskins' playoff run.

First, there were the Bears in Chicago, where Green wrote another chapter of Redskins history. In the third quarter, with the score tied at 14–14, Green went back to field a punt. He took it at his own 48-yard line and then hurdled Cap Boso at the Chicago 30-yard line. When Green did that, he tore some rib cartilage, but he managed to make it all the way to the end zone while holding his side for a 21–14 Washington lead. The Bears added a field goal, but Washington came away with a 21–17 win.

The Redskins were heading for the NFC title game in a rematch with the Vikings, this time at RFK Stadium, and Green would make the defining play in that game as well. Washington led 17–10. There were about fifty seconds left in the game. The Vikings had the ball at the Washington 6-yard line, and it was fourth down. The pass from Wade Wilson to Anthony Carter fell incomplete, as Green, covering Carter, put a hit on him that forced him to bobble the pass. Washington was heading to the Super Bowl for the third time in six years.

All the buzz before the game against the Denver Broncos, who were repeat AFC champions and determined to avenge their defeat to the Giants the year before, was about Doug Williams being the first black quarterback to play in the Super Bowl. But in Washington there were more pressing matters, such as who would start as running back. George Rogers had been struggling, so Gibbs opted to play unheralded rookie running back Timmy Smith.

The players felt they had been well prepared to face the Broncos.

Charles Mann   "Our defensive coaches had us very well prepared. In my last few years, I was so smart because of Torgy Torgeson. If I read all my keys and everything, I knew where the play was going to go. It was almost that easy. That was because of Torgy Torgeson and the other coaches breaking down the films for us. They broke down the films of the Denver Broncos, and we had cards of all the plays. We were practicing their plays, and on the very first day in practice, they came at us with a quarterback throwback. Reggie Branch was playing Steve Sewell, and I think Stan Humphries may have been playing

John Elway. He got the snap, and he handed it to Reggie Branch. Reggie went one way and Stan went the other, and Reggie threw the pass back to him. We got in the huddle, and we said to ourselves that we are going to see this play. They ran it only once during the season, early in the year, week two or three, and here it is, the end of the season, and our coaching staff knew beyond a shadow of a doubt that we would see that play. So we ran it every day in practice. The first day it burned Dexter. The second day he got caught off guard on it a little bit, but he caught up on it. We are in our defensive linemen meetings, and Torgy told me, 'You need to get Dexter on top of this so he sees this.' I took it upon myself to alert Dexter when I saw Elway in the shotgun to watch out for the quarterback throwback.

"Fast forward to Sunday, the second series of the game. Now, teams are not going to change what got them to the Super Bowl. They are not going to make wholesale changes, but what they will do is tweak the plays you are going to see. So we are on the field, the second series, Elway is in the shotgun, I see it, and I am yelling at Dexter, 'Quarterback is in the shotgun.' He looks at me like, 'Huh?' I yell again, 'The quarterback is in the shotgun,' and he looks at me again like, 'Huh?' I am pointing to the backfield, and he shakes his head, 'Yeah, yeah, yeah, okay.' He gets down in his stance, and the pass comes my way, and I am thinking, 'Oh, no.' I turn and run with everything I have, but it seems like slow motion, and I am thinking, 'I'm getting burned in the Super Bowl.' I am running, and thank God Alvin Walton and I were able to get Elway down at the 10-yard line, and they had to kick a field goal, which made it 10–0. If they had scored on that, 14-0, I think we might have been struggling. They flip-flopped that, play and ran it toward me. I had Dexter all prepared for it, and who did they run it on? Me. And I didn't recognize it initially, being so worried about playing nursemaid to Dexter.

"After that we shut them down. We changed our cleats because guys were slipping on the field. We didn't have great footing, and Joe Gibbs called [equipment manager] Joe Brunetti, 'Get these guys some new cleats.' We changed to longer cleats so that we wouldn't be sliding all over the place. Denver wasn't sliding, but on defense we were slipping all over the place, so we made the change."

At first, it looked as if John Elway and company would get the redemption they sought at Jack Murphy Stadium in San Diego on

January 31, 1988. The first time Elway got his hands on the ball, he hit Ricky Nattiel for a 56-yard touchdown pass. Denver's next possession resulted in a 24-yard field goal by Rich Karlis, and the Broncos already had a 10–0 lead after the first quarter.

Then Doug Williams stepped into history and took the Redskins with him. In the span of the final six minutes of the first half–5 minutes and 47 seconds of football, to be exact–Williams hit Ricky Sanders on an 80-yard touchdown pass. Then he connected with Gary Clark on a 27-yard score. The next Washington possession resulted in a 58-yard touchdown run by Timmy Smith, and Washington led 21–10. Williams wasn't done, though. He hit Sanders on a 50-yard touchdown pass and Clint Didier with an 8-yarder, and the Redskins led 35–10 halftime. They added another touchdown with a 4-yard run by Smith in the fourth quarter, but once the first half ended, it was a Redskin party, with the Broncos paying the tab. Washington had broken nineteen Super Bowl records and tied ten others, including most yards gained in one quarter (356), most points scored in one quarter (35), most yards passing in one quarter (228), and most yards receiving in one quarter (Sanders, with 193). By the end of the game, Jay Schroeder was an afterthought.

Joe Jacoby   "Playing over twenty years, in high school, college, and the pros, I had never been involved in anything like I had seen in that fifteen minutes of football. I remember one play toward the end of the game, when we scored our last touchdown. We were on the goal line, and we ran one of our goal-line plays, but the left guard, Raleigh McKenzie, had the wrong play. I was the only one who pulled, and we still scored. On the second long touchdown run by Timmy Smith, you could see the look of dejection on their faces. They had been up 10–0 and now they were down 35–10 at halftime."

Raleigh McKenzie   "I don't think there was a quarterback divide on the team. I think Coach Gibbs handled it better than any coach would have. But once they went back to Doug for the final switch, Coach Gibbs made the right decision. Doug had the offense moving. He may not have been able to run around, like Jay did, but for then, he was the right choice for our offense and had the ability to rally the team together.

"It was great playing for Doug. I was always an admirer of him. I grew up watching him play college football at Grambling and then with the Tampa Bay Bucs, I tried to follow his career. Once he joined the team from the USFL, I knew he was something special. He fit right in and was a good team leader. He wasn't a selfish guy. He was a team guy, and it showed in the way he played. We rallied around him not just because of his talent but also because of his ability to lead.

"When we were down 10–0 to Denver in the Super Bowl, our offense still felt that we could move the ball on those guys. I don't think anyone panicked on offense. We knew what we could do. We needed to get Charles and Dexter and those guys on defense going. Once we had a drive, the defense turned it up a notch. They started keeping Elway off the field, and then the offense started coming in bunches for us. The line, after the first few series, we picked up on what they were doing, and the way Coach Gibbs made the calls and the way we were blocking then, all the running backs had to do was run, and all the receivers had to do was catch the ball that Doug was throwing. Look at what Tim Smith did that day. That was one of the best games that our offensive line ever played. We had played two tough games going into that Super Bowl, against Chicago and Minnesota. We played well in both of those games, and I think that was one of the reasons we didn't push the panic button in the Super Bowl; we knew we had just beat two very good teams to get there."

Tight end Don Warren   "Jay Schroeder was talented, probably one of the strongest arms I have ever seen. He always told us that when he was a high school catcher, he could throw the ball over the fence in centerfield from sitting behind home plate. I could believe it, with the arm he had. He was very intelligent, with a lot of talent. The one thing we didn't like about Jay was that he always started to get fidgety feet and always went right, rather than stand in the pocket. Teams knew that. With Bugel and Gibbs, there were times to get out of the pocket and times to stay there. When Bugel and Gibbs built protection, everyone needed to be on the same page. That was one of our main beefs with Jay. He would always fly out of there and go right because he was right-handed. Jake [Joe Jacoby] would be in the huddle giving him crap about it. He did not have as much leadership ability as Joe T. [Theismann]. Joe T. was a hell of a leader. Ryp [Mark Rypien] was a good leader, too, better than Jay.

"Doug Williams was also a great leader. He couldn't run. He was basically a statue, and everybody knew that. But he was one of the toughest statues I ever played with. He got hammered in his days at Tampa Bay. He would wait until the last minute to get rid of the ball. He would wait and wait for a receiver to get open and then he would get slammed. He had no fear. He didn't care about getting hit. He cared about putting the ball in the right person's hands. He was one of the toughest guys I ever played with. That was why the pocket schemes and boot schemes worked well with him. He was one of the better deep throwers that the Redskins ever had. He could throw the ball deep, and he could throw it on the money."

Receiver Gary Clark   "In that Super Bowl it took us a quarter to settle down, but once we did, nobody was going to beat us that day. We were just invincible. Everybody was on point, to the point where offensive linemen were saying where the play was going and stop it if you can. When you are telling the opposing team what you are going to do and they still can't do anything to stop it, that is a pretty good game and a pretty good team.

"Doug was a great leader and a smart football player. Jay was a good quarterback for us, but that tells you the kind of quarterback Doug was for us. He took advantage of that situation."

That game solidified Doug Williams's legacy as a quarterback. He had taken a beating for years as the Tampa Bay Buccaneers quarterback and had led them to their first playoff appearance. But it was as a Redskin that people woke up to what kind of quarterback—and person—Williams was.

It was also Timmy Smith's time in the sun, but it would be brief, like a shooting star. His record-setting performance—22 carries for 204 yards—would be a footnote. Smith was soon out of football, never fulfilling his potential, and in September 2005 he was arrested, along with his brother, Chris, in Colorado after allegedly delivering 20 ounces of cocaine to an undercover drug agent in a restaurant parking lot.

Joe Gibbs had now taken two different teams to Super Bowl titles, showing an ability to adapt to change. It would serve him well as the decade wound down and the final decade of the century was about to begin.

9

The Final Run

The 1988 season for the Washington Redskins would be a first for Joe Gibbs: a losing season. They posted a 7-9 record, in a season where the Redskins were fighting to survive, let alone win.

Linebacker Wilbur Marshall arrived as a rare free agent, costing the Redskins two number-one draft picks. Dexter Manley was suspended for drug use and back in rehabilitation during training camp. Unhappy quarterback Jay Schroeder was traded in September to the Raiders for tackle Jim Lachey. Doug Williams would undergo an emergency appendectomy, and an untested sixth-round draft choice who carried a clipboard around since the 1986 season would get to start. They brought in a rookie kicker, Chip Lohmiller. And at the end of the season, general manager Bobby Beathard would leave.

After going 2-1 in the first three games, Williams was hospitalized, and Mark Rypien, the clipboard carrier, got the call.

Quarterback Mark Rypien "I was brought in under the best circumstances you could for a young quarterback. When I came in, I was actually the fourth quarterback. Babe Laufenberg was there and third, Doug Williams would come and be second, and Jay Schroeder was the starter.

"I was fortunate because Jerry Rhome was my quarterback coach. Joe did most of the offense, but when it came to position Rhome was my coach, and he spent every day from when I got there in May until the first day of training camp in Carlisle at quarterback school with me, working on throws on the sideline, giving me a better understanding of the offense until I was capable enough of playing in the preseason and then comfortable enough to jump into a game situation. I was brought along a lot differently than quarterbacks are brought along today. I was very blessed with having an opportunity to learn the system, watch the guys ahead of me perform, and understand what we were trying to do offensively and what we were all about, so when my day did come, I was either going to get it done because I could physically or I couldn't get it done because I couldn't physically. It wasn't going to be because I didn't know what we were doing or what our philosophy was.

"In 1988, I got a call at about eleven at night saying get ready, Doug just went through an emergency appendectomy, and you're the guy. I didn't sleep well that night, nervous and excited about getting the opportunity. We were playing the Phoenix Cardinals in Phoenix. My wife, Annette, was about eight months pregnant. We were moving into our new house, all in the same week that I am playing in my first regular season professional game as a Redskin. So there were a lot of things going on at the time. I played fairly well. I threw three touchdown passes. Then I was rolling out near the end of the game and got hit from the backside and fumbled and lost the ball. It was a sour way to end what was a pretty good day. But I think the coaches thought they saw someone who showed some promise. I came back to have some good numbers, sharing the job with Doug. And the following year the job was mine. I had some good numbers again, but I had some issues with holding onto the football. Once I got that under control, we got our first playoff win in 1990, and then the big year in 1991."

Williams would come back later that season, but he would struggle and be benched in favor of Rypien after the team posted a 6-6 mark and was about to face Cleveland. But after a 17–13 loss to the Browns and a close 20–19 victory over the Eagles, Gibbs went back to Williams for the final two games of the season—both losses (24–17 to Dallas and 20–17 to Cincinnati). What was noteworthy about the Bengals game was the record-setting performance of the brother of a running back who had given the Redskins fits over the years: Jamie Morris, the brother of New York Giants running back Joe Morris.

Jamie Morris carried the ball 45 times—nearly one-quarter of all the carries he would have in his NFL career. Morris got the carries because Gibbs was struggling to find a running back he could count on. Neither Timmy Smith nor Kelvin Bryant were those backs, but for this one day, Morris, a rookie, who had rushed for 437 yards that year, was a back he could count on against the Bengals, who would be heading to the Super Bowl that season. Morris had 152 yards rushing, and the Redskins thought they might have their running back for 1989. But he was small, and Gibbs liked his backs big; Morris would be traded, and the Redskins would bring in Gerald Riggs and Earnest Byner in deals before the start of the new season.

Gibbs didn't find his running back in 1988, but he certainly found a new tackle in Lachey, who would be an anchor on the offensive line for years to come.

Tackle Jim Lachey   "I got traded from the Chargers to the Raiders as training camp was about ready to start. We played the Redskins in an exhibition game, and we got our butts kicked. Not long after that they started talking to the Redskins for a trade. The Raiders needed a quarterback, the Redskins had Jay Schroeder, and the next thing you know, my name is being circulated in trades, but I didn't believe it, because I had just been traded. The Redskins had gotten burned on a trade a few years earlier with the Raiders when they got a receiver named Calvin Muhammad, who was damaged goods and never worked out. Beathard didn't trust the Raiders. So when they offered up a few other guys for Schroeder, he said no, we want Lachey. When they told me about it, I said no, I like it here. I was getting to know everyone and learning the playbook, and we had just beaten the Chargers, the team I had played for. But within twenty-four hours of that first game, I was traded to the Redskins for Schroeder. I played right tackle for a few games, and then they switched me to left tackle after the fourth or fifth week I was there, and that was where I spent the rest of my career.

"I knew Joe Gibbs and the Redskins were winners, and I knew he had come from San Diego. Coming off an All-Pro year in the AFC . . . I knew Dan Riley, the one contact I had there. We were kind of disciples of the same kind of training.

"I played on a Sunday, flew across the country on my day off, showed up there on a Tuesday, met with Gibbs and Joe Bugel. Gibbs said, 'You don't look too excited about being a Redskin.' I said, 'Coach give me a day or two.' They were thinking, 'This guy isn't happy to be here.' I was, but I just needed to figure out where I was. I had stayed in a hotel for eight weeks already, and I was going to be staying in another one for three or four weeks until I found a place to live in Washington. It all worked out."

It worked out, but Lachey found he would get a workout in the brutal NFC East, particularly when he had to face Lawrence Taylor at least twice a year, or more, in the playoffs.

Jim Lachey   "When you have to line up against L.T., you don't ever forget it, and that is why Joe Gibbs said they got me, to block Lawrence Taylor. They said that was the reason I was there. We lost a tough one—the first one was at 24–23—but we came back and got them later on in the year. In 1989, we opened the season on Monday night. I had one of my best games ever against L.T. that night, but we still lost the game. Next thing you know we were 4-6, then we won the next six. For a long time that I played we never beat the Giants, then we beat them 17–14 in 1991. I will never forget that I was so physically drained after the game, so worn out, and I thought, 'This is how you have to be to be able to beat the Giants.' L.T. and I had a mutual respect. I ran into him at a golf tournament after my first year of playing against him in 1989, and we talked. He said he had a lot of respect for me, even though I was a young guy. If you are going go up against L.T., you have to be relentless because he was relentless. You had to stay on him.

"You never got a day off in the NFC. Bruce Smith is not an easy task in the Super Bowl, but after you've had to go up against L.T., Charles Haley, or Ken Harvey twice a year each, you are prepared for it."

Charley Casserly—the former high school football coach who wrote George Allen for a job and worked for nothing when he first got to Redskin Park—would take over as general manager. Doug Williams was sidelined with a bad back, so Rypien was the starter going into the 1989 season. Washington bounced back from their losing season, posting a 10-6 mark. It was still not good enough to make the playoffs, but there were positives to take into the next season. Rypien emerged as a quality NFL starter, throwing 22 touchdown passes with just 13 interceptions and 3,768 yards. And Gary Clark emerged as the leader of one of the most talented receiving corps ever to take the field. Clark, Art Monk, and Ricky Sanders combined for 377 catches for 4,476 yards, and Clark had the most yardage of the trio, catching 79 passes for 1,229 yards, a 15.6-yard-per-catch average and 9 touchdowns. Clark stood out among the Redskins not for his outstanding play, though. He was clearly the most volatile and demonstrative player on the field for Washington and could often be seen on the sidelines engaging teammates and coaches in arguments—a totally different persona from the one he had away from the field.

Receiver Gary Clark "I think for a lot of guys who are shy, sports is their outlet to allow them not to be shy. I grew up a shy kid. I don't like talking to big crowds or a lot of people. But on the field, I was able to come out and say and do what I wanted to. I did not like losing. I am not a good loser. People say now, it's okay to lose, it's how you play the game. I didn't grow up like that. And I didn't like to play bad or cause my teammates to lose because of something I was doing. I gave it to myself if I played bad, and I would give it to my teammates as well if I didn't think they were playing like they should be. They knew it was never personal. I was just trying to win the football game. I was definitely two personalities. I spoke my mind on the field and was very quiet off the field.

"With Joe, it was more like a father-son than a player-coach. I was always the son who would wind up in his office on Tuesday for something I said during a game on Sunday. But we had a good relationship. There is nothing I wouldn't do for the guy. He understood me and the way I went out to play. There are probably a lot of coaches who wouldn't have understood the way that I went out to play and the things that came out of my mouth when I was playing.

"I wouldn't talk trash unless someone was talking trash to me. But if they started it, I would sure damn finish it. Joe was a great manager of people. You had Art on one side, who was quiet on and off the field, and you had me, where you never quite knew what was coming out of my mouth. I never knew what was coming out. It depended on the situation, if we were playing good or bad, or if I was playing good or bad. My relationship with Joe is probably kind of like he had with [race car driver] Tony Stewart. We had very similar personalities.

"Me, Art, and Rickie got along great. We all lockered together. Art talked to us. He talked to his teammates all the time. Anybody outside of the football family, he was just quiet and shy. Art would speak when he had something to say, and when he did speak, people listened. It meant something. A lot of times he let his actions on the field speak for themselves."

His teammates would often be a target of his wrath, but they understood it was also what drove Clark to excel on the field.

Guard Raleigh McKenzie "Nobody pushed himself more than Gary Clark. He was his own worst critic. If the offense was struggling, he took it upon himself to try to do something about it. He was kind of like Art off the field, sort of quiet and low key, but on the field he certainly wasn't quiet like Art. On game day, he was hollering at linemen and hollering at the defense, yelling at the quarterback, calling passing plays, yelling at Coach Gibbs. That was Gary. He would challenge anybody."

Quarterback Jeff Rutledge "Gary was very excitable. He would yell at me in the huddle. I remember once when I first got there, before we even started the season . . . I think it was in a minicamp. Joe had a lot of verbiage in his plays, and I was having trouble calling them half the time. When I had to call it all in the huddle, I messed up some. I remember him yelling at me once, 'Just get the play called,' and I was taken aback. I had been in the league longer than he had. He was a competitor. He wanted to do well and wanted the team to do well."

Tight end Ron Middleton "Gary was very emotional, a fierce competitor. He was the rebel in the group. He wasn't that approachable. A lot of those guys, the stars, had nice cars and big houses, but Gary had two or three nice cars; you know what I am saying. He was fiery. We got into it a few times. He didn't back down from nobody. I don't mean this in a negative way, it was just how he was."

No one could get a handle on what drove Dexter Manley, but whatever it was, it drove him from the Redskins after the 1989 season. The team released the former star defensive end, having lost patience with his personal indulgences. Many of his teammates still wonder to this day what might have been if Manley could have realized his potential and if they could have helped him.

Cornerback Vernon Dean   "Dexter was an outstanding athlete with tremendous strength and tremendous explosion off the line. His combination of speed, quickness, and strength made him one of the better pass rushers of all time. He had that kind of talent, sprinter's speed at that position. He was a freak for the position. People talked about Jevon Kearse being a freak, about how big and fast he was, but Dexter was bigger and just as fast."

Running back Joe Washington   "I knew Dexter real well. He and his girlfriend at the time and my wife and I, we were all good friends. It was hard not to like Dexter Manley. Dexter used to come over to the house, and my wife is a psychiatric therapist, and I never had any idea that he had some problems, but I knew when something was taking place after the first time. I knew when he was in trouble because he would want to talk to my wife. He would call me and said, 'Hey Go-Go, let me talk to Meadowlark [Washington's wife].' They would talk a little bit, and I knew he was having some issues to deal with."

Defensive end Charles Mann   "I had a great relationship with Dexter. We were staunch competitors. But off the field, after the lights had dimmed and we would leave, I would try to give him a ride home, because I think that year his license was taken from him. He couldn't drive, so I would try to give him a ride home and try to encourage him not to go out to the clubs. I was always, 'Hey, let me give you a ride home,' and he would say, 'No, I'm gonna go out.' I was always after him, trying to keep him on the up-and-up, trying to encourage him.

"He would be on the plane saying, 'I got you, Charles, I got you,' when he was ahead of me in sacks. Once we were heading to Philly, and I was leading briefly, with 8 sacks, and he had 7½ or something like that, and then coming back he had me by a half, and he said, 'I got you Charles, I got you.' He was sitting a row ahead of me and turned around and said that to me. He would try to push my buttons, but it was friendly. We respected each other. I knew he was one of the greatest defensive ends to ever play the game, and he knew I was a solid run blocker, something that he didn't care too much about, yet we also competed every week on the sacks. We admired and respected each

other, but we had a great competition. I look back on some of the pictures I have from Nate Fine, and in almost all of the pictures Dexter
and I are in, we are smiling. We must have had some fun, because we
always had a smile on our faces. But it is easy to smile when you are
winning.

"His problems were apparent. What was tough for me was that I
couldn't help him, as much as I tried. He didn't want my help, and
would say he was okay. I wouldn't call him a drug addict, from what
I saw. Most of the time he was drinking, and half a beer would make
him crazy. He couldn't handle alcohol. A little bit in his system, and he
would go crazy. It was frustrating. He was a team project. Everyone
wanted to be there for Dexter, to help him. I love Dexter to death. He
is hard not to like."

Defensive end Dexter Manley   "I had this beast on my shoulder,
and the beast was cocaine. It destroyed my life. I never felt like I got
the recognition that I could have because of the beast. Because of that,
I didn't live up to my expectations or the expectations of other people.
I disappointed so many people. I didn't know. I was just having fun.

"I am the all-time sacks leader for the Redskins. I had sixty-five
sacks in four seasons. No other player was doing that then.

"I never took drugs until I got into pro football. I grew up in a
drug-infested neighborhood, but I had such great determination to
get out of Houston's Third Ward and do something with my life.

"There was an All-Pro defensive player with the Redskins early in
my career. I'm not going to say who it was. I went to his house, and he
had all these girls in his house. There was this white guy there who
drove a Corvette. He dropped off a package, and I really didn't know
what it was then. I was so impressionable, and this player was impressive. He had money, clothes and women, and I really looked up to
that. I thought this is what they do in the National Football League. He
was always with different women, two at a time. I never had that in my
life. I was setting myself up. Bobby Beathard sent Art Monk to talk to
me and tell me not to socialize with that guy.

"The beast would tell me that it was okay to use drugs, that I could
handle it. But here I was, the Redskins Player of the Year, and Attorney General Ed Meese came to make the presentation at a luncheon,
but I never showed up because I had such a bad hangover. I subjected

myself to so much embarrassment and humiliation. I had such denial. How did I let myself get that way?

"Anytime you use a mood-altering chemical, you are at your worst. You are powerless. I never heard that until I went into a program. I used to feel powerful, but I was really powerless because the beast would always call me. And I was such a binger. I could go four or five months and not use drugs. But when I did use, I would get into so much trouble. I would pass out somewhere.

"I thought nothing could beat me. I was Dexter Manley, the main ingredient. I lived in the sun. I went to all these high-powered luncheons and dinners in places like Duke Ziebert's. I was a showman, and I loved to be in the spotlight. Everyone in town knew me. So I had to step up to the plate. It was the greatest city in the world to play in. There is no more powerful city in the world, and during football season everything revolves around the Redskins. I was a young man visiting the White House and meeting Alexander Haig and George Schultz and President Ronald Reagan. These people knew me. That was amazing.

"Joe Gibbs spent a lot of time with me. We would get together every Friday morning. The organization did all they could to help me, but the best thing they probably did was let me go after I was suspended for a year, telling me to move on. It was hard, but it was an act to separate the men from the boys, and I needed to grow up to be a man."

Manley is still growing up. His personal woes have been on public display since he stepped into the "sun," as he referred to it. There was his tearful testimony in Congress when he revealed he had gone through life unable to read because of dyslexia. His addiction has made news since he was suspended from the NFL in 1989 after testing positive for drug use.

After Washington released him, Manley played for the Arizona Cardinals for one year, then for the Tampa Bay Buccaneers in 1991. He was banned from the NFL for life after he failed a drug test for the fourth time and played in the Canadian Football League in 1993.

He was done with football then, but not drugs. Manley was arrested four times for crack cocaine possession between November 1994 and July 1995. He served fifteen months of a four-year sentence and was paroled in November 1996. He finally appeared to have gotten his life in order after that, staying clean for five years until his arrest in 2001 for failing to show up for a court-ordered hearing and because of his long history of drug-related arrests. He came out of prison in 2004 and has worked to stay sober.

The 1990 season saw the departure of Joe Bugel, who took a head coaching job with the Arizona Cardinals, and the arrival of Jim Hanifan, a former Cardinals head coach, to take Bugel's place. He would fit right in after he was given an initiation at Carlisle by the Hogs that illustrated life in training camp when professional football players got bored.

Tight end Don Warren   "We used to frequent the establishments up there [in Carlisle] to have a couple of beers after practice. It was probably the worst thing you could do after sweating everything out all day and you want to replenish your body, and you go drink beer. But, as professional athletes, we decided to go to the Fireside. We pretty much would go there after every practice, stop for an hour or so and have a few beers. This one night Joe Jacoby and Russ Grimm had a line meeting scheduled later that night. They had all the rookies and veterans there at the bar, and the tight ends. After about an hour or so of drinking, Russ and Jake decided, 'We're not going to the meeting. We're just going to hold out.' Now there are about five or six rookies in there who are thinking, 'I'm not doing that. I'm trying to make this team, and you're telling me not to go to a meeting?' I go to eat. I always went to the special teams meeting, which met before the group meeting and before the offensive line meeting. First was special teams, then Gibbs came in, and we had a group meeting, and then we were supposed to have a line meeting. But Russ and Jake locked the place up and weren't letting anyone go to the line meeting. They guarded the door. They are bonding.

"We are at the team meeting, and Gibbs doesn't notice that all these guys are not there. He is talking about this motivational stuff, getting ready for a preseason game. He is in the front of the room talking, and after about ten minutes, we break. We get up, and Gibbs has the big room, and the quarterbacks and running backs stay there. The tight ends and linemen are supposed to go next door, so [Clint] Didier and I walk in, and Rennie Simmons, the tight end coach, and Jim Hanifan are in there. It's me, Clint, and Rick Walker in there.

Rennie asks, 'Where is everybody?' I said, 'Rennie, the last time I saw Jacoby, Russ, and Mayday [Mark May], they weren't letting any linemen out of the Fireside.' Hanifan starts laughing. He has been through all this stuff. But Rennie says, 'That does it. You go back there right now and tell them it is $500 for every minute they miss.'

"So Dids and I get in my truck and we go racing back to the Fireside. I'm banging on the door. It is locked. They eventually let us in. The rookies are scared to death. They're asking, 'What did the coaches say?' I say, 'They are pissed. Rennie was really pissed and said for every minute you are late, you're going to be fined $500.' Their jaws hit the floor. Back then, you only made about $400 a week. You got paid when you made the team. These guys are going, 'Oh my God, we've got to go.' But Russ and Jake wouldn't let them leave, and none of these guys would challenge them.

"Russ looks at me and says, 'Are you guys in or are you guys out?' I said, 'Yeah, we're in.' He says, 'Go back and tell Hanny we are staying here. We're not going to the meeting.' So we go back. Hanny and Rennie are looking at films by themselves, grading practice. I walk in the door and Rennie says, 'What did they say?' I said, 'They said nobody is leaving, and nobody did, and they said to come back here and tell you that nobody is coming back tonight.' Rennie was furious. He slammed his book down and went storming off, and I knew he was going straight to Gibbs to tell him what happened.

"They never did come back. We are sitting in there with Hanny, and he says, 'Boys, there's not too much we can do here. You might as well go back and have a couple of beers. I can't do anything here. There's only two of you, and Rennie left.' Gibbs knew about it, so the next day he tells Hanny, 'Make it miserable on those guys. We're fining them. They're going to run their tails off.' Normally, we just ran in afternoon practice, but after morning practice, they've got the cones out, ready to run. Most of the linemen will tell you that all their running is done during practice. If you are sprinting 20 yards every time on running plays during practice, you got your running in. Gibbs wasn't a firm believer in sprinting after practice. If you gave your best effort during practice, there was no running after practice.

"So they are lining up the cones for 10-yard dashes, 20-yard dashes, and 30-yard dashes, and they start running. Now, these boys are hung over from the night before. They are dying. After about five sprints, Ed Simmons stops. Hanny yells, 'Ed, why are you stopping?'

Ed says, 'You can fine me or you can run me, but you ain't getting both out of me. If I stop now, you can fine me. But you ain't doing both.' The way this ended up shows what Gibbs is all about. They never got fined. Gibbs used that. A lot of these coaches like players to bond together and get close, and I think he knew how important this was, and that little hour and a half they missed in meetings was not as important as how they grew together that night."

Jim Lachey   "I think I spent forty weeks of my life in Carlisle, Pennsylvania, on the campus of Dickinson College in a dorm room. It was a great place, with great people. Russ [Grimm] always had the attitude, and he would get the guys to back him up. If he could skip out of a drill, he would. If he could hide behind a goalpost, which was hard for him because he was a big guy, he would, especially early on, when we would be doing the chutes and stuff, which is kind of mundane, but you have to do it. Russ would try to skip those. One night Russ and I were out having a little fun, and we decided to go out on the field, take the chutes, and make them disappear, so we wouldn't have to do them anymore. So we went there and started disposing of some of the chutes and the heavy sandbags, the twenty-five-pound bags that we used to have to hold up and punch out with them, and they would make your elbows and fingers hurt. The next morning we had kind of half forgotten about it. It was one of those nights. Hanifan is all pissed off, yelling, 'Where is my stuff. It better be back here by this afternoon.' We had hid them . . . some of it got bent up a little bit somehow, I don't know how that happened. Russ and I had a little fun. I don't think it was ever really known who did it.

"We had an offensive line rebellion meeting, it was Hanny's first year. We were all sitting around the bar. I was eating a basket of pretzels, and Russ and I were talking, and he said, 'Let's boycott the meeting.' I said, 'Okay, I'm on board, but we have to get everyone's keys, because one of these rookies will try to sneak out.' So I jumped up and went around the room yelling to everyone, 'Put your keys in here. We're not going back.' We were upset because we had a lot of rushing output after one preseason game, and there was a lot of talk about the offensive line and doubts, so we boycotted the meeting to show that we were all right, and we got about 150 yards the next game. It was a lot of fun."

. . .

Other new faces included two defensive tackles who came in by trade, Eric Williams and Tim Johnson, and Brian Mitchell, a 5-foot-10, 190-pound rookie quarterback out of Southwest Louisiana who was going to be used as a running back and kick returner. Mitchell, selected in the fifth round of the draft, made everyone sit up and take notice the first time he touched the ball in a preseason game against the Atlanta Falcons: he returned a kickoff 92 yards for a touchdown. He was intelligent and tough, and sometimes the toughness got in the way of the intelligence.

Raleigh McKenzie "Brian Mitchell was a little boisterous when he was a rookie. Some rookies come in and think they are seven-year veterans, and Brian was one of those guys. One time in training camp he was popping off, and for some reason he wanted to challenge Jumpy Geathers [6-foot-7, 290 pounds] after practice once. Jumpy had him all tied up. They were both Louisiana guys. That was funny. They tussled, it was quick, and Jumpy grabbed him, and then it was all over. Jumpy was a big, strong man."

Running back Brian Mitchell "I got into a fight with Jumpy Geathers. It was my second year. We had been joking back and forth with each other, and I kind of won that joking battle, and then we got into practice and he came up behind me and elbowed me. I twisted my ankle, and that was when they brought in Ricky Ervins, and the talk that year was that I really had to battle for my job. So I'm thinking if I sprain my ankle, I'll really be in trouble, so I picked up a football and drilled it at the side of his head, and we got into a scuffle. I held my own. He got stitches, I didn't. There were some punches thrown, and he ended up with a gash under his eye. It made me look like a maniac. I was the youngest of seven kids. My Dad was in the army for twenty years, and he boxed, and he had me box my older brothers. He taught me that you don't have to be scared of anyone. There is a tactic for everything."

Washington finished with the same 10-6 in 1990 that it had in 1989, but this time it was good enough to make the playoffs for the first time in three years. Rypien had missed six games because of an injured knee, which gave Stan Humphries a chance to play. Rypien, though, was Gibbs's choice as quarterback, and Humphries would be dealt to the San Diego Chargers, where he would eventually flourish and lead the Chargers to their first Super Bowl. Byner emerged as the Redskins primary ball carrier, rushing for 1,219 yards, while Gerald Riggs began filling the role as a short yardage back. Rypien threw 16 touchdowns and 2,070 yards, but he missed two of the most eventful games for the Redskins that season: November 4 against the Lions at the Pontiac Silverdome and November 12 in Philadelphia against the Eagles.

The game against the Lions was a disaster in the making, as Detroit built up a 35–14 lead. Gibbs replaced Humphries, who had three interceptions, with thirty-three-year-old backup quarterback Jeff Rutledge, whose primary role to that point had been as Chip Lohmiller's holder on kicks. Rutledge, near the end of his career, had one more big game left, though. He marched the Redskins down the field 63 yards, ending with a 3-yard Riggs run for a touchdown to cut the Lions' lead to 35–21. Detroit added a field goal, but their offense shut down after Eric Williams knocked Detroit quarterback Rodney Peete out of the game. Rutledge got the offense in position for another score, a Lohmiller field goal, and now it was a 38–24 game. When Washington got the ball back again, Rutledge hit Clark with a 34-yard scoring pass, and then, with eighteen seconds left in regulation and Washington near the Lions' end zone, Rutledge ran a gutsy quarterback draw for 12 yards, and the point after tied the game at 38–38. Both teams failed to do anything with the ball in their first overtime possession, but on his second try, Rutledge, on third down and 15 at their own 5-yard line, connected with Monk on a 40-yard pass. They kept the drive going until they got in Lohmiller's range, and with about six minutes left in overtime, he hit a 34-yard field goal for the game winner, capping off one of the greatest comebacks in franchise history.

Rutledge had completed 30 of 42 passes for 365 yards, threw for 1 touchdown, and ran for another.

Jeff Rutledge   "I still have the tape from that game and put it in to watch it from time to time to remember that game and what I did. To be able to bring them back was a great experience. We had a great offensive line. They protected me a lot, because I was throwing almost every down. I threw the ball forty-two times in a matter of a quarter and a half. The defense played great during that. They kept stopping them and getting us back the ball. When you get to my age now, and still have that moment, it is great to have a game like that to look back on.

"The Lions thought by the time the score was 35–14 the game was over. After all, they had Barry Sanders, and they were running the run-and-shoot offense back then. They took Rodney Peete out and put Bob Gagliano in. But Gary Clark and Art [Monk] made some great plays, and it was a great team win. Coach Gibbs and all the coaches came over and congratulated me. I was thrilled. I had been in the league for twelve years, and I didn't have a lot of playing time over my career, so that was exciting for me to do that."

It wasn't so great being the Redskins quarterback one week later in Philadelphia, where Washington lost 28–14 in the game now known as the "body bag game." The Eagles had a punishing defense, led by Reggie White and Clyde Simmons, that pummeled the Redskins that night. The score at halftime was tied 7–7, and they had knocked nine Redskins, including two quarterbacks, out of the game. Five Redskins had to be carried off the field. And there was insult added to injury when the Eagles started taunting the Redskins by yelling, "Do you guys need any more body bags?" and "You guys are going to need an extra bus just to carry all the stretchers." After the game, Philadelphia defensive tackle Jerome Brown told writers, "They acted like they didn't want to play us anymore."

It was so bad that Mitchell had to finish the game as quarterback.

Brian Mitchell "A lot of guys got hurt, and someone came to me in the sidelines and said, 'Brian, you're in there.' And I said, 'In what?' They said, 'Playing quarterback.' But I was thinking more about it being a *Monday Night* game and so many of my friends and family getting a chance to see me play quarterback in the NFL in that game, I wasn't really worried about going in. I wasn't scared. I was happy to have that opportunity."

The Redskins had their revenge, though. They traveled to Philadelphia to face the Eagles in the first round of the playoffs. The

Eagles scored first with two field goals for a 6–0 lead, but that was all the Washington defense would give up. Rypien put his team up 7–6 with a 16-yard touchdown pass to Monk and then a 20-yard field goal by Lohmiller for a 10–7 lead at halftime. Washington added 10 more in the third quarter with a 19-yard Lohmiller field goal and a 3-yard scoring pass from Rypien to Clark for a 20–6 win.

Jim Lachey   "They had our number. But when it really counted down the road in the playoffs, we were able to knock them out of it. That was sweet redemption. I remember that [body-bag] game. There was a lot of talk on the field and from the fans in Philly, and a lot of talk in the locker room after the game. I remember Joe telling us not to sink down to their level, and that we will get a chance to get them again. We all bit our tongues in the interviews after the game, but we had a lot pent up inside of us and let it out during the playoffs."

Washington lost in the next round to San Francisco 28–10, but the stage was set for what would be the final run of the Joe Gibbs Redskins.

Russ Grimm started it by announcing it would his final season. There was a feeling that time was running out and that this might be the last, best chance for this Redskins unit to taste Super Bowl glory again.

There was also another development that would play a significant role in the history of the Redskins franchise: Gibbs, an avid racing fan, announced he was forming a NASCAR racing team.

Rypien was healthy and in his prime, and it showed from the start of the season, a 45–0 beating of the Lions on *Monday Night Football*. They got a break when Barry Sanders bowed out of the game during warm-ups because of sore ribs and a groin injury, and they made the most of that break by ringing up 35 first-half points. Rypien had 2 touchdown passes, Mitchell returned a punt 69 yards for a touchdown, and even Earnest Byner had a touchdown pass on a halfback option. Darrell Green had 2 first-half interceptions, and both the offense and the defense served notice on the rest of the league in this season opener at RFK Stadium.

The Cowboys, their opponent the following week, didn't appear to be impressed. In front of the crowd at Texas Stadium, the Cowboys, led by quarterback Troy Aikman and running back Emmitt Smith, took a 14–7 lead in the first quarter. But thanks to the special teams play coached by Wayne Sevier, the Redskins would come out on top by the score of 33–31 when the clock ran out. Chip Lohmiller had 4 field goals, including a 53- and 52-yarder, and Brian Mitchell set up a touchdown when he ran on a fake punt on fourth and 1 for a first down on a play called by Sevier.

Off to a 2-0 start, Washington seemed unbeatable by the third game of the season, a 34–0 win over the Phoenix Cardinals at RFK Stadium. So far, Redskins fans had yet to see a team score a point in 1991 off the Redskins defense during a home game. Linebacker Wilbur Marshall intercepted a pass from Cardinals quarterback Tom Tupa and ran 54 yards for a touchdown, one of 2 interceptions he had that day. Safety Brad Edwards also intercepted a pass, and the Hogs pushed the Cardinals defense all over the field, as Byner rushed for 109 yards and backup running backs Ricky Ervins and Gerald Riggs rushed for 53 yards.

It would be closer the next week in Cincinnati. Washington got off to a 27–10 lead over the Bengals going into the second half on 2 field goals by Lohmiller, two drives that led to short yardage touchdown scores by Riggs–who would be pressed into more action because of a hurting Byner and wound up with 61 yards rushing that day–and a 66-yard punt return by Mitchell. The Bengals, using a no-huddle offense, confused the Redskins defense, causing 100 yards on penalties, with 80 of them coming on drives of 92 and 90 yards. But in what could have been the game-winning drive for Cincinnati, linebacker Andre Collins knocked the ball loose from tight end Mike Barber on a fourth down in the final minutes, preserving a 34–27 Redskins victory.

Linebacker Andre Collins "That Super Bowl year, our offense made life easy. Rypien had an amazing season. Gary Clark was outstanding, Art was outstanding, Ricky Sanders was outstanding, our running game was strong. Defensively, I know we finished in the top five. That was a really fun year. It was something special. When you watched us on film, especially for those first eleven games, it was like a pack of wild dogs defensively going after a piece of meat, and that meat was the ball carrier. We were relentless on defense. You had to make plays to win, and we had some playmakers."

. . .

The "wild dogs" turned in their third shutout of the year in week five, a 23–0 beating of the Eagles–again leaving the home crowd at RFK Stadium watching a defense that they had yet to see scored upon in person. The win was more amazing because Rypien had four turnovers–2 interceptions and 2 fumbles, in the worst game he would play that year–but the Hogs were on a mission, leading a running game that rushed for 157 yards. With Randall Cunningham injured, the Redskins defense teed off on a Philadelphia offense led by Jim McMahon and held them to just 89 yards of total offense.

Tackle Joe Jacoby   "We started something special from the fifth game on. The older guys, we had our own meetings every Saturday, after we met as a team and talked about things, about how important this is and all that. We kept going week after week. We were on a mission, and we were playing so well, it would have been a shame if we didn't win it all. We had an offensive line that gave up only nine sacks all year. We had a good running game with Earnest Byner and Ricky Ervins, and Mark Rypien was hot that year. Everything he threw got caught."

The machine was rolling. The Redskins beat the Bears at Soldier Field, 20–7. The Redskins defense intercepted Jim Harbaugh 3 times in a wind-filled game where Rypien connected on 18 of 31 passes, including 2 touchdowns to Monk. They were now 6-0 and going back home, where Redskins fans finally saw an opponent score on their defense when the Browns scored in the first quarter. It was a novelty, though, irrelevant to the outcome, a 42–17 Washington win. Art Monk would catch career pass number 751, passing Charlie Joiner for second place on the NFL's career reception list. And a fresh-legged Ricky Ervins ran for 133 yards on just 13 carries, including a 65-yard touchdown jaunt. Now they faced the defending Super Bowl champion New York Giants at Giants Stadium, and it looked like the undefeated season was going to end going into the locker room at halftime, as the Giants led 13–0. But the second half was a complete reversal. Clark caught 2 touchdown passes from Rypien, a 7-yarder and a 54-yard completion, and Lohmiller finished the Giants off with a 35-yard field goal. The Redskins won 17–13.

Coming back home, Washington was 8-0, and the talk was starting to center on the question of an undefeated season–accomplished, ironically, by the 1972 Miami Dolphins, who achieved this record by defeating the Redskins 14–7 in the Super Bowl. The talk continued after a 16–13 win over Houston and a 56–17 victory over the Atlanta Falcons and their outspoken coach, Jerry Glanville, at RFK Stadium, though the talk that November 10 day was more about Rypien than the undefeated Redskins. The Washington quarterback threw 6 touchdown passes, tying the franchise record held by Sammy Baugh, and threw for 442 yards, 4 shy of Baugh's record. He could have easily passed it, but he came out of the game before he had a chance, giving Rutledge the mop-up duty. He ran for one touchdown as well, becoming the first Redskins quarterback to account for 7 touchdowns in a game. Art Monk and Gary Clark combined for 11 catches, 5 of them touchdowns, for 367 yards. They were 10-0 and looking like the best team that ever wore the Redskins uniform. The winning continued in Pittsburgh the following week, with a 41–14 victory over the Steelers.

Game number twelve was extra special: Dallas week at RFK Stadium. A second victory over the hated Cowboys would make this magical season shine even more. The Cowboys led 14–7 at halftime, and, when Charles Mann and Jumpy Geathers sacked Troy Aikman and knocked him out of the game, it seemed as if Washington caught a break. But backup quarterback Steve Beuerlein came in and completed 7 of 12 passes for 109 yards and 1 touchdown, leading Dallas to a 24–21 win over Washington. The talk of an undefeated season was over, but it stung particularly because the dream ended at the hands of the Cowboys. Washington should have seen it coming. They lost to Dallas in their one defeat during the strike-shortened 1982 season, and again in 1983, when that powerful Redskins squad opened the season that year.

Gibbs had started using the no-huddle offense the previous two weeks, and he employed it again against the Los Angeles Rams the following week by putting 14 points on the board in the third quarter on their way to a 27–6 win at Anaheim Stadium and a 12–1 record. That record appeared in jeopardy in Phoenix when Washington was down 14–0 to the Cardinals and their old Hogs coach, Joe Bugel, at halftime. But Rypien and the Hogs led a second-half comeback with touchdown passes to tight end Terry Orr and Ricky Sanders to tie the game in the third quarter, and field goals of 42 and 27 yards by Lohmiller in the final quarter for a 20–14 win. They ran over the Giants the next week—153 yards combined by Byner and Ervins— for a 34–17 win. They had a chance to finish the 1991 season with a

15-1 record in the season finale in Philadelphia against the Eagles, but there was little to gain from that prestige. They had already clinched home-field advantage, and one loss in a year was not nearly as glamorous as an undefeated year. So when Washington led 13–7 at halftime, Gibbs began resting his regulars, keeping them off the hard Veterans Stadium surface and playing the backups. The Eagles came back to score 17 fourth-quarter points for a 24–22 win, which left Washington with a 14-2 record for the regular season, matching the 1983 squad's mark—the team that the 1991 squad has been compared to the most over the years.

In the first round of the playoffs, Washington welcomed back the Falcons team they had thoroughly embarrassed earlier that season. The win this time was not by nearly as wide a margin on the scoreboard, but was, for all intents and purposes, a sound defeat. In a rainstorm, the Falcons mustered just 7 points, while the Redskins fought it out on the ground, with 2 touchdowns by Riggs and another by Ervins in a 24–7 win before 55,000 wet but elated fans at RFK Stadium. They were drier and happier the following week as the Redskins finished how they started the season, with a shellacking of the Detroit Lions, this time by the score of 41–10. But there had been a scary moment during the week when everyone thought their star quarterback was hurt in practice.

Ron Middleton "We were getting ready for the playoffs in 1991, and we were having a blitz pickup period. A wide blitzer came off my side, and I went out to block him. Somehow I stumbled and rolled up on Ryp. I was laying face down, and I knew I had hit him. This was a practice before the NFC championship game. My face was in the mud and I was lying on my belly, and all I could say, and I didn't even know I was saying it out loud, but Coach Hanifan heard it, "Oh, God, please let him get up, please let him get up.'"

Rypien got up and showed no physical woes in the NFC title game. He had 2 touchdown passes, a 45-yard reception by Clark and a 21-yard scoring pass to Monk. Riggs carried the ball over twice for touchdowns, Lohmiller had two field goals, and Darrell Green intercepted an Erik Kramer pass and ran it back 32 yards for a touchdown.

The mission this team had set out on from week one was nearly accomplished. They would have to travel to Minneapolis for a cold-weather, albeit indoors, Super Bowl to finish the job, going up against the perennial bridesmaids who were on their own mission to finally win a Super Bowl: the AFC champion Buffalo Bills. But, as in years past, this was not the Bills' year. Buffalo running back Thurman Thomas couldn't start the game because he couldn't find his helmet.

Linebacker Monte Coleman "What sticks out for me was that we came into that Super Bowl as underdogs. They didn't give us any credit. They were debating on the sideline who was going to be MVP of the game, Bruce Smith or Thurman Thomas. There was a lot of talk from their camp, and we were just business as usual. But we had a lot of confidence, and there was nothing that was going to hold us back from winning that game."

After a scoreless first quarter, the Redskins offense poured it on. Lohmiller scored a 34-yard field goal. Rypien started a 51-yard drive that ended with a 10-yard touchdown pass to Byner. Darrell Green intercepted a bomb that Bills quarterback Jim Kelly intended for James Lofton, and another drive ended with a Washington touchdown, this one a 1-yard run by Riggs. Washington led 17–0 at halftime and never looked back. Redskins linebacker Kurt Gouveia intercepted Kelly's pass on the first play of the second half and took it back to the Buffalo 2-yard line. Riggs took it over for the score, and now it was a 24–0 Redskins lead. Buffalo attempted to mount a comeback by scoring 10 points on a 21-yard field goal by Scott Norwood and a 1-yard plunge by Thomas, but it was just a tease. Rypien found Clark on a 30-yard scoring pass, and Lohmiller followed with 2 field goals for a 37–10 lead in the fourth quarter. The Bills managed 2 touchdowns in the final minutes to make the score of 37–24 appear less embarrassing in the papers the next day.

Andre Collins "I remember being so tired in the Super Bowl, because they went to their no-huddle offense, and for a minute it was as if we were just trying to hang on. If that game had been an hour longer, they probably would have been able to come back and beat us. At one point, when they went to that no-huddle offense, I was terrified. Monte Coleman had gotten hurt, and there just weren't a whole lot of linebacker substitutes. I remember being so tired, and when we won, it was a feeling of relief. We had been the best team all year, so it was nice to be able to get out of that game with a win."

This was the coronation that never took place for the 1983 team that lost to the Raiders in the Super Bowl. This 1991 Redskins team separated themselves from the pack as the greatest team in franchise history with its Super Bowl championship win, the third for Gibbs in ten years.

The 1991 Redskins team had scored 485 points, compared to the 1983 squad's 541. But the 1991 defense is what truly made this the best all-around unit, holding opponents to 224 points, compared to 332 points given up by the 1983 squad. Joe Theismann and Rypien had nearly identical years: Theismann with 29 touchdowns, 11 interceptions, and 3,714 yards, and Rypien with 28 touchdowns, 11 interceptions, and 3,564 yards.

Brian Mitchell   "Mark Rypien was an overachiever. People didn't expect that he could take the team as far as he had. The year he had in 1991, he was deadly accurate, and he threw a better long ball than anyone I ever saw that year, and he knew how to run the offense."

There were seven Pro Bowlers on the 1983 team and eight on the 1991 team. But the 1991 team had a trophy, and in the NFL, that is how success is measured.

General manager Charley Casserly   "That 1991 team was the greatest in Redskins history, in my opinion. We led the league in scoring. We were second in defensive points allowed. You have to go back to the 1940s to find a championship team that won games by as many points on an average that we did. We're 14-1 going into the final game of the season. We're ahead, and Joe pulls [Mark] Rypien from the game. Philadelphia comes back and beats us on a last-second field goal. That's how close we were to 15-1."

Jim Lachey   "When we played the Rams early in December, we were able to secure home-field advantage. We had a good run and played good football. We just rolled; everything was just working. It is nice to be in a position in the third quarter to just kill the clock and not turn the ball over. It is especially rewarding for fans, who got a chance to enjoy it, and it gave us a chance to enjoy it with them for a quarter. We were on a mission that year, and we got it down."

Gibbs had many moments to cherish from his three Super Bowl championships. But the ones he cherished the most were on the field after the game.

Coach Joe Gibbs "When you talk about special moments, I grabbed my kids after two of those Super Bowls, and I've got pictures of that, one with J. D. and one with Coy. Then for the third one we were all together on the sidelines. I remember those moments the most."

The value Gibbs placed on those times were a signal of what was to come for this Redskins franchise—the end of an era.

10

Changes

There were all sorts of signs at training camp in Carlisle that 1992 would be a tough year for the Washington Redskins. First of all, Russ Grimm–Carlisle hell-raiser extraordinaire–was a coach, not a Hog. In some ways, it was difficult to imagine Grimm as management. But in other ways, he was always a coach of sorts on the field.

Quarterback Joe Theismann "Russ Grimm was the most versatile of our offensive linemen. Russ could have been an All-Pro at any position. Clay Matthews, who played for Cleveland . . . Bruce Matthews, who played for the Houston Oilers and Tennessee Titans, he played center, guard, and tackle. Russ Grimm was that kind of a football player. We were playing the Eagles, I believe, and toward the end of the game, and we have to score a touchdown, and we are down around the 3- or 4-yard line. I call a play that Joe had sent in, and Russ said, 'Hey Joe, look. If you run a quarterback draw, there won't be anyone within yards of you. Both of those tackles are charging out, Jeff [Bostic] will block the middle linebacker, it will be a walk in.' I said, 'Russ, that's a great idea, but we don't have a quarterback draw in our offense.' It wasn't part of it. He said, 'Yeah, I know, but it will still work.' So I became middle management. I was stuck in the middle. I've got my guy on the field telling me something that will work, and I've got the executives over there telling me what they want. I go in the huddle, and I picked up some rocks, and diagrammed a quarterback draw in the dirt. We wound up scoring a touchdown. I walked to the sidelines, and Joe Gibbs had this strange look on his face. He is looking down at his play sheet. He says, 'What was that?' I said, 'That was a quarterback draw.' He said, 'We don't have a quarterback draw.'"

In 1992, the Redskins didn't have a quarterback, either, at least not when camp opened in Carlisle. Mark Rypien was engaged in a bitter holdout. It got so ugly that he made an appearance in a Canadian Football League game, raising speculation that he would be signed by flamboyant Toronto Argonauts owner Bruce McNall.

Rypien wasn't the only one absent from camp. Jim Lachey, Darrell Green, and first-round draft choice Desmond Howard were all out of camp with contract disputes. None would fare very well this coming season. There was more being written about agents and contract disputes than football. Plus, there was the distraction of a preseason game played in London.

Rypien eventually signed the deal he was looking for—a four-year, $12 million contract, capitalizing on his championship season—but he would never approach those 1991 numbers again, and he struggled throughout the 1992 season. Howard, Lachey, and Green would all report to camp, but Green and Lachey got hurt early in the season, and Howard—the Heisman Trophy winner and the number-one pick in the draft—was not nearly the pro player they thought he would be.

There was one change that would be viewed as positive: the team was moving into a new practice facility, a new state-of-the-art Redskin Park in Ashburn, Virginia, near Dulles Airport and their old location.

Washington opened with the Cowboys at Texas Stadium, and the game would be a preview of two teams going in different directions: the Cowboys, young, fast, and on the rise, led by coach Jimmy Johnson and their offensive trio of quarterback Troy Aikman, receiver Michael Ervin, and running back Emmitt Smith, and the Redskins, old and on the decline.

The Cowboys offense amassed 390 yards of offense, but it was an all-around beating. They scored on a 79-yard punt return by Kelvin Martin and a safety when Dallas cornerback Isaac Holt blocked a Redskins punt.

Washington bounced back at home the following week against the Falcons, and the hometown fans were buzzing about the second-quarter play on an Atlanta kickoff when Brian Mitchell took the ball and lateraled to Howard, who took it for a 55-yard touchdown return on the way to a 24–17 victory. This was what Redskins fans were hoping for from the team's highest draft pick. Little did they know this would be the highlight of Desmond Howard's career with the Redskins.

The Redskins struggled to beat the Lions 16–13, then lost to Joe Bugel and the Cardinals in Phoenix 27–24, blowing a 24–6 lead. Jeff Bostic was sidelined the rest of the season with a rotator cuff injury. Lachey went out again for a month with a knee injury. The team's play continued to be erratic. But there was one moment where the team could step back and celebrate not just the accomplishments of one of its greatest players but also perhaps one final acknowledgment of the finish of a glorious run.

In a 34–3 win over the Denver Broncos at RFK Stadium on October 12, Art Monk broke Steve Largent's career reception record with his 820th catch. Monk came into the game needing seven catches to break the record. He got three straight passes to him in the fourth quarter to break the record, the 820th one a 10-yarder. His teammates mobbed him, but even in his greatest moment, Monk remained subdued. He had always been reluctant to call attention to himself, refusing to talk to reporters throughout much of his career.

Joe Theismann   "I think that Art Monk was Jerry Rice before there was Jerry Rice. He had a work ethic that was incredible. A clutch receiver. From a passing standpoint, he was the one who made the big plays. He was the one we counted on. I've always said this about Art, if you spent any time with him, you would improve the quality of your life by 10 percent. Forget the football player, he was that kind of a man. There is no reason why he should not be in the Hall of Fame. I nicknamed him Big Money. He used to wear a dollar sign on a chain. To me, he was money. He was our money guy."

Kicker Mark Moseley   "Art was quiet even with his teammates. He kept to himself, but he was a super nice guy. His work habits made Art what he was. He was one of the hardest workers I had ever been around. I think Terry Metcalf had a big influence on Art early on in his career. He and Art worked out together. He made a big impression on Art and his work habits. Art passed it on to Darrell Green, and that made him the player he was. They did a tremendous workout in the off season."

One of the teammates who knew Monk best was linebacker Monte Coleman. He remembers a story that shows a side of the stoic Art Monk that fans never saw.

Linebacker Monte Coleman   "Art Monk was a very good friend of mine. He was like a brother. In Carlisle, after morning practice, instead of a siesta time after lunch, he and I would go fishing. One day we went to the bait and tackle store to find a place to fish, and they gave us directions to get there. They told us to turn one way, then another, and go down a hill. We would see a big cave, an old cave. We went down the hill and saw this big cave. There were lots of footprints around it. We weren't Lewis and Clark, we didn't discover anything. But it was kind of spooky, with these footprints. Who knew what was in there? We fished a little, and decided to leave when we weren't catching anything. We started back up the hill and there were a couple of squirrels in the trees. I stopped and was throwing rocks at the squirrels. Art keeps going. I hear screaming, like a woman. The first thing that popped into my mind was that something came out of the cave and grabbed Art. I am running through the woods to get to him to see what is wrong. I get there and ask him, 'What's wrong?' He said, 'I've got a spider web on me.' He was screaming."

The Monk record-breaking catch appeared to at least give the Redskins some momentum for the next two weeks. They didn't perform well offensively, but they still managed to beat the Eagles 16–12 and the Vikings 15–13. But the inconsistency continued. They lost to the Giants 24–17, beat Seattle 16–3, and lost to the Saints 20–3. They destroyed the Cardinals in the rematch at RFK Stadium 41–3. But, with a record of 7–5, it appeared Washington was in the driver's seat for a playoff berth with consecutive wins over the Giants by the score of 28–10 and the Cowboys 20–17. But they lost the final two games of the year, one a 17–13 defeat to the Eagles and the season finale a bizarre 21–20 loss to the Raiders at RFK Stadium at the hands of thirty-seven-year-old backup quarterback Vince Evans.

They slinked into the playoffs and surprised everyone when they traveled to Minneapolis and played perhaps their best game of the season, beating the Vikings 24–7. The key was using kick returner Brian Mitchell more in the game plan as a running back, and the talented and tough former college quarterback rushed for 109 on just 16 carries.

They had to travel to San Francisco to play their 1980s' nemesis— now led by Steve Young—but there was optimism that Washington had finally gotten on track at the right time for a playoff run. However, the 49ers jumped out to a 17–3 lead at halftime, and it appeared the Redskins' hopes were dashed. But with the score 17–6, Young fumbled at his 15-yard line, and Rypien took the ball over several plays later to cut San Francisco's lead to 17–13. The momentum had changed, and Washington was driving down the field, heading for the 49ers' end zone, when Rypien and Mitchell mishandled a handoff, and San Francisco recovered the ball. The 49ers engineered a long drive to run out the clock and added a field goal for a 20–13 win and a chance to play the Cowboys in the NFC championship game.

Running back Brian Mitchell   "In that San Francisco game, everyone thought I had fumbled the ball, when in fact I actually never got the ball. The ball slipped out of Mark Rypien's hands and hit me on my thigh. Everyone thought I should have held onto it, but I never got it, and you could see that in the replays and photos. I was looking ahead, which is what we were taught—keep looking ahead and not at the ball. The week before I had a chance to play running back, Earnest was hurt and Ricky [Ervins] was out. I had more than 100 yards and had a chance to play again the next week. I think I showed that I could do more than return kicks."

Guard Raleigh McKenzie   "If it weren't for the 49ers, we probably would have won three Super Bowls in a row—1990, 1991, and 1992. In 1992, the magic wasn't there like it was in the latter part of 1990 and then in the 1991 season. We had some injuries in 1992, but we made it into the playoffs, and we knew going out against San Francisco we had a chance. But we also knew that we weren't the same team that we were in 1991. We didn't have the same depth on defense that we had in 1991. But here we were, in that same situation, because Joe Gibbs was an amazing coach. He and Richie Petitbon really coached us up that year to get us in that position."

Gibbs's players had no idea how much coaching them that year had exhausted him. He had been suffering from a series of medical problems that worsened as the season went on. He took a vacation with his family, but the problems—lack of sleep, headaches, and pain in his arms—persisted. He went for a series of tests that showed he had diabetes and was told to eat better and get more rest. For a man who subsisted on fast food and a few hours' sleep a night on a cot at Redskin Park, this was going to be a problem.

Gibbs had been struggling with the feeling that time with his family—his wife Pat, and two sons, Coy and J. D.—was slipping away, and he wanted to spend more time with them. Three years before, his father, a deputy sheriff from Mockville, North Carolina, told Gibbs as he was dying that he felt bad he had not been around for his sons.

Coach Joe Gibbs   "I had my dad tell me, 'Joe, I'm sorry I wasn't there for you and your brother.' My dad was a great guy, a tough guy, who ran around the hills of North Carolina as a sheriff, fist fighting. But a lot of times he was caught up in other things. He wasn't there a lot. I started thinking about those things. I thought how much longer do I have to enjoy those other things? After twenty-five years of doing what I was doing, I was getting a little tired of doing the same thing."

Gibbs was also enjoying success in his newfound venture and first love from the days of growing up in North Carolina: stock car racing. His NASCAR team, with Dale Jarrett driving, won the Daytona 500 on February 14, 1993. So he began to lay the groundwork for a move that would stun his players and fans alike: Joe Gibbs, at the age of fifty-two, was quitting.

He flew to Washington and met with owner Jack Kent Cooke and general manager Charley Casserly, who were taken by surprise at Gibbs's decision and tried to get him to take more time and reconsider. But when it was clear that Gibbs had made up his mind, they moved quickly to say good-bye to Gibbs and to hire longtime assistant head coach and defensive guru Richie Petitbon.

During an emotional press conference at Redskin Park, Cooke declared that he knew when he first met Gibbs that Gibbs was the right choice to coach the Redskins.

"You know, Joe and I met in New York some twelve years ago," Cooke said. "I would say I don't know how many minutes, because I wasn't counting the minutes, but I would say within thirty or forty minutes I knew that this man possessed a unique talent, which is not vouchsafe to most of us. He had an intensity of purpose, a burning, unquenchable fire, almost an obsession, to succeed.   And so help me, and he'll confirm this, I knew within thirty minutes after meeting him that this man, Joe Gibbs, the unheralded Joe Gibbs, was to be the coach, the head coach of the Washington Redskins. Since then, there has actually been a father-son relationship between the two of us. Some of you may find this hard to believe, but there's never been a cross word between us in those twelve years, not even at contract-signing time, not a murmur, not a whisper of discontent on his part."

Players were, like everyone else, caught by surprise at the news and voiced their admiration for the coach who had led the franchise to three Super Bowl championships.

Linebacker Andre Collins   "Coach Gibbs called several players before he announced he was going to retire, and I was one of them. That made me feel special. He said, 'I just want to thank you for all the hard work you did and the big plays. Hang in there. You never know—I may be back someday.' It blew my mind, but maybe it was a good time for him to take a break, because the game really did change going into that next season—the first year of free agency. The game and the players drastically changed right at that point. I could under-stand why he did it. Sometimes you have success and then you want to move on. But for us he was the spirit of the team. It forced us to try to find another way to do things."

Tackle Jim Lachey   "Sitting in meetings and listening to him go over game plans, it was like listening to [Vince] Lombardi. He instilled so much confidence in us. We believed what he said would work, and it did. And the way he handled players, he would never degrade anyone in a meeting. He would talk to you privately, and if he called you for one of those, it was either good or bad. I had a few, and fortunately they were good. He would tell me that he wanted me to be one of his core guys. I've seen some guys go in there and a week later they would be gone. That was the way he would do it if you didn't produce. He gave you an opportunity, and that is all you can ask. We had a lot of different personalities on those teams, and whenever he walked into a room, everyone would get quiet and sit down and focus on football. If you liked football, there was no better place to play than the Washington Redskins, with Joe Gibbs as the coach."

Quarterback Jeff Rutledge   "Gibbs was a real workaholic. Quarterbacks got in earlier than most guys, and you would see him at the coffee machine after he has slept there. He wouldn't say a word. Then at the end of the year he came up and said to me, 'Jeff, remember all those times at the coffee machine when I didn't say anything. I knew you were there.' It was like the season was over, and he could relax. He was so intense, but a class guy, who believed in the same principles that I believed in.

"He was in chapel with everyone else, and it was great to finish my career with a coach like that. He didn't force it on anyone, but he was very devoted to his beliefs, and I shared that with him."

Brian Mitchell   "It was shocking when Joe Gibbs resigned. We always had the feeling that as long as he was the coach, we had a chance to win, because he was a genius offensive mind and he knew how to get the best out of his players. If you look at those Gibbs teams, it was not like there was a superstar at every position. There were some guys who were very good, but you had a lot of lesser-known guys who played their roles perfectly. So him leaving was a total shock. We had won the Super Bowl the year before, and came close that last year, and then, boom, he's gone."

It was an abrupt change, which was all the more reason to believe that Richie Petitbon was the right choice. He was more Redskin than Joe Gibbs, having come to Washington as part of the Ramskins, when George Allen brought a bunch of Rams players to Washington in trades in 1971, and then came back as a defensive coach for Jack Pardee in 1978 and had been on the staff ever since. He had been mentioned as a head coaching candidate in numerous other vacancies, and was nearly hired by one of his old teams, the Bears, just a few weeks before Gibbs resigned. And it seemed that the Redskins weren't going to miss a beat in the opening game, a stunning 35–16 win over the defending Super Bowl champion Dallas Cowboys on *Monday Night Football*. It seemed as if the Gibbs era would continue, only with Petitbon carrying on the success. Things were good in Washington.

They wouldn't be that good again for the rest of the year, and, much to the dismay of Redskins fans, who didn't realize they were about to fall into the category of long-suffering, not that good again for quite a while.

This was an old team falling apart, while the game was changing with the new age of free agency. There were too many changes, and the Redskins couldn't adjust. Gary Clark, Wilber Marshall, safety Martin Mayhew, and defensive linemen Fred Stokes and Jumpy Geathers were gone, and the Redskins failed to fill in those losses adequately. Their first dip in the free-agency pool—wide receiver Tim McGee, defensive end Al Noga, and linebackers Carl Banks and Rick Graf—was a dismal failure. Rypien injured his knee in the 17–10 loss to Phoenix in the second game of the season, leaving Washington with young unproven Cary Conklin as quarterback. The Redskins lost six straight and would win just three more that year for a 4-12 record. Unlike Gibbs's 0-5 start, Cooke was not standing behind Petitbon for long; he fired him at the end of the season. It was a sad ending to what had been a great career as the Redskins defensive coach who had never gotten the credit he deserved because the team had an offensive personality under Gibbs.

Monte Coleman "It was a joy to play for Richie Petitbon, and it was sad when he got fired. I didn't feel that he got a fair chance as head coach. I thought he should have been given another year. It was the first year of free agency. We had lost a lot of veteran players, and lost a lot of character when we lost those guys. We brought in a lot of players who had been in other places who didn't fit in."

Brian Mitchell "In 1993, a few guys left, and the next year, when Norv [Turner] came, a ton of people left. Richie was a guy who could handle the defense, and Joe was a guy who could keep the team together, handle the media, run the offense, and still pay attention to the defense. That what was so impressive about Joe: he delegated authority, but he was still on top of what was happening with the whole team. Richie now had to do more than handle the defense, so it took more out of him. When you lose a guy like Joe Gibbs on the sidelines, calling the plays, you lose a lot."

Defensive end Charles Mann   "I loved Richie Petitbon. Richie Petitbon did not want to put Joe Gibbs and his offense in a hole. His goal was to keep the other team at 17 points or less, and we did that fairly often. That meant Joe Gibbs and the offense would only have to score 18 points to win most of the time. We wanted to get pressure on the quarterback without blitzing. There was an era here where we had great defensive ends, Dexter and myself. I am going to say that. I never got a sack without anybody blocking me. I am still waiting for the day that I can get the quarterback without running through somebody. We had to pressure the quarterback without any dogs from the linebackers or blitzes from the safeties. The defensive line had to beat their man. Because we did that pretty consistently, Richie could play sound, fundamental defense, and didn't have to gamble. That is not to say that Richie didn't bring the heat, didn't bring corner blitzes and the dogs, but we didn't do it too much. And because we didn't, people don't remember us as a great defense. I've had to endure the talk about the Ravens a few years ago, and when people start talking about the great defenses of the past, and people always were impressed with the ones that blitzed like crazy. Those defenses stick out in people's minds as great defenses. But from 1983 to 1993, I think we had one of great defenses of all time, but we don't get that recognition because all we did was show up and shut people down every week.

"Everything he taught was so fundamental, and what really carved his niche as far as greatness as a defensive coordinator was his ability to adjust his defense according to players' strengths. We had Wilbur Marshall, a linebacker who had great abilities, but sometimes he would do things opposite of what Richie was trying to do. Wilbur would rush when he was supposed to be dropping back, and vice versa. Richie took the defense down to another level. For example, a play now would be called in the huddle, 43 Jet, Wilbur free, Wilbur rush, or Wilbur drop to the flat. He just broke it down to its elementary form. He also saw Wilbur had a knack for beating running backs. Richie saw he needed to get Wilbur running on the edge, so he had about nine sacks one year because he was just killing the running backs.

"He was a great guy, and he treated us like men. He played the game. He had been where we were, and done it all, at a high level in the pros. You respect somebody like that. He was a player's coach, but he wasn't easy on us. I remember in Carlisle once during training camp . . . I was an avid moviegoer, and the last years I was on the team, I took a few liberties in camp. A new movie comes out, I'm going to see it. One time Fred Stokes and I went out to see a movie, but we were not going to get back before curfew. We are sitting in the movie theatre, and someone says, 'Hey, Charles, how are you doing?' I look up, and it's Richie Petitbon and another coach. Fred and I wanted to crawl out of the theater, but we stayed. Now somebody had to let us in from inside the building, because the doors are locked after curfew. We would call someone to let us in, but for some reason on this night we couldn't get a hold of anyone to let us in. We are standing at the dorm door, trying to figure out how to get in after the movie, when Richie walks up, and says to us, 'Hey, studs.' He opens the door and we all walk in together, past curfew. I couldn't look at him the next day because I knew we were wrong, but he never said anything."

The Redskins would commit what some fans would consider a nearly sacrilegious act with the choice to replace Petitbon. They picked the hottest offensive coordinator in football, whose team had just won two straight Super Bowls. The problem was, though, that Norv Turner was a Dallas Cowboy and now he would coach the Washington Redskins.

Years later, some might consider the Redskins franchise cursed for that decision.

Like Joe Gibbs, Turner was born in North Carolina but grew up in California. He played quarterback at the University of Oregon, where he had been recruited by assistant coaches John Robinson and George Seifert. Turner became a graduate assistant at Oregon after playing there, and in 1976 he went to the University of Southern California, where Robinson had taken the head coaching job, to work on Robinson's staff. He eventually moved up to be offensive coordinator of the 1984 team that defeated Ohio State in the Rose Bowl. When Robinson took the head coaching job with the Rams, he brought Turner with him, where he was a successful receivers coach before Jimmy Johnson brought him to Dallas in 1991 as his offensive coordinator.

Turner gained a reputation as an offensive mastermind with the Cowboys, coordinating a system with Troy Aikman, Michael Ervin, and Emmitt Smith, all of whom swore that Turner was a big part of the Cowboys' two Super Bowl championships. "He is the major reason we have been so successful," Smith said.

The same thing was said about Gibbs when he came to Washington from San Diego. The similarities ended there.

Considered a quarterback guru, Turner made one of his biggest blunders right from the start by pushing for the team to draft quarterback Heath Shuler out of Tennessee, who would take his place among the greatest draft busts in NFL history. Shuler was unable to grasp NFL offenses and after the 1996 season, the Redskins released him. He would be out of football two years later, suffering from a severe foot injury.

There were all sorts of new faces in 1994. Joe Jacoby was gone, having retired, and Rypien left, replaced by Shuler and two more new quarterbacks, John Friesz and another rookie named Gus Frerotte. Other arrivals included former Rams receiver Henry Ellard, former Giants defensive tackle Leonard Marshall, and a host of others, in what would be a revolving door of players at Redskin Park for years to come, given the nature of free agency and the failures of Redskins teams from one year to another.

One player who came to Washington with high hopes was standout Cardinals linebacker Ken Harvey.

Linebacker Ken Harvey   "Washington made me a very good offer, but another reason I came here was because of the tradition of the Redskins and winning football. As a player, I would see the stands shaking when they played at RFK Stadium and how much the fans cared about football here, and that was a big difference from Phoenix, so I wanted to come someplace where they had a lot of passion about the team. I thought I could be a part of that. They had lost the year before, and I thought I could help turn things around."

He didn't. Washington was one game worse under Turner than they were under Petitbon, going 3-13, and not winning a single home game. It wasn't the same, and it was difficult for those who had experienced success under Gibbs to live with the change in atmosphere under Turner at Redskin Park.

. . .

Andre Collins   "The Norv Turner year wasn't a fun year for me. My biggest fear became a reality. When a new coach comes with a new agenda, players sometimes don't survive that. For me, the Redskins tradition and the Redskins way was something I believed in. This is how naive I was, because the game was changing, players were going everywhere, the loyalty wasn't there with free agency, coaches were moving around, and that is standard today. But it wasn't at that point. So when we were going to hire a Cowboys coach, that blew my mind. How could this organization hire a Dallas Cowboy coach to come in and coach this team. For me, I just didn't get that. Norv was the kind of coach who wanted to have a relationship with the players, and personally, I didn't understand that. I played for Joe Paterno, and he was like, 'Do what I say and you will be okay.' Gibbs was a lot like that. I didn't need to spend time in the coach's office. Norv wanted that relationship with the players, and that wasn't what I was used to. So I really didn't get off on the right foot with him. The 1994 season was my most productive as a pro, bar none, but for whatever reason, Norv didn't see me as the type of guy who he wanted on his club, and he didn't think I could help them win. My football life changed dramatically when the 1994 season was over. I was sad to tears to leave Washington and go to Cincinnati."

The 1995 season didn't seem to be going much better. First, the team had training camp in very unfamiliar territory. They had made a deal to operate training camp at Frostburg State University in western Maryland, about three hours from the District, leaving Dickinson College in Carlisle after thirty-three years—perhaps leaving something behind there they would never capture again. There would be no tale of glory days and good times in Frostburg.

After winning the season opener 27–7 over Arizona, they won just two of their next eleven games. However, the team finished strong, winning three of its final four games, including a 24–17 victory over the Cowboys in Dallas, and even though they finished with a 6-10 record, there was hope going into the 1996 season. Gus Frerotte, with 13 touchdown passes and 2,751 yards, had emerged as a surprising solid quarterback, while Shuler struggled with injuries and a lack of progress. Their number-one draft choice, star receiver Michael

Westbrook out of Colorado, showed some promise, catching 34 balls for 522 yards, a 15.4-yard-per-catch average. Former Minnesota back Terry Allen came back from his knee surgeries to rush for 1,309 yards. Brian Mitchell continued to shine as the premier kick returner in the league, with a league-leading 25.6-yard per average return on kickoffs and a 12.6-yard per average on punt returns, second in the league.

There was a lot of hope and emotion going into the 1996 season. It would be the last one at RFK Stadium, as Jack Kent Cooke's new stadium would open in Landover, Maryland, the following season. Those hopes rose shortly after an opening 17–14 loss to the Eagles at RFK. The Redskins won their next seven games, decimating the opposition—31–10 over the Giants, 31–16 over the Jets, and 31–16 over the Colts—during that stretch. Then another team seemed to take the field, and that one looked nothing like the first-half Redskins. They lost six of their next seven games, and the Redskins, who had been 7-1, were now out of the playoffs picture and fighting just to come away with a winning season. Washington managed to soften the embarrassment slightly by not saying good-bye to RFK Stadium on a losing note, winning the final game there, 37–10, appropriately, over the Cowboys. The Redskins finished 9-7 that year—their first winning season since Joe Gibbs left—and left RFK with a home record of 173-102-3, including 11-1 in the playoffs, since the stadium opened in 1961.

Ken Harvey   "We win seven of our first eight games and we think we have turned the corner. This was it. Sometimes, though, that can hurt a team, thinking everything had changed, instead of taking it one game at a time. You start thinking we are playing so good that we can't lose, and that's not good. Losing can become a habit just as much as winning. We were a good team, but we were not a great team. The great teams have to play great every game, and we stopped doing that. We played tough against Arizona, but they found a way to win, and that's what was happening. Other teams were finding a way to win, and we were not. It wasn't to say that guys didn't try, but there comes that point where someone has to step up and make a big play, where something has to happen, and that didn't happen. We had meetings and tried to find a way to stop the losing, and sometimes you can play not to lose instead of to win, and I think we did that a lot.

"The last game at RFK was a great memory for me. You really got a sense of how much the community loved the team. We were getting flowers and gifts and really showing how much they cared. That was cool. I've had people give me gifts that you know they worked extremely hard on, handmade gifts, like a sewn blanket or something like that."

They were leaving RFK Stadium behind and about to move into Jack Kent Cooke's new $250 million home, paid for by the owner himself (with more than $100 million in accompanying infrastructure by the state of Maryland) after he failed to make a deal with district officials to build a new stadium in the city. They were called the Washington Redskins, they trained in Ashburn, Virginia, and they played in Raljon, Maryland—yes, Raljon, a name created by Cooke, who combined the first names of his sons Ralph and John, as an address for his suburban Maryland ballpark. Ironically, while the Redskins were moving out there, the NBA Wizards and NHL Capitals, owned by Abe Pollin, were vacating nearby U.S. Airways Arena and moving to Washington to the new MCI Center. The John Kent Cooke (JKC) Stadium held 80,000 people, about 25,000 more than RFK Stadium, yet the legend of a lengthy list of season ticket holders—some stories proclaimed people waited twenty years or more for their turn to come up—would continue, since the team decided not to include several thousand empty club seats in that claim.

But the owner did not get a chance to see a game in his new stadium. Jack Kent Cooke—whose friends used to joke that he was too rich to die—passed away from congestive heart failure at the age of eighty-four on April 6, 1997. In Washington, his death was treated as though a head of state had died.

Cooke had been one of those larger than life figures—illustrated by the fact that he owned the Chrysler Building, bred horses that ran in the Kentucky Derby, and owned the Redskins. He had made his money in the newspaper business in Canada, and the first team he owned was the Toronto Maple Leafs minor league baseball team in 1951. One year later, he was named Minor League Executive of the Year. He came to the United States and set up shop in Los Angeles, purchasing the NBA Lakers and NHL Kings and building the new sports arena in Los Angeles known as The Forum. He owned the Lakers when Wilt Chamberlain and Jerry West won the NBA championship in 1972. He also put up the $5 million for the legendary first fight between Muhammad Ali and Joe Frazier in 1971. Ten years later, he had purchased some shares of the Washington Redskins from Milton King. He eventually took over operation of the team from Edward Bennett Williams and presided over the greatest era in Redskins history.

Cooke was flamboyant, abrasive, charming, difficult, loyal, funny, and intimidating.

Tackle Dave Butz "Jack Kent Cooke once said he was going to do the negotiations for my contract. So I come in during the off season, I leave my suitcase in my locker, and I go out to Middlebrook, Virginia, to sit down with Mr. Jack Kent Cooke. He has three rows of secretaries, and I think all they are doing is adding up his money. We start negotiating, and the phone rings. He says, 'Just a minute. When this phone rings, I have to answer it.' He says, 'Yes, okay $14 million. Sell it.' We start up again and the phone rings again. He picks it up, and is talking, and says, "$23 million," and then he starts quibbling about a $100 bonus for knocking down passes. I spent the day there, and we didn't get anywhere. So my plane ticket said for me to go home. I went back to Redskin Park, and Bubba Tyer, the trainer, had hidden my suitcase from me. He took it out of my locker and hid it, like that was going to keep me from leaving. There was nothing in there that I needed, so I was out of there. I get home, and Jack Kent Cooke calls and wonders why I didn't come back out there, and I said, 'Hey, you said negotiations were over.' So I got out of there."

Monte Coleman "I had a lot of respect for Mr. Cooke. The conversations I had with him on the practice field—he would call me over and introduce his friends to me. One day I was having dinner with my agent at Duke Ziebert's. Mr. Cooke came in and paid me a compliment. He said that he admired me for my work ethic and for my loyalty to the team. I took it as a great compliment coming from a great man."

Charles Mann "I know I didn't want Mr. Cooke slapping me. He would do that to people, affectionately, you know, 'Hey, how are you doing, nice to see you,' and slap you right in your face. I saw him do that to a few people, and I was hoping that wouldn't happen. I remember my first year. I went back home after the draft and came back for the minicamp a few weeks later. We had to run a twelve-minute run back in those days. After the run, [Cooke] called me over to be introduced to his wife. I was already dead tired from the run. 'Charles Mann, come over here.' I ran over and introduced myself. I went back home and told my girlfriend that Mr. Cooke invited me over, and he knew who I was. I was very excited. He was really into the game."

Cooke's legacy to the team, though, would be one of confusion. His will did not leave the team to his son, John, who had been operating as executive vice president and was considered the natural heir for the team. Instead, the unpredictable Redskins owner ordered the team be sold and the proceeds go to a scholarship fund. That decision certainly changed the future of the franchise and sent it into a tumultuous period.

If there was a symbol of the turmoil the Redskins were about to face, it was an incident that took place during training camp in 1997 in Frostburg. Michael Westbrook had a disappointing 1996 season by showing no growth and much immaturity and clashing with coaches and teammates. He had drawn the wrath of the fans for his play and personality and was not very well liked in the locker room, either. In late August, Westbrook attacked running back Stephen Davis in camp and gave him a brutal beating while Davis laid on the ground. Westbrook was fined $50,000 by the team for his actions, but would be tolerated by the team until 2001, when he was released. After a brief stay with the Bengals, Westbrook was out of football after 2002 and resurfaced in 2005 as a competitive cage fighter, in a pay-per-view bout against former Giants running back Jared Bunch.

In an interview before that event, Westbrook gave his version of what happened that day in Frostburg. "I was telling those guys they were jealous of me," Westbrook said. "I said, 'You come into my house and you go, "Wow." You see my car and you go, "Wow." Then every time I come into the locker room, you want to get quiet. I know everything you say about me.'" Then Westbrook said Davis came over, described what Westbrook was saying as nonsense, and made reference to him with a homosexual slur, "and then I punched him."

He was not exactly Art Monk.

Ken Harvey "Michael Westbrook had a lot of talent, but the maturity level wasn't there. Sometimes young players need someone to be hard on them, and Westbrook, because everyone wanted him to be a superstar because he had so much potential, it was like sometimes he was more popular than the coaches. Coaches sometimes have to reel in a player. There are different styles of coaching. He had potential, but potential sits on the sideline if you don't do anything with it."

Brian Mitchell   "Mike's mind-set was that I'm from a big-time program like Colorado, I caught the game-winning touchdown, I'm a number-one draft pick, and I should automatically be the number-one guy on the team. He had a problem that guys like me and Leslie Shepherd were more popular in D.C. But I had been there for a while, was on the Super Bowl team, had won the respect of the fans, and they liked the way I played. Leslie Shepherd was a hometown boy from D.C, and they will always support someone like that. A lot of players who come into the league talk and act a certain way to try to become popular players, instead of just going out and doing their jobs. If you go out and play well, fans will like you. When you go out and try too hard, it doesn't work. Fans can sense if you are real or not, and you won't get the respect that you want."

The Redskins showed no progress in 1997, posting an 8-7-1 record, including one particular embarrassing game at JKC Stadium on November 23, a Sunday night nationally televised embarrassment that after five quarters ended in a 7–7 tie against the New York Giants. This was the game where Gus Frerotte cemented his legacy in Washington by banging his head against a cement wall, albeit a padded one. After crossing the goal line on a 1-yard run to go ahead 7–0 in the second quarter, Frerotte celebrated by butting his head against the padded wall in the end zone, jamming his neck and forcing him to leave the game and go to the hospital. Then, with time running out in the overtime period, backup quarterback Jeff Hostetler completed a pass to Westbrook, who was ruled out of bounds at the Giants' 30-yard line. He took off his helmet in anger and was called for unsportsmanlike conduct, which put the ball back in Washington territory—too far for Redskins kicker Scott Blanton, whose 54-yard field goal attempt fell short as time was running out.

What was worse in 1998—Turner's fifth year—not only did the Redskins not show any progress but they also took a step back, going 6-10. It was the exact opposite of the 1996 season. This time the team started the year by losing its first seven games, then wound up 6-3 the rest of the season. The only saving grace should have been that they found a quarterback in Trent Green, who replaced Frerotte in the first game of the season, a 31–24 loss to the Giants. Green would have the best passing year since Rypien's championship season. Green threw 23 touchdowns, with 11 interceptions, and 3,441 yards.

They weren't able to keep him, though. Wanting to cash in on his season, Green sought a big contract and, given the uncertainty of the Redskins ownership, Charley Casserly was unable to offer him one, so Green left, signing as a free agent with the St. Louis Rams.

Guard Rod Milstead   "In 1998, we lost three quarterbacks. We lost Gus, and we ended up with Trent Green. He had a great year, and the players were upset to see Trent leave for the Rams. We thought that was a terrible decision. Trent would fight for you. He would get hit, get hit hard, and then would jump up and say, 'We'll get them next time.' He was that kind of quarterback. We enjoyed playing for him. He is doing real well now.

"It was terrible to lose those first seven games. The morale was so low in the building. A lot of players were injured that year, and it was a bad situation all around, from the coaches on down. It got so bad that we, as the offensive linemen, told the media if they had any questions to direct them to Russ Grimm [offensive line coach]. It became that bad. We decided we would pull together and not talk to the media for a while. What else could we say? We were going to let our play speak for itself. Why dig a hole for ourselves? Send all the questions to him, he gets paid to answer all the questions. We needed to shut our mouths and concentrate on doing our jobs.

"Trent had a lot to do with the turnaround, but finally it hit the point where we had to put up or shut up and just go out there and play. Whoever was on the field needed to play, period. The second half was a lot more fun. It was more fun to go to practice, to be in the building. When you are winning, everything is fun. When you are losing, everything boils down to trying to find a way to win.

"When the season ended and we saw what we could do, we dedicated ourselves in the off season for the 1999 season. We saw things turning around."

. . .

The sale of the franchise dominated the news for months, as trustees for the Cooke estate went through a lengthy process. They entertained bids from a number of prospective buyers, including one that Redskins fans were very excited about: businessman Sam Grossman, whose partner was the icon of the franchise, former coach Joe Gibbs. There was also a lot of local sentiment in favor of John Kent Cooke, who, despite his father's failure to set up his will to leave him the team, put together a bid to buy the team from the estate. He was also the favorite of fellow NFL owners.

Instead, Daniel Snyder, a brash young upstart who grew up wearing a Redskins belt buckle in suburban Maryland and passionately following the Redskins, wound up being the new owner of the Washington Redskins in a record-setting sale. But it would be a difficult process for Snyder, the founder, chairman, and CEO of Snyder Communications, who at the time was the youngest ever CEO of a New York Stock Exchange company. He partnered with Howard Milstein, a Long Island real estate developer who owned the NHL New York Islanders. They were believed to have been the highest bid, but the NFL rejected the bid, having problems with the way it was structured. Milstein bitterly fought the rejection and wound up suing John Kent Cooke and Casserly. But Snyder rebounded and came back with a new bid—a record $800 million—that was accepted by the NFL.

Casserly lost Green, but managed to make a trade to bring in quarterback Brad Johnson, who would lead the team to their first playoff appearance since 1992. Stephen Davis emerged as a star running back, rushing for 1,405 yards and a 4.8-yard-per-carry average. Westbrook finally had the sort of season that had been expected of him, catching 65 balls for 1,191 yards, an 18.3-yard-per-catch average. And he was not even the leading receiver. Free agent running back Larry Centers became a key figure catching the ball out of the backfield, pulling down 69 receptions. And Johnson made everyone forget about losing Green, throwing 24 touchdowns with 13 interceptions and 4,005 yards while leading Washington on to a 10-6 record and the NFC East title.

The Redskins hosted the first playoff game at JKC Stadium—now called FedEx Field, a symbol of the marketing and promotion that Snyder would use to take the Redskins brand and turn it into one of the most profitable and high-profile sports franchises in the world—and defeated the Detroit Lions 27–13. The Lions were led by former Redskins quarterback Gus Frerotte, who threw two interceptions and was beaten up by his former teammates throughout the game.

The season ended the following week in Tampa Bay against a powerful Bucs defense led by defensive tackle Warren Sapp. Washington led 13–0 in the third quarter, thanks to two Brett Conway field goals and a 100-yard kickoff return by Brian Mitchell, who had come under some criticism within the organization by new owner Dan Snyder for his play on the field and his attitude off it. The Mitchell flap was a good indication of the problems the franchise would face under Snyder, as would the play that ended the game against Tampa Bay. The Bucs came back when Bucs safety John Lynch intercepted a Brad Johnson pass and the subsequent drive led to a 2-yard Mike Alstott touchdown run in the third quarter. Then Johnson fumbled when he was sacked, and that possession turned into another score, a 1-yard pass from rookie passer Shaun King to tight end John Davis, and Tampa Bay led 14–13.

Washington got the ball back with about three minutes left and got into position for a last-gasp 52-yard field goal attempt with 1:17 left to play. But the hike from long snapper Dan Turk, the brother (and agent) of Redskins punter Matt Turk, rolled on the ground, and the kick never came off. The Redskins lost 14–13, but once the dust settled, there was much to be positive about. The team had finally responded to Turner and made it back to the playoffs, and there was good reason to think they had turned the corner.

The owner, though, did not buy the team just to sit back and let things remain the same. Snyder had given a preview of what was to come when he took over the team and immediately fired about thirty employees, some of whom had been with the franchise for more than twenty years. He fired Casserly and hired former 49ers director of player personnel Vinny Cerrato, who would become very close to Snyder—often referred to as Snyder's "racquetball" buddy. The aggressive style that had served Snyder well in the business world would not play well in the NFL.

He had a team that had achieved more than any since Gibbs last coached them, yet Snyder felt compelled to bring in a host of high-profile free agents who would destroy the chemistry that came together in 1999. They had a great draft, bringing in linebacker LaVar Arrington and guard Chris Samuels. Snyder also brought in cornerback Deion Sanders, safety Mark Carrier, defensive end Bruce Smith, and the most controversial of all additions, quarterback Jeff George. He also let Brian Mitchell go, and the changes would create turmoil within the team the likes of which it had never seen before.

Brian Mitchell "If you look at my entire last year in 1999, it was always in the papers—sources say that Brian Mitchell has lost a step, sources say this, sources say that. I talked to the guy who was writing those articles and found out who those sources were, and they were Dan Snyder and Vinny Cerrato. At the end of the season, after that playoff game against Tampa, I said that step that I lost, I must have found it somewhere. I said I would love to have a meeting with Dan Snyder to discuss my future. This was in January. I finally got that meeting right before June 1, which is the day they can release you and not get a salary cap hit. It was a strange meeting. Snyder was there, and Vinnie was sitting there, and Darrell Green was there as well. This was a meeting about my future, and I didn't think that another player should be in there. It was strange. They told me that I would always be a Redskin, blah, blah, blah. I also remember during that year my wife was on bed rest for ten weeks because my daughter was born premature, right before the Thanksgiving game against the Eagles. I had a big return to set up a touchdown. He calls me into his suite, introduces me to some people, congratulates me on the game, and says I will always be a Redskin. I felt okay, but then I was gone.

"I was gone because they wanted to bring in Deion Sanders. They felt they could market Deion Sanders. I proved I didn't lose a step, and in the two games the following year prior to playing the Redskins, when I was playing for the Eagles, I ran back two kicks, a 94-yarder, and an 89-yarder or something like that. Then they said I was a bad influence on the younger players. That baffles me. I was the guy who showed up early and stayed late, and who always performed at his best, whether we were losing or winning. I was the guy who did everything I had to do. Later, I learned that came from a particular player that they trusted, and it bothered me that they took his word and didn't come to me to talk to me about it or talk to other players about it. They wanted to bring in Deion Sanders, and Dan being a marketing guy thought he could promote the team with stars. You saw they brought in all these star players that year, and they didn't do well. I was given a second chance by the Eagles, and I made something of it.

And since I left, all of the returners they have had in Washington put together didn't do the things that I did when I was there."

There were reports that Mitchell and Darrell Green, who had become a favorite of Snyder, had some locker room conflicts, and when Mitchell went to meet with Snyder after the season was over, Green was in the room.

Brian Mitchell   "I don't know why Darrell Green would be in a meeting about my future. He was in the back supposedly on the phone making some kind of deal. I was sitting out in the lobby waiting for about an hour and a half for the meeting. I get in there. He had been meeting with Darrell. I wasn't going to say I didn't want to meet with Darrell in there, but I was uneasy about it. When I left, I felt like I didn't know what went down. Dan said all of this stuff is not personal, but I said it sure seems personal. I've been attacked personally all year. When I go on the football field, it is another paragraph on my resume. I don't have to like my coach. I don't have to like my owner. This was my future. But it was tough playing that year, with my wife, the premature birth, and reading in the paper that I probably wouldn't be there next year, but I still performed.

"I never thought I had a conflict with Darrell. I don't know what is true or not. I've heard a lot of things that were said. Since I left I've heard from a lot of people I was close to, both players and people who were in the organization, that they heard some comments about things that were said about me, and it all led back to him. I don't know what the deal was. I never said anything to him about it, and I probably never will, because my mom always told me if you know someone doesn't like you, now you have the upper hand because you know who is saying bad things about you, so you kill them with kindness. Whenever we run into each other, I am always nice. I am always cool."

Rod Milstead   "Ownership really doesn't have that much of a direct effect on the players. It's more like the trickle-down effect. You have the general manager and the coaching staff and then us, and by the time it gets to us, it is often diluted. But with Snyder, it was totally different. It hit hard, like a knife. He was a fan before he was an owner, and he was more attracted to some players than others. Dan Snyder was more attracted to a Darrell Green than a Rod Milstead, because he was probably a Darrell Green fan growing up. He was a Deion fan, flying him all around and taking him out. But generally that is as far as it goes. The owner is someone you respect because he signs the checks.

"Brian Mitchell, he was the type of guy in the locker room who demanded and commanded respect. I don't know anyone in the locker room who didn't like Brian Mitchell. That was a dagger when they let him leave. He was very outspoken. He could get those guys to believe everything he was saying, and supposedly that was one of the reasons they got rid of him. They couldn't put a muzzle on him. He could rally people about something he believed in. He should have been a Redskin for life."

All the big names—and the circus of holding training camp at Redskin Park, charging fans $10—destroyed what had been built the year before and turned the Redskins into a laughingstock soap opera. Snyder's reputation as a meddling, overbearing owner was solidified this year. He constantly battled with Turner over decisions. He sent vanilla ice cream to defensive coordinator Mike Nolan to illustrate he thought the coach's defenses were vanilla. After a 27–21 loss to the Cowboys at FedEx Field, he came into the locker room and reamed Turner out in front of the players. After a 9–7 loss to the Giants in week thirteen, Turner was fired, despite his team's 7-6 record. What happened the following week only proved to strengthen Snyder's reputation as a fantasy football owner gone wild. There was a point in the hours following the firing of Turner that Snyder and fellow owner Fred Drasner considered hiring Pepper Johnson, a confidant of Snyder's. The choice would have brought more ridicule than what had already been heaped on the team, since Johnson would have been, to put it mildly, overmatched in the job. Instead, they gave it to offensive coordinator Terry Robiskie, who presided over two losses, including an embarrassing 32–12 defeat to the Cowboys, during which Jeff George was grabbed by his facemask and dragged on the field by a Dallas lineman, with no teammate coming to his aid. The Redskins managed to win the season finale against Arizona by 20–3.

Brian Mitchell "Norv and I had a good relationship. But I think where Norv missed the boat was that I was a rah-rah type of guy. I felt the team was everybody's team, as much my team as anyone else's, and if someone messed up, I would let them know about it. When I came into the league, the veteran guys showed me that if you messed up, you had to answer to them. So I picked up that same attitude. But Norv told me he wanted the coaches to handle that, and I said, okay, I'll let the coaches handle it, but if it doesn't work, I'm going back to the way it was. That was where he missed the boat. Joe knew who the leaders of his team were, and he let those guys help him police the team. Norv missed that boat. I don't know if it was a competitive thing or what, but I think he was scared that some players had more control than the coaches did, and he wanted to maintain that control, instead of partnering with his players. I promise you, if he would have come to myself or Tre Johnson or Leslie Shepherd, we didn't have the reputation of Darrell Green, but when you came down to it, the nuts and bolts of it, we were the motivational leaders of that team in the locker room. We were the rah-rah guys who would get on your butt if you were messing up, and we associated with everyone. Norv began to lose the team one by one. The Michael Westbrook incident was a big mistake by Norv. By not being tougher on Mike, he lost a tremendous amount of respect on the team. He suspended him for a preseason game. Well, nobody wants to play a preseason game anyway. It should have been a lot worse. That situation was totally uncalled for. Norv did not have the toughness to punish a supposed star guy, but he would jump on a guy who didn't have any kind of clout. Joe Gibbs didn't care who you were. If you messed up, you would hear about it, and if you did a great job, you would hear about it, also."

Linebacker Eddie Mason "When I got here [in 1999], we didn't have a lot of big names on the team. We didn't have a lot of egos. We had a bunch of guys who played well together, and were tight like a family. We knew how to win and come together. That is what it takes. We had guys who cared about each other and who wanted to play football. We were one game away from being in the NFC championship. It was a tremendous feeling.

"I will tell this to Mr. Snyder or anybody, and I always try to stay positive. The inexperience that Mr. Snyder had when he came in as the owner, he didn't fully understand what he was doing. He was a great businessman, and he proved that in his field, but football is more than business. It is about people. You have to learn how to put the right kind of people together to win. Names and stars don't do it. You have to create the right team chemistry. You have to put the right people in place who can get the type of players to build around your philosophy and where you are trying to go. Under Mr. Snyder, I don't think the team ever had a real identity, philosophy, or direction. Everyone wants to win the Super Bowl, but you have to have a vision to get there.

"All of the off-season acquisitions that were made in 2000, with the Bruce Smith signing, Mark Carrier, Deion Sanders, Jeff George . . . and we cut a lot of guys who may not have been big names but were guys who were good solid football players. We had good chemistry, and we didn't need to break that up. When he broke that team up and maxed out the salary cap, the team has been reeling from that ever since. All they had to do was let what they had develop, and build from within.

"If Mr. Snyder would have done a little more research, and understood . . . he was what, thirty-six, when he purchased the team. He was a young billionaire and it was probably fun for him, buying guys and doing what he wants. It is like a twenty-year-old first-round draft pick signing a big contract. He hits the Lotto, and the first couple of years he is spending, spending, spending. I think that was his mind-set when he first owned the Washington Redskins. 'I'm the owner of the Washington Redskins. I can buy Bruce Smith.' That was probably exciting for him, so you can't really fault him for it.

"But we were one play away from being in the NFC championship game, and you don't want to break that up. That is very difficult for a player to swallow, because when you put out all your blood, sweat, and tears working all year round, that is hard for players. When you are in the game for the right reasons, and that is to win a championship, which is why I played the game, it is very hard. You know you only have so much time, and when you have the opportunity to do it, you hope your owner and the people running the team will make the right personnel decisions, keep the right people on the team, and put that team in the best position to get there. That didn't happen, and it was very difficult for me and the other guys to handle. I know it was hard during that period. We were gutting it out.

"In 2000, it was not like the same place. Some of the stuff that happened, it was like we couldn't believe it was happening. If you are going to hire a coach, let him do his job and coach. If you are going to reprimand him, don't do it in front of the players. I think that was ego more than anything. Mr. Snyder was this young billionaire, the owner of the Washington Redskins, one of the most storied franchises in football. It was a tremendous accomplishment for someone so young. But you have to bring humility with you. It comes with the territory. Wayne Weaver in Jacksonville was a tremendous owner—so nice and friendly to everyone. Everybody in the organization knew him. He would come into the locker room and be one of the guys. He had no airs or ego. I know there are different personality types, and people have different management styles. Mr. Snyder may be a nice man, but I guess he wanted to project this image of being the tough boss. He wanted to be the guy to keep his coaches on pins and needles—show that he was in control. He ran the show, not the coaches. But I think honey works better than vinegar, and I think that is where he made a lot of mistakes, with some of his coaching choices, and his decision-making in 2000 and even 2001, when he hired Marty Schottenheimer. He wanted people to perceive him a certain way, and I don't think that is who he really is. I've seen him outside of football, and that is not the way he is. All he had to do was be who he really was. People would rather have had that Mr. Snyder than the one we saw and the one who the fans really turned against."

Snyder's image had taken such a hit—he was featured as a cartoon character in the comic strip "Tank McNamara"—that he felt obliged to bring in a coach to try to defuse the situation. So he courted former Cleveland Browns and Kansas City Chiefs coach Marty Schottenheimer, who was working as an analyst for ESPN. Surprisingly, Schottenheimer agreed to work for Snyder, but under the condition that Snyder would not get involved in any of the football operations.

Schottenheimer was a no-nonsense disciplinarian, and his methods angered some of the veterans, particularly when he tried to coach Darrell Green on playing cornerback. Deion Sanders, whose $8 million signing bonus would prove to be an albatross around the Redskins' salary cap for several years, refused to play for Schottenheimer. Bruce Smith chafed at some of Schottenheimer's practice methods. Two weeks into the season, Schottenheimer cut Jeff George. But after a 0-5 start, the team responded to Schottenheimer—as it did to Gibbs after his 0-5 start in 1981—and finished the final 11 games with an 8-3 record, a remarkable achievement considering the quarterback was journeyman Tony Banks. Winning wouldn't be enough for Snyder, though. He couldn't enjoy it without being in the middle of it, so Schottenheimer was fired in January 2002, even though he had three years left on a $10 million contract.

Schottenheimer made it clear to reporters the issue was that Snyder had reneged on his promise of total control for the coach. "The issue we could not resolve was the process of selecting players to make up the Washington Redskins roster," Schottenheimer said. "The opportunity to determine the composition of the Washington Redskins was the single most important element of my taking the job here last January. It was my belief that my way would have been the most successful, but Daniel Snyder owns the Washington Redskins. He made the commitment to the organization and he is entitled to make any decision he chooses."

The decision Snyder made was to hire the coach he claimed he wanted all along: University of Florida coach Steve Spurrier. The Gators coach, outspoken and successful, had been the target of pro teams before, but Snyder was able to convince him to leave Florida and take a five-year, $25 million deal to coach the Redskins. It seemed inconceivable that things could get worse, but they did.

Spurrier was ill prepared for the demands of NFL coaching. He was often out-coached and seemed in a daze at times. His 2002 team went 7-9, and then dropped to 5-11 in 2003, and the soap opera continued with questions about whether Spurrier would quit or be fired. He resigned in embarrassment, and the once-proud Redskins franchise had hit rock bottom. Snyder was perhaps the most vilified owner in football—certainly in Washington—and there didn't appear to be anything he could do to dig his way out of it.

There was one thing he could do, though, and he did it. He convinced Joe Gibbs to come back and coach the Washington Redskins. The former coach had built a successful career for himself as a NASCAR team owner, but he always entertained the possibility of coming back. He had a relationship with new Atlanta Falcons owner Arthur Blank as a NASCAR partner, and he was a minority investor in the Falcons: there was even talk about Gibbs coaching the Falcons. But in the end, if he was going to come back and coach in the NFL, he couldn't see himself doing it anyplace but back in Washington. So

Snyder shocked the sports world and with one fell swoop changed the whole landscape by bringing back a sports deity to Washington on January 9, 2004.

Fans flocked to Redskin Park to welcome Gibbs back home. He arrived in a five-limousine procession. The practice facility was filled with media, former players, and others who were there to rejoice in Gibbs's return. At a fifty-minute news conference, Gibbs vowed to work hard to regain success for the franchise.

"I didn't wear my Super Bowl ring," said Gibbs, who signed a five-year, $28.5 million contract to return. "We're focused on the future. We want to try to do something great here. It's a whole new deal. I've got to prove myself all over again. I love the challenge of doing something that's almost undoable. Certainly, this is as close to that as you can get. I come here with the most humble spirit. I'm coming into this with my eyes wide open."

Since then, Snyder has been low key, and in an interview with the *Washington Times*, he said he has learned from his mistakes. "I've learned an awful lot," Snyder said. "I wasn't as patient then as I am now. I've developed more patience, an understanding of the continuity of the game and continuity on the business side as well."

There was much hope with Gibbs's arrival—the hope that the Redskins could reclaim their glory and "Hail Victory" once again.

Epilogue

In 2004, the hope inspired by the return of three-time Super Bowl champion coach Joe Gibbs was buttressed by a 16–10 victory over Tampa Bay in the season opener, but it collapsed slowly from that point onward.

Gibbs had brought in some veteran big-name talent to lead his team: former Jacksonville quarterback Mark Brunell and running back Clinton Portis from Denver, who had averaged 5.5 yards per carry in his first two seasons with the Broncos and rushed for more than 3,000 yards over that two-year span. He also brought back some familiar names to the coaching staff, including former offensive line coach Joe Bugel and offensive coordinators Don Breaux and Jack Burns, and recruited former Buffalo Bills head coach Gregg Williams to be his defensive coordinator.

But the team struggled as they had under former coach Steve Spurrier, going 6-10. At the age of thirty-four, Brunell had been a disaster; not fully recovered from an elbow injury in 2003, he started just nine games, throwing 7 touchdowns and 6 interceptions. Patrick Ramsey—whom Gibbs inherited and had shown no inclination toward being particularly thrilled with—threw 10 passes and 11 interceptions. Portis rushed for 1,315 yards, but it was not a clear indication of how much he struggled in Gibbs's offense. His 3.8-yard-per-carry average was more than a yard below his career average, and he did not seem to fit in. The entire offense was dismal, scoring just 240 points over 16 games.

So there was not a lot of optimism going into the 2005 season—particularly when two fan favorites and "core" Redskins—cornerback Fred Smoot and linebacker Antonio Pierce—were lost to free agency. Then safety Sean Taylor, their star problem child, was arrested on assault charges in Florida in an incident involving a gun that he was alleged to have used in a dispute. Plus, there was the salary bonus battle going on with linebacker LaVar Arrington and his slow recovery from a knee injury in 2004. There were two positives, though. Wide receiver Laveranues Coles was sent back to the Jets in exchange for receiver Santana Moss, and Bill Musgraves was hired as quarterback coach.

Washington opened the 2005 season at home against the Chicago Bears, a team not very highly regarded and led by a rookie quarterback. The Redskins won 9–7, but it was hardly a confidence-building victory, with just 9 points scored. Ramsey, who had been named the starting quarterback, was knocked out of the game and replaced by Brunell, whom Gibbs then named as the starter for game two, which was against the Cowboys in Dallas on *Monday Night Football.*

That night, in the final 3:46 of the game, everything changed for the Redskins, both for the season and the direction of the franchise. Down 13–0, Brunell hit Moss with 2 touchdown passes, a 39-yarder and a 70-yarder, to pull out a 14–13 win, the first time they had beaten the Cowboys at Texas Stadium since 1995. Gibbs had managed to change the culture at Redskin Park to one where players didn't quit or put their own agendas ahead of the team, and it was finally showing up in the results on the field.

They beat the Seattle Seahawks the following week at FedEx Field, 20–17 in overtime, on a field goal by substitute kicker Nick Novak. Brunell completed 20 of 36 passes for 226 yards and 2 touchdowns, and Portis ran for 90 yards. It was the best the offense looked so far this year. "It's a process," Brunell told reporters. "What you saw today was improvement."

Little did anyone realize this would be a preview of a future NFC playoff game.

The Redskins didn't get much of a chance to work on improvement. Their next two games were at the hardest places to win in the league: Denver and Kansas City. Washington played tough against the Broncos, one of the AFC's top teams, but lost 21–19. The Redskins nearly pulled it out in the last minute when Brunell attempted a pass to an open David Patten in the end zone, but the ball was tipped and fell incomplete. Then they lost 28–21 to the Chiefs in a mistake-filled contest that saw 3 Washington fumbles, wasting strong performances by Brunell (331 yards passing) and Moss (10 catches).

The Redskins returned home the following week and hosted a house party for their fans—a 52–17 beating of the San Francisco 49ers. This win put Washington on top of the NFC in a tie with the New York Giants and the Philadelphia Eagles. "Everything was clicking today and we got a big win and a win we needed," Brunell told reporters. It was the most points for a Redskins team since a 56–17 victory over the Atlanta Falcons in 1991.

But they followed their biggest win with their biggest loss—a 36–0 beating at the hands of the Giants in the Meadowlands. It was the first time a Gibbs team had been shut out since 1987. "That was as bad a performance as I've been a part of in my whole life," offensive tackle Jon Jansen said after the game. "From not protecting the quarterback and turning it over to giving up big plays and making stupid penalties, it was a bad day all around."

Fortunately for Washington, they caught a break the following week when they faced the division rival Eagles, who were a team in turmoil. This was the week that Terrell Owens was suspended and subsequently kicked off the team for comments he made about Donovan McNabb and team management. Without Owens, the Eagles didn't have any weapons, and Washington won the Sunday night contest 17–10. The Redskins had been erratic to date, but still had a 5-3 record, and were looking for two winnable games in the next three games—at least on paper. It didn't work out that way, however.

Washington went through its worst stretch of the season by losing 36–35 to the Bucs in Tampa and their inexperienced quarterback, Chris Simms. Then they came home and suffered the embarrassment of losing to a bad Oakland Raiders team, 16–13, led by their former coach, Norv Turner, who would be fired at the end of the season. They then suffered another home loss to another former coach, Marty Schottenheimer, and the San Diego Chargers, who beat the Redskins 23–17. At 5-6, it appeared Washington's season was over, and they were indeed heading for their second straight losing season under Gibbs.

But the work the Hall of Fame coach had done to bring in quality character players and to change the culture of losing within the franchise paid off, as the Redskins reeled off five straight wins for a 10–6 regular season mark to capture a wild-card position in the playoffs, their first appearance in postseason play since 1999. The three final victories were particularly sweet, coming against NFC East opponents. They thoroughly embarrassed the Cowboys 35–7 at FedEx Field. "It was one of those nights that you dream about," Gibbs told reporters after the game. "The last two years I can't remember coming close to this." Then there was an avenging of the earlier defeat to the Giants by beating New York 35–20, also a home win that saw Brunell go down with a sprained right knee and Ramsey come in and throw a 72-yard touchdown pass to Moss in the third quarter. And the season finale was the playoff-clinching 31–20 victory over the Eagles in Philadelphia. They had been down 20–17 but rallied with a 22-yard touchdown run by Portis, set up by an interception by linebacker Lemar Marshall, and a 39-yard fumble return for the final score by safety Sean Taylor. "At halftime, we talked about going out and trying to find a way to win or we were going to be cleaning out our lockers," Portis said. "I wasn't ready to clean out my locker. I don't think any of the other guys were, either."

Ironically, their return to the playoffs would happen at the same place they last appeared in the playoffs: Raymond James Stadium in Tampa, where in 1999 they lost in the second round 14–13. This would also be a rematch of the regular season game against the Bucs that made Chris Simms an NFL quarterback in a 36–25 win over Washington.

The Redskins defense didn't let Simms build on his reputation. The defense intercepted Simms twice—one by Arrington that set up a touchdown run by Portis and a second by linebacker Marcus Washington, who in turn fumbled, with the ball picked up by Taylor, who ran it 51 yards for a touchdown and a 17–10 Redskins victory. The defense saved the woeful offense—just 41 yards passing by Brunell and 53 yards rushing by Portis—and a stupid act by Taylor, who was tossed from the game late in the third quarter for spitting in the face of Bucs running back Michael Pittman.

"We were very fortunate," Jon Jansen said in the victorious locker room. "Our defense outscored their defense and that's why we won the game."

Still, they did win a playoff game, if by nothing else but grit and determination—a major turnaround for this franchise, something they had never been credited with since Gibbs left after the 1992 season. That, more than anything, was the evidence of Gibbs's handiwork. "We have a lot of guys who have a lot of fight in them and say, 'I'm not going to give up no matter what the circumstances,'" Gibbs said.

Now, they were one game away from reaching the NFC championship game. All they had to do was go to Seattle and beat a team they had already beaten earlier in the season. The catch was that Seattle had improved and, with a 13–3 record, it was considered to be the best team in the conference. The Redskins would need more of a showing from the offense to pull off their seventh straight win, but they wouldn't get it, in a 20–10 loss to the Seahawks. Portis rushed for just 41 yards, and while Brunell completed 22 of 37 for 242 yards, they were, for the most part, inconsequential yards. It was a disappointing loss, but no one felt cheated. "We hit a rough point this year when we were 5-6 and guys could have pointed fingers," Portis said. "But nobody did. We won a tough one last week and lost a tough one today. We've got more to look forward to next year."

There was also much to look back on with pride. Portis turned in the kind of season that made him a star in the league his first two seasons in Denver, breaking the single season franchise rushing record with 1,516 yards. Moss, with 1,483 receiving yards, also set a new team record, pulling down 84 catches. H-back Chris Cooley became a vital weapon in the offense, catching 71 passes for 774 yards and making 7 touchdowns. Gregg Williams's defense turned in a second straight strong season, finishing sixth in the conference. And Brunell had recovered from his dismal first year in Washington to throw 23 touchdowns, though he appeared to have run out of gas by the end of the season. "We certainly accomplished a lot this year," Gibbs said. "We were 6-10 last year, and the facts speak for themselves this year. We got a lot of good things done."

The biggest thing they got done was to bring credibility and respectability back to the one of the most popular and proud franchises in the NFL: the Washington Redskins.

PHOTO CREDITS

INDEX